STUDIES IN PHILOSOPHY AND HEALTH POLICY

JUST HEALTH CARE

STUDIES IN PHILOSOPHY AND HEALTH POLICY

Edited by
DANIEL I. WIKLER
Program in Medical Ethics, University of Wisconsin Medical School

Advisory editors
RUDOLPH KLEIN, MARY WARNOCK,
DAVID P. WILLIS, UWE REINHARDT

The books in this series will address the conceptual issues and moral problems arising from health policy and the practice of medicine. Issues of a social and political nature facing policymakers and administrations, as well as issues primarily affecting individuals in medical relationships, will be discussed. The series will include works by philosophers and by philosophically inclined writers from other disciplines whose distinctive methods can be brought to bear on the questions. Only in this way will a proper understanding of the problems be achieved, as a basis for sound policies and decisions.

JUST HEALTH CARE

NORMAN DANIELS

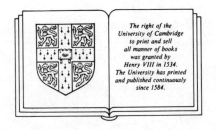

The right of the
University of Cambridge
to print and sell
all manner of books
was granted by
Henry VIII in 1534.
The University has printed
and published continuously
since 1584.

CAMBRIDGE UNIVERSITY PRESS

CAMBRIDGE

LONDON   NEW YORK   NEW ROCHELLE
MELBOURNE   SYDNEY

Published by the Press Syndicate of the University of Cambridge
The Pitt Building, Trumpington Street, Cambridge CB2 1RP
32 East 57th Street, New York, NY 10022, USA
10 Stamford Road, Oakleigh, Melbourne 3166, Australia

© Cambridge University Press 1985

First published 1985

Printed in Great Britain at the University Press, Cambridge

Library of Congress catalogue card number: 84-23807

British Library Cataloguing in Publication Data
Daniels, Norman, *1942–*
Just health care. – (Studies in philosophy
and health policy)
1. Medical care – Philosophy
I. Title   II. Series
362.1′01   RA394

ISBN 0 521 23608 8 hard covers
ISBN 0 521 31794 0 paperback

wv

For Anne and Noah

CONTENTS

vii

Contents

PREFACE

This book is about justice in the design of a health-care system. The term 'health care' is used broadly to include personal medical services, preventive medical and public health measures, including health and safety regulation, and certain social support services for the chronically ill or disabled. So a health-care system involves a diverse set of institutions which have a major impact on the level and distribution of our welfare. A theory of justice articulates the general principles which should govern this system. It is not merely a catalog of its features we think in advance to be just. To find such principles of justice for health care we must address questions such as these:

> What kind of a social good is health care? What are its functions and do these make it different from other commodities?
>
> Are there social obligations to provide health care?
>
> What inequalities in its distribution are morally acceptable?
>
> What limits do provider autonomy and individual liberties of physicians or patients place on the just distribution of health care?

A theory of justice for health care is not just the fare of philosophers and political theorists. It concerns us all. Quite simply, distributive justice concerns who ought to get what. How our health-care institutions distribute various goods and services has a direct bearing on our welfare, and all of us take an interest in comparing how well off we are with how well off we ought to be. But the conception of just health care developed in this book is of special importance to the many social scientists, planners, policy makers, legislators, administrators, and providers who tend to the day-to-day functioning of our health-care delivery system. Often it is these people who wonder, to themselves and out loud, what justice requires of them. The philosophical arguments and positions developed here will not directly answer their most immediate and pressing questions about how to improve the system, but they should help explain why these questions arise, how they are connected, and what in general would have to change for satisfactory answers to be given.

ix

Preface

About eight years ago, when I first became interested in the literature on medical ethics, I was struck by the relative absence of philosophical work on the distribution of health care.[1] The more dramatic topics of abortion, euthanasia, and organ transplantation seemed to hog the philosophical stage, and with few exceptions, and an occasional comment on 'rights to health care', no one analyzed what kind of social good health care is or investigated the principles that should govern its distribution. Even in such a young area of philosophical inquiry, the absence was surprising because so much work was being done on the general theory of justice. This book was written over the last five years in an effort to fill that gap.

In the first three chapters, I motivate the search for a theory of justice for health care and develop a particular approach, the 'fair equality of opportunity account'. In chapters 4 and 5, I apply the theory to the problems of access to personal medical services and the distribution of health-care resources between the young and the old. In chapters 6–8, I illustrate possible conflicts between liberty and equality through a discussion of provider autonomy and health hazard regulation in the workplace. Chapter 9 contains more general remarks on applying the theory of just health care to public policy issues. Though some of the chapters may be read as self-contained studies, my intention has been to bring unity to the discussion of issues which generally have been discussed separately.

When work on the material for this book began in 1978, there was still public discussion in the US about instituting a more comprehensive national health insurance scheme and continuing public efforts to improve access to health care begun in the mid 1960s. The public perception was that justice required improved access to health care. In that context, investigating more generally what the principles required for the just distribution of health-care services would look like did not seem overly idealistic and had the virtue of timeliness. Central to the planner or legislator designing such a financing scheme were the questions, How much equality should there be? What inequalities in access to care are morally acceptable? How should the burdens of achieving that equality be distributed? My hope was that principles of justice for health-care institutions could give practical guidance to what I perceived as an effort to reform a major system of institutions. I might add that such principles are also of importance in countries such as Great Britain,

[1] Important early efforts to address of justice include Outka (1974), Jonsen and Hellegers (1974), Jonsen (1976a and b), and Branson and Veatch (1976).

where the debate runs in the opposite direction and the controversy concerns dismantling a relatively egalitarian system. Though my examples are largely drawn from the context of US institutions, the issues they illustrate are perfectly general. When I refer to 'our' system, I may have US institutions most immediately in mind, though I intend the discussion to be quite general.

But even as I became more aware of the complexities of the problem of just health care, the focus of public discussion in the US began to shift. Constraining rapidly rising health-care costs became the main item on the health-care agenda, and though issues of equity still arise in this context, there is little pretext that the just redesign of a health-care system is a current national objective. Were this an essay in policy analysis, the shift in the national political agenda would be more than embarrassing. But this is an essay in applied philosophy, and the issues it addresses are not less important or relevant because of the – probably temporary – shift in the political agenda. Timeliness is nice, but it is not a central virtue even for applied philosophy.

An essay in applied philosophy has its risks – it risks frustrating both the professional philosopher and specialists in the area of application. I must in this book avoid discussing certain abstract issues in the general theory of justice, which are of considerable interest to me and other moral philosophers. For some of them, this discussion starts a bit too close to the ground to really fly, even though, all admit, we learn much about the adequacy of moral theories by attempting to apply them. At the same time, this discussion does not contain the detailed empirical investigation that gives the policy analyst, planner, or legislator his nuts and bolts. For some of them, this discussion is never down to earth enough. My intended audience includes all those who think it worth while to explore that intermediate space in which we try to look at real social institutions with some philosophical vision.

ACKNOWLEDGEMENTS

Many debts have accrued in the time I have worked on this project, and though I cannot discharge them here, I would like to acknowledge them. Much of the research involved in this book was supported by the National Center for Health Services Research, Grant No. HS03097, OASH, which provided me with valuable time-release from teaching duties and summer support during 1978–82. A Tufts sabbatical leave in 1978–9 permitted my full attention to this project early in its conception, and the opportunity to give a seminar on some of this material at Brown University in the spring of 1979 was provided by the Commonwealth Fund. Material for the chapters on equity of access (Chapter 4) and health care for the elderly (Chapter 5) was prepared originally for the President's Commission for the Study of Ethical Problems in Medicine and Biomedical and Behavioral Research. Some reworking of the material on health care for the elderly has been supported by recent grants from the Retirement Research Foundation and the National Endowment for the Humanities (NEH). Material in Chapter 8, 'Risk and Opportunity' is substantially based on 'Biological monitoring: ethical issues that arise from individual variation in susceptibility to risk in the workplace', copyright for which resides with Michael Baram and Robert Field. The original essay was commissioned for a National Science Foundation Project, 'Ethical, legal, and policy issues in the use of biological monitoring for occupational health' (No. ISP–8114738). The material incorporated here is used with the permission of the copyright holders.

I have also been aided, especially during the early years of this project, by various members of the Hastings Center Institute of Society, Ethics, and the Life Sciences. In particular, Ron Bayer, Art Caplan, and Ruth Macklin were especially generous with comments and criticism during the course of a project on Ethics and Health Policy funded by the Kaiser Foundation. I am also indebted to the members of an NEH Summer Seminar for Health Care Teachers which I directed in the summer of 1981; their provocative discussion forced me to develop earlier versions of this material. I received invaluable help from staff members of the President's Commission for the Study of Ethical Problems in Medicine and Biomedical and Behavioral Research. In particular, I would like to thank Mary Anne Bailey, Alan Weisbard, and, especially, Dan Brock, Allan Buchanan, and Daniel Wikler, who helped greatly in the development of material for chapters 4 and 5. Daniel Wikler has also provided detailed editorial comments on an earlier draft of the whole manuscript, improving it in many ways.

Other individuals also provided me with valuable and constructive criticism. I wish to thank Jacob Adler, Jerry Avorn, Hugo Bedau, Christine Bishop, Richard Brandt, Christopher Cherniak, Josh Cohen, Daniel Dennett, David Gauthier, Allan Gibbard, Amy Gutmann, George Smith, Larry Stern, and the editors of *Philosophy and Public Affairs*. I also owe a special debt to John Rawls, whose work on the theory of justice has left its mark on my thinking in many ways and whose discussion of early versions of some of this material was most helpful. His work also shows how far short of offering a comprehensive theory of justice my effort in this essay falls. I would also like to thank Barbara Keesey Simkowski, Julie Roberts, and Teresa Salvato for their help in manuscript preparation at various stages in this project.

My wife Anne served as a sounding board and critic of many of these pages, and to her I offer my thanks for accepting in good spirit the many intrusions into our lives caused by this work.

Several of the chapters draw heavily on previously published articles. I wish to thank the relevant editors and publishers for permission to use material from the following articles:

On the picket line: are doctors' strikes ethical? *Hasting Center Report* 8:1 (1978):24–30

Rights to health care and distributive justice: programmatic worries. *Journal of Medicine and Philosophy* 4:2 (1979): 174–91

Health care needs and distributive justice. *Philosophy and Public Affairs* 10:2 (1981): 146–79

Conflicting objectives and the priorities problem. In Peter G. Brown, Conrad Johnson, and Paul Vernier (eds.), *Income Support: Conceptual and Policy Issues*, pp. 147–64. Totowa, NJ: Rowman and Littlefield, 1981

Cost-effectiveness and patient welfare. In Marc Basson (ed.), *Rights and Responsibilities in Modern Medicine*, vol. 2 pp. 159–70. New York: Alan R. Liss, Inc., 1981

What is the obligation of the medical profession in the distribution of health care? *Social Science and Medicine* 15F (1981):129–35

Equity of access to health care: some conceptual and ethical issues. *Milbank Memorial Fund Quarterly Health and Society* 60:1 (1982):51–81

Am I my parents' keeper? *Midwest Studies in Philosophy* 7 (1982):517–40

1 · Is health care special?

Micro and macro

Medical ethics, a child of the 1970s, has thrived on the exotic. It has fed on new life-and-death dramas: Should aggressive treatment be stopped for a terminal patient with metastasized bone cancer, or started for a hydrocephalic newborn with open spinal lesions? Which of several medically eligible patients should receive the life-saving liver transplant? Should a leukemic child's parents be allowed to switch him from chemotherapy to laetrile? These dramas are modern morality plays. They feature the patient as Everyman who must find his way in a land of mystical medical powers, ruled by the High Priest Technology. These real dramas are reenacted in classroom case studies, or in the media, where they have the flavor of TV soaps: the villain, the paternalistic doctor, threatens Everyman's autonomy, until he is rescued by the good Doctor Informed Consent. There are many variations on the plot. Is the geriatic patient with Alzheimer's disease competent to agree to amputation of his foot and commitment to a nursing home? Should a physician tell one of his female patients that her fiancé, who is also one of his patients, is homosexual or is sterile? Though exotic, these dramas have a universal appeal. It is easy to imagine participating in them first hand, as a patient, family member, or practitioner. Moreover, these problems of *individual* or *micro* decision-making are forced on us by biology, technology, and very general moral concerns. They might arise in any health-care system and seem to be part of our self-made human condition.

Though this is an essay in medical ethics, it draws on a different menu. I shall be concerned entirely with the *social* or *macro* level of decision-making – a macro-bioethical diet, if you will. Though less dramatic than micro decisions, macro decisions in a society have an even greater impact on the general health status of its members. I do not mean, however, to draw this line between macro and micro levels of decision-making too sharply. Some questions I have characterized as micro have systematic implications for the behavior of individuals throughout an institution, and thus resemble macro issues; similarly, some macro issues have implications for the behavior of individuals working in an institution, and so resemble micro issues. For my purposes, it is enough to say that the macro level concerns the scope and design of *basic health-care institutions*, the central institutions and social practices which form a health-care system.

Most visible and familiar among these institutions is the complex system for delivering and financing the personal medical services that comprise acute care and a few individually focused preventive techniques. I include here our system of high-technology hospital and clinic-based medicine, the training institutions for physicians, nurses and allied professionals, and the research and development institutions supporting these forms of health-care services. Less visible and less glamorous, but extremely important in their effect on collective health status, are the various public health agencies concerned with preventive programs. I include here the laws and agencies responsible for the control of infectious diseases, nutrition and health education, drug and food protection, consumer product safety, and the regulation of health hazards in the environment, including the provision for clean water and for proper sanitation and other waste disposal. The health-care system also involves institutions responsible for social support and personal care services needed by the mentally and physically disabled or the chronically ill. Personal medical care services alone involve about 10% of the total goods and services included in the US Gross National Product, so when we add the public agencies concerned with preventive health care in all its forms, we are talking about institutions which account for well over the frequently bemoaned 10% figure. Somewhat lower, but still comparable, figures reveal the size and importance of these institutions in other industrialized countries.

Macro decisions determine (1) what kinds of health-care services will exist in a society, (2) who will get them and on what basis, (3) who will deliver them, (4) how the burdens of financing them will be distributed, and (5) how the power and control of these services will be distributed. These decisions affect the *level* and *distribution* of the risk of our getting sick, the likelihood of our being cured, and the degree to which others will help us when we become impaired or dysfunctional. Because these macro decisions critically affect the level and distribution of our well-being, they involve issues of social justice. Indeed, they poignantly combine some of our most intimate and personal concerns, for our mental and physical health, with our public passion, our concern for the social order and our fair treatment in it.

Public concern and debate about justice is triggered by perceptions of inequality, which is often taken to imply inequity. Indeed, in the US health care system, it is easy to perceive persistent inequality; and inequality in access to personal medical services is measurable in various dimensions. Despite major improvements in access by the very poor and the elderly following the introduction of public medical insurance schemes such as Medicaid and Medicare in the mid 1960s, between 22 and 25 million Americans, some 11–12.6% of the noninstitutionalized population, have *no* health-care insurance, and about 20 million more have inadequate coverage (President's Commission 1983a: 92–3). Those without coverage tend to be the poor, the near poor, members of racial and ethnic minorities, and rural residents.

Lack of insurance coverage, combined with other features of the delivery system, have a systematic effect on the utilization of health services, on whether one has a regular source of care, and on the point in illness at which care is sought. If we control for health status, we can see these effects on the use of services: In 1976–8 in the US, whites below the poverty line (many of whom are ineligible for Medicaid) and below age seventeen whose health status was poor to fair averaged 9–14 physician visits a year, whereas those whose family income was twice poverty level averaged 17.16 visits a year. For blacks, the figures were 5.18 and 10.67 visits, respectively, so that poor blacks and relatively disadvantaged whites, all in poor to fair health, differed over 250% in their use of physicians (Bayer, Caplan, and Daniels 1983:xviii). Thus there are serious inequalities in the US in access to personal medical services which are correlated with both class and race. I shall return to these matters in more detail in Chapter 4.

Inequalities in the risk of getting sick also correlate with class and race in ways that suggest unequal protection from the health-care system. Large groups of industrial workers, for example, are far more likely to get serious respiratory and other diseases, like cancer, than other population groups because of exposure to occupational hazards. The lack of prenatal care is partly responsible for an infant mortality rate among blacks which in the US was 200% that of whites in 1977. When asked to judge their own health status, 10.9% of whites responded 'fair' or 'poor', while 20.8% of blacks did. And this perception is not illusory: the number of bed-disability days, a restrictive measure of illness, was 6.6 for whites in 1977 and 8.9 for blacks (Bayer, Caplan, and Daniels 1983:xiv).

These inequalities – whether or not they are injustices – are the direct results of features in the design of our basic health-care institutions.

3

Macro decisions which lead to them, no less than decisions about health care at the micro level, should be made in accordance with acceptable moral principles. If the glaring inequalities in access in the US are justifiable, it must be because acceptable general moral principles provide justification for them. For the kinds of macro decisions that concern us, we are concerned with only certain moral principles, the principles of justice, for these principles should serve as a public and final basis for resolving disagreements about how basic institutions, such as health-care institutions, should be designed. These principles provide a general framework within which planners and legislators can make more specific public policy decisions. Without agreement on such a framework, policy decisions are especially difficult to make because there is no principled way to resolve the conflicting claims advanced by different groups. These conflicts reflect the fundamental differences in interest that exist between providers and consumers of health care, between different groups of providers or consumers, or between different economic classes, who bear the benefits and burdens of policy decisions differently. At one extreme, the moral principle might be simply to accept as just the (expedient) outcome of any legislative and judicial process which is itself constitutional or otherwise determined to be procedurally acceptable. Such a principle – if it were itself acceptable – might justify existing inequalities. Other principles of justice act as more direct constraints on acceptable outcomes of the political process. I will urge we accept certain principles of justice which do act as direct, substantive constraints on the political process and on political expediency.

Rights to health care

Faced with significant inequalities in the distribution of health-care services, many start by invoking the notion of individual rights and assert that a violation of basic rights is involved. They believe that a just redesign of health-care institutions can be effected by appealing to such notions. In doing so, some mean to claim justiciable welfare rights. Such claims may implicitly assume that health care is more like certain other social goods, say certain liberties, to which we assert right claims, than it is like other goods, such as computers or automobiles, to which we do not (except as they may derive from property rights in general). However, others who assert a right to health care have in mind no particular theoretical account of its foundations – its grounds or justification – or its limits. The assertion of a right may simply be the natural or only way that comes to mind to argue for just reform and to insist that the health-care system eliminate the particular inequalities found objectionable. After all, if we can agree to acknowledge such a right, then perhaps we can unite behind the desired reform, which may be a proposal for a more comprehensive national health insurance scheme.

One problem with this somewhat pragmatic appeal to rights is that it does not carry us past our disagreements and uncertainties about the scope and limits of such right claims. And, of course, the pragmatism leaves us well short of determining which beliefs and theories count as an adequate justification for them. My working assumption in this essay is that the appeal to a right to health care is not an appropriate starting point for an inquiry into just health care. Rights are not moral fruits that spring up from bare earth, fully ripened, without cultivation. Rather, we are justified in claiming a right to health care only if it can be harvested from an acceptable, general theory of distributive justice, or, more particularly, from a theory of justice for health care. Such a theory would tell us which kinds of right claims are legitimately viewed as rights. It would also help us specify the scope and limits of justified right claims.

Taken this generally, my working assumption borders on a philosophical commonplace, despite the more general 'lay' practice of claiming rights wherever strong interests are felt. The utilitarian countenances right claims only if they can be derived, at an appropriate level within his theory, from utilitarian considerations. A libertarian, like Nozick (1974), or a contractarian, like Rawls (1971), allows them only if they are compatible with the rest of the general distributive theory. And intuitionists and some natural rights theorists will countenance a right to health care only if the claim can be justified given their theory of how we come to know or discover such rights. Much of the work of this book, especially in chapters 2 and 3, will reveal what support of this commonplace commits us to in the way of theory construction.

I would like to motivate my support of the commonplace by pointing to some vagaries about the notion of a right to health care. I have already indicated that health care is an exceedingly broad notion, at least as I am using it. I include not only certain personal medical services but also a range of health-related services, including public health and preventive measures. Thus claiming a right to health care is excessively vague unless the services being claimed are further specified.

I take the expression, 'right to health', to be elliptical for the expression, 'right to health care', but this needs some comment. Some suggest that a 'right to health' is a negative right – a claim that others refrain from actions that threaten health. One might then try to see how much health care – as I use the term – might be required on the basis of this negative right. But advocates of a right to health often treat it *both* as negative and positive, requiring people to take positive steps to improve conditions that threaten health, so forcing the expression into this negative mold does not capture what is being said. Some philosophers have remarked that the expression 'right to health' embodies a confusion about the kind of thing which can be the object of a right claim. Health is an inappropriate object, but health care, action which promotes health, is appropriate. If my poor health is not the result of anyone's doing – or failing to do – something for, or to, me that might have prevented, or might cure, my condition, then it is hard to see how any right of mine is violated. The issue seems more pressing if we embed a concern for equality in the expression, claiming, say, an 'equal right to health', or worse, 'a right to equal health'. The latter, and perhaps the former, suggest that if everything possible were done to maintain my health, but it failed anyway, then some right to equality would still be violated. Unless this is a misleading way to press a demand for compensation for damages (not insurance), it is hard to make sense of it at all.

Someone who claims a right to health, therefore, should be understood to be claiming that certain individuals or groups (or society as a whole) are obliged to perform certain actions which promote or maintain his good health and are obliged to refrain from actions which interfere with it. The reference to *health* should be construed as a handy way to characterize *functionally* the category of actions about which one is making a claim. This classification allows us to see why some advocates have insisted on a 'right to *health*' and not just on a 'right to (certain) health-care services'. They want their right claim to include a broad range of actions that affect health – say, protection of the environment – even if these actions are not normally construed as health-care services.

In a widely anthologized article, Charles Fried (1975, 1976) complains about the expression 'right to health' through an analogy to the right to free speech. The right to free speech, he suggests, is a person's right to be free of certain constraints on the speaking he wishes to do. Who one is or what one wants to say should not be bases for denying a person the right to speak. Such equality of free speech, he urges, should not imply that all have an equal right to be effective in their speech, say, by having equal access to the mass media. That would be the same confusion, he insists, as thinking that guaranteeing equal access to health care implies we are committed to guaranteeing equality of health.

Fried's analogy is multiply confused. First, the appropriate free-speech analogue to guaranteeing equality of access to health care *would* be to guarantee people equality of access to the means of disseminating their views, e.g., the mass media. But this is just what Fried denies an equal right to free speech involves. One problem here is that Fried construes freedom of speech as a negative liberty which imposes constraints on the ways others may interfere with our speech. In contrast, the right to equal access to health care requires a positive contribution of others to our health maintenance – through their providing or financing the services.

Second, Fried confuses guaranteeing equality of access to the means of delivering speech with guaranteeing equally *effective* speech. Those who might protest that Fried's construal of freedom of speech fails to guarantee real opportunity to speak are not demanding a right to be equally effective. They assert only a right to the *opportunity* to be equally effective in their speech. Fried, not the proponent of equal access to the means of speech, seems to conflate the opportunity to be effective with a guarantee of effectiveness.

Finally, if the equal right to health care were made strictly parallel to Fried's description of an equal (negative) right to speech, then all it would require is that one not be discriminated against in his effort to seek health care because of *who* he is. But I might still be denied access to health-care service if I could not pay for it, just as I may be denied access to a full-page ad in the *New York Times* if I cannot pay for it.

Despite the confused analogy, however, Fried's main point is correct: a right claim to equal *health* is best construed as a demand for equality of access or entitlement to health *services* – where these may include preventive and environmental measures. In fairness to Fried, his way of characterizing free speech is not idiosyncratic but is the standard analysis. My complaint is partly with that analysis (see Daniels 1975).

Those who claim a right to health care often gloss over another important distinction. They may intend only a system-relative claim to health care: whatever health-care services are available to any within the given health-care system should be accessible to all. Such a claim may be met by removing services accessible only to a privileged few from the system. This equality of access demand is not a demand for an independently determined level of health care, only for equality relative to whatever level of services the relevant system provides. Contrast this right claim with one that requires that some specifiable range of health-care services be made available to all (and perhaps that any additional services be made available to some only if they are available to all). Such a substantive demand might require specific expansion or contraction of the existing health-care system, not just in terms of *who* is treated, but in terms of *what services* are offered. The two right claims may have vastly different implications for reform of a given system; also, it is not obvious which demand is more 'radical' or 'conservative'.

Quite different theoretical issues may underlie justification of the two different right claims – and this would be true even if they happen to require exactly the same reform of a given health care system! The right claim to equal access may ultimately best be defended by considerations that depend, not on the special nature of health or health care, but rather on more general considerations of equality itself. For example, it might be argued that the public nature of health-care institutions – their dependence on public subsidies for training and facilities – requires that each person is due 'equal protection'. This argument is compatible with there being no basic right to any particular level of health services (as with the legal right to public education, where 'due process' requires equality in its provision, but not that it be provided). In contrast, a right claim to some particular level of health care may require for its justification a theory of basic needs (of the sort discussed in chapters 2 and 3). Moreover, a right claim to equality of health care at a level that exceeds satisfaction of our 'basic needs' may require a different type of justification – it may be justifiable only on moral grounds which are different from rights to have basic needs met (see Chapter 4, pp. 83–5). In general, right claims to different kinds of health services may require different justifications (the issue is sometimes fudged by inflating the notion of needs).

Talk about a 'right to health care' can thus imply quite different things, both with regard to the *scope* of what is being claimed and with regard to the type of justification it needs. This fact may be more perspicuously represented by the following *sketch* of an analysis of a right to health care. Claiming a 'right to health care' reduces to a composite of other rights and claims, among them: (1) society has the duty to its members to allocate an adequate share of its total resources to health-related needs, such as the protection of the environment and the provision of medical services; (2) society has the duty to provide a just allocation of different types of health services, taking into account the competing claims of different types of health needs; (3) each person is entitled to a fair share of such services, where a 'fair share' includes an answer to the question, Who should pay for the services?

But what share of total resources is adequate for servicing health needs? How should such a share be divided among the different types of health needs? What is an individual's fair share of such health services? Asserting that there is a 'right to health care' answers none of these questions. It only brings us face to face with them. Even if all that is ordinarily intended by the assertion of a right is that citizens have a claim on the state for much routine health care, too much is left indeterminate. In particular, claiming this vaguely specified right does not help us settle the complex problems about how health services are to be financed, let alone what they should be. National health insurance is not an immediate consequence of asserting a right to health care. To answer the difficult questions suggested by this sketch of what a right to health care might include, we need a systematic theory of distributive justice for health-related needs. That is what underlies the philosophical commonplace I noted earlier about the importance of systematic theory.

General theories of justice

We are seeking principles of justice to govern the design of basic health-care institutions, but we must dig much deeper than direct appeals to health-care rights. To specify a right to health care – and to justify it – we need a more comprehensive account of distributive justice for health care. A natural place to seek such an account is to examine general theories of justice, which have been a major area of philosophical investigation during the last fifteen years. Libertarian, utilitarian, and contractarian theories, for example, all contain more general principles governing the distribution of rights, opportunities, and wealth. Perhaps the principles we seek for health care are but straightforward applications of more general principles from such a theory. If we agreed, for example, that one of these general theories was the preferred one, then we might expect its application to health problems would give us the desired principles for our health-care institutions. Even if we could not agree which general theory was best, by great good luck it might still turn out that the theories do not diverge with regard to distributive principles for health care. For example, the connection of health care to the protection of liberty and its connection to the maximization of utility might be such that libertarianism and utilitarianism agree on distributive principles for health care even if they agree on other such principles, which I think is unlikely (for an excellent review, see Buchanan 1981).

Unfortunately the issue is not quite so simple, for we run into a general issue in ethical theory: How should we 'test' the adequacy of a theory of justice? If one of the theories contained principles which matched our considered judgments about what just health care required, we might think it the most plausible theory, though even here mere match with considered judgments is not all there is to justifying a moral theory (Daniels 1979c, 1980). But the problem is more complicated. It is much more likely that we do not all agree what justice requires in health care, so that some theories will match the views of some people best, while others best match those of other people. The strategy of choosing the best theory of just health care by seeing which general theory yields results closest to 'our' views is not going to yield a unique answer. Somehow, we must find arguments which at the same time make one theory seem better and give us reasons to revise our initial considered moral judgments about just health care. But this quite general problem of theory acceptance in ethics is not one it is appropriate to try to solve here, and I say little about it in what follows.

I turn instead to the optimistic assumption that we know how to apply general distributive theories to problems in the design of health-care institutions. I certainly shared this assumption when I began work on justice in health care. My first effort (Daniels 1979b) was to examine a theory that seemed amenable to generating a right to health care, Rawls's (1971) theory of justice as fairness, to see what implications it had for health care. After examining four approaches to extending the theory, I drew the rather pessimistic conclusion that there was no very promising way to apply it to the design of health-care institutions. I had learned that there was a central difficulty with the strategy I was pursuing.

In order to apply such general theories to health care, we need to know what kind of a social good health care is. We need to know what its functions and effects are and why we might think these make it differ in moral importance from other things which improve our quality of life in various ways. An analysis of this problem cannot be provided by appeal to the theories of justice themselves. What looks like the natural way, from within each general theory, to make such an application, usually presupposes a particular view of the kind of social good health care is. One way to see the point is to ask whether health-care services, say personal medical services, should be viewed as we view other *commodities* – things we agree to buy and sell in a market – in our society. Should we allow *inequalities* in the access to health-care services to vary with whatever economic inequalities are permissible according to more general principles of distributive justice? Or is health care 'special' and not to be assimilated to other commodities, like cars or personal computers, whose distribution we allow to be governed by market exchanges among economic unequals? Put generally, this is the question, Is health care special?

The difficulty, I believe, can be overcome, and the strategy to be followed in the early chapters of this book is to focus first on this general question about the nature of health care. To answer it, we will have to analyze the notion of health-care *needs* and to distinguish needs from mere *preferences*. We shall explain the moral importance of these needs by noting their effects on *opportunity*. This result suggests that a general principle of justice governing the distribution of opportunity can be extended so that it governs the design and function of health-care institutions and practices. Before taking up these theoretical issues in chapters 2 and 3, it will be useful to confirm that the question, Is health care special?, is really a central one. To do so, it will be useful to examine how public controversy about health-care delivery focuses, in diverse ways, on this question.

Some public policy issues

Issues of distributive justice, and controversy about the nature of health care as a social good, lie at the center of much current debate about health-care delivery. Demands for more equal access to personal medical services, which shaped US health-care financing reforms in the Johnson and Nixon period, were clearly influenced by the view that health care is special and should be treated differently from many other social goods. Specifically, even in a society that tolerates (and glorifies) significant and pervasive inequalities in the distribution of most social goods, many people feel there are reasons of justice for distributing health care more equally. But views about the special nature of health care have also played a role in recent efforts to regulate capital investment in health care, to constrain health-care costs through cost-sharing and budget-capping proposals, and to restrict the autonomy of providers in order to insure cost control and quality accountability. Consider some examples.

Access to care

The issue of access to health care is really two issues: access for whom? and access to what? To many the first question has a very simple answer. There should be access to medical services for anyone in *medical need*. Specifically, non-medical features of individuals – their race, sex, geographical location, or ability to pay – should not determine whether or not they have access to care. Sometimes the point is asserted as a right claim: individuals have a right to health care and a wrong is done to them if their medical needs are not met. Minimally, what is demanded is that certain non-medical barriers to care should be eliminated, e.g., that society has an obligation to provide medical services on the basis of medical need, regardless of ability to pay or other non-medical factors. As I noted earlier, Medicaid and Medicare can be seen as explicit responses to this view that health care is special, but so too was the effort to fund neighborhood health centers and mental health centers, and the effort through various programs to place physicians and other providers in medically 'underserved' areas.

To support such a view, some offer what we may call the Argument from Function: (1) The function of medical services is to meet medical needs; (2) The sole rational basis for distributing a good that functions to meet certain needs is in proportion to those needs; (3) Therefore, the sole rational basis for distributing medical services is to meet medical needs; (4) Health status should determine access to medical services. (I discuss an application of this argument in Chapter 4.) But this argument will not do as it stands. The *function* of food processors is to meet vegetable slicing needs. But no one insists that willingness to pay for food processors is an inappropriate basis for distributing them and that access to them should be subsidized for those who cannot pay. Similarly, no one insists on a 'right' to the best brand of food processor. Clearly, if the Argument from Function has any merit, it is only with regard to a special class of needs and things that function to meet them. Similarly, if there is a right to health care, it is because of the *kind* of social good health care is, the *kind* of needs it meets. (Nozick (1974:233–5) makes a related point but draws a different conclusion; so too does Walzer (1983:88).) We are back to our question, Is health care special?

It is useful to put this recent concern about access to health care in historical perspective, for health care was not always thought so special. Prior to the emergence of scientific, efficacious medicine, medical care had relatively little effect on health status. (Major decreases in mortality and morbidity in the late nineteenth and early twentieth centuries were primarily the results of better nutrition and sanitation, although scientific medicine usually gets the lion's share of credit.) Access to medical care was clearly less important or urgent, for physicians had little effect on the course of most diseases, however important the comfort, caring, and occasional placebo effect they may have provided. But the increased scientific and technological basis for medical services not only increased efficacy, altering the doctor–patient relationship in the process, but it dramatically increased its costs. As a result, access to it became far more difficult for large classes of people beginning in the middle part of this century.

A rational way to distribute the burden of facing such expensive but important services is to pool the risks and costs through public or private insurance schemes. In the US, private, 'third-party payer' schemes grew after the Second World War to replace a system of direct patient payments to physicians and hospitals. This growth took place largely in the form of 'tax-sheltered' group insurance plans for employees of large corporations covered by union contracts. But insurance does not help the poor or near poor unless they can pay premiums, and by the mid 1960s the gaps in insurance coverage were glaring. I have already noted that important gaps remain, even after the establishment of Medicaid and Medicare.

But as public policy has moved in the direction of reducing some important barriers to access to care, it has had to face more directly the question, *access to what*? Health-care services are *non-homogeneous*. Some services save or extend lives; others improve its quality. Some functions are more important, more basic, or more urgent than others. Should we guarantee access to *all* the services offered anywhere in our health-care system? Is there a social obligation to provide access to all services or only to a basic minimum? Mrs Nadir, a mother in Boston's Bromley Heath housing project who receives 'welfare' payments for the poor, is not fed or sheltered as well as Mr Zenith, a hospital administrator living in expensive Chestnut Hill. Should Medicaid nevertheless guarantee that her access to health care be equal to his?

It is when we get to the details of public policy concerning access that we see the tension in our attitudes toward the special nature of health care. On the one hand, Medicaid was introduced as a system for reimbursing regular health-care providers, not just some special public welfare layer of providers, in order to avoid establishing a 'two-class' system. In theory, Mrs Nadir would be able to buy health care of the same quality – from the same providers – as Mr Zenith, even though the food stamps (vouchers) she has do not let her set the same table he does. In part, this difference in our welfare system for food and health care reflects a difference between food and health care: it seems easier to draw up a budget for meeting basic nutritional needs than it is to characterize basic health-care needs, and it seems easier to characterize nutritional needs and distinguish them from mere preferences or tastes than it is to distinguish health-care needs from mere preferences. But it is also possible that some people – reasonably or not – think health care so special or urgent that they insist it be distributed even more equally than food.

The controversy about how special health care is is revealed when we see that Medicaid has important reimbursement features which are concessions to the power and autonomy of medical providers. Physicians are *not required* to accept Medicaid patients, so many providers are, after all, inaccessible to the very poor. Moreover, the very low reimbursement rates for certain services give providers an incentive not to accept Medicaid patients – higher rates can be obtained through other third-party payers, including Medicare. Medicaid expresses, at best, an ambiguous statement about the specialness of health care. Similarly, current efforts to control rising health-care costs through increased cost-sharing also suggest that many legislators believe the mechanisms for marketing other commodities are also appropriate for health care. For example, out-of-pocket payments for medical care by Medicare patients have risen dramatically since its inception. Again, there is a mixed message here about how special health care is, though interpreting this message is complicated by various factors (I return to these issues in Chapter 4).

Resource allocation and rationing

The question, *access to what?*, already raises some issues about resource allocation and rationing, but the problem is more general. So far, in inquiring about access, we have taken the medical services provided in our health-care system as a given. But we can ask an even more basic question: What kinds of services should the system provide? And, if not all services can be provided because resources are restricted, then which are the most important to provide? Should we concentrate on delivering a liver transplant to a jaundiced infant and an artificial heart to an adult in his prime? Or should we restore recent cuts in funding for prenatal and maternal care? Or should we revitalize enforcement of existing workplace health hazard regulations governing lead, asbestos, and cotton dust, which has been lax because of the anti-regulation stance of recent US federal legislatures and administrations?

In general, many critics of our health-care system have argued that it is biased in favor of high-technology acute care and that it ignores preventive measures, which are of comparable or greater importance, even if less glamorous or profitable. It is safe to say that cost-constraint measures, such as the effort to plan capital expansion of health-care facilities regionally and to require 'certificates of need' before costly expansion is permitted, have had little effect on the priority given acute care. Other critics complain of a similar bias in favor of acute care over other kinds of personal care and social support services. Thus Mr Styx, dying of colon cancer, has had lavished on his seventy-eight-year-old body the full range of exotic, hospital-based care which his physician has ordered and his family has insisted on. But Mrs Frail, who is seventy-five and partially disabled, faces a critical absence of adequate long-term care or home-care services. Similarly, while Mr Styx was having his death prolonged, eligibility requirements for Medicaid recipients were being raised and budget ceilings imposed. We seem more willing to impose cutbacks on a program most of whose recipients are poor young women and children, or to cut back on preventive measures, like nutritional programs in the schools or environmental protection and enforcement, than to alter our practices with regard to the chronically ill and dying elderly. The issue here is not just one of old versus young, but reflects a prominent view in our class-divided society about who are the 'deserving' poor.

Even if we decide that access to health care should be based on need for services, which needs should we meet when we cannot meet all? Here we need guidance in deciding which health-care services are *more special* than others. This question is not faced squarely by current proposals to control Medicare costs by increasing the proportion of 'cost-sharing' or 'out-of-pocket' payments. Mrs Angst, who was hospitalized twice last year for brief periods, is frightened that she will be forced to 'stick it out' at home when the next episode of her illness strikes.

Provider responsibilities and autonomy
Just as there is no 'free lunch', and whatever health care society provides must be paid for by someone, so too it must be prepared and served by someone. Issues of access and demands about resource allocation both have a bearing on the traditional roles and responsibilities of health-care providers. We already saw this point when we observed that current public subsidy programs in the US, such as Medicaid, do *not* require physicians to accept patients covered by them: the physician has the power to determine his patient mix in ways that suit his interests. Moreover, low Medicaid reimbursement rates, an effort at cost-containment, serve as a disincentive for providers to accept the very patients for whom access is most a problem.

This tension between protecting provider autonomy, power, and interests and treating health care as *special* is clearly not resolved in many delivery contexts. If people believe government must guarantee access to medical services to the rural and inner-city poor, then some physicians, nurses, and technicians must be there to deliver them. If people insist that certain medical services must be available, such as more primary care for the elderly, then some physicians will have to have geriatric training and forego other specialities. If people believe that diagnostic and therapeutic services must be delivered in a 'cost-effective' fashion, and they insist physicians take such costs into account in their medical decision-making, then we may have to modify the traditional view that physicians should do everything possible to pursue their patients' best interests.

These examples point to possible conflicts between traditional liberties, privileges, and responsibilities of providers and the requirements of justice. It is the belief of many that health care is special which forces us to examine the reasons we have for extending to providers their traditional autonomy and power. These issues will be discussed in greater detail in Chapter 6, but it is enough here to see that concern and controversy about the specialness of health care is at the core of public policy debate about the powers of providers.

Health hazard regulation

The special nature of health care is an issue in preventive and not just acute-care contexts. The Occupational Safety and Health Act of 1970 calls for eliminating health risks to workers to the extent it is 'technologically feasible' to do so. This requirement has been the focus of much controversy and litigation. Advocates of stringent regulation see this limit as a vital feature of preventive regulation, for it seems to place the protection of health above direct calculations of the cost-effectiveness of undertaking particular protective measures, and thus avoids the interminable debates about costs that would take place between employees and regulators. Critics of regulative approaches argue that all such regulative measures should be tested to make sure they are cost-beneficial. Further, they insist that such rigorous standards may value the protection of health at a far higher dollar level than it is reasonable to do so. Indeed, they suggest workers themselves might well believe that where such measures are instituted at the expense of wage and benefit packages or job security, they may constitute an unduly paternalistic protection of worker health. Health protection may be special to the regulators but not so special to the very workers it is intended to protect.

Here, and elsewhere in health-care contexts, we have a challenge raised to those who insist that health care is special and that there are social obligations to provide it. The risks individuals want to take with their lives and their health are also a matter for *individual* determination: the consequences of risk-taking are, after all, consequences for individuals. So we need to be clear just when protecting health interferes in unjustifiable ways with individual liberty. In the acute-care context, there has been much discussion of this conflict, and there is an extensive body of literature on paternalism and informed consent. But there has been relatively little discussion of these issues in the public health context. I return in chapters 7 and 8 to discuss these claims that, however special health care is, it cannot be allowed to interfere with individual liberty or opportunity.

Is health care special?

Some of the public policy controversy noted in these examples reflects a simple conflict of interest between providers and consumers. Providers have vested interests in a system that has traditionally guaranteed them enormous power and autonomy, as well as healthy incomes and profits (see Starr 1982). Some of the controversy about these issues reflects class conflict: if redistributive financing of health care is a social obligation, it is the middle and upper income groups who will bear the burden of increased costs. If workplaces are to made cleaner and safer, it may cut into profits. But these sources of economic and political conflict are also interwoven with moral disagreement.

Much of the controversy in these public policy examples reflects conflicting views about the nature of health care as a social good or about the requirements of justice in general. Even in the US, which has a much less egalitarian health-care system than many other industrialized capitalist or socialist countries, there is the belief that health care should be distributed more equally than many other social goods. What explains this special importance or urgency we attribute to health care? Why should preferences for health care be treated differently from other kinds of preferences? Is there a function or effect of health care which explains the importance we attribute to it? Can we explain our belief that some kinds of health care are more important than others? Does the explanation for the special importance of health care show the relationship between health care and other, general kinds of social goods which are the subject matter of general theories of distributive justice? I have used the question, Is health care special?, as shorthand for this constellation of questions about the nature of health care as a social good. Answering them will require a theory of health-care needs.

2 · Health-care needs

Why a theory of health-care needs?

A theory of health-care needs should serve two central purposes. First, it should illuminate the sense in which many of us think health care is *special* and should be treated differently from other social goods. A theory of health-care needs should show how these needs are connected to other central notions in an acceptable theory of justice. It should help us see what kind of social good health care is by properly relating it to social goods whose importance is similar and for which we may have a clearer grasp of appropriate distributive principles.

Second, such a theory should provide a basis for distinguishing the more from the less important among the many kinds of things health care does for us. It should tell us which health-care services are more special than others – which is why I start with a theory of needs, not services. Thus a broad category of health-services functions to improve quality of life, not to extend or save it. Some of these services restore or compensate for diminished capacities and functions; others improve life quality in other ways. We do draw distinctions about the urgency and importance of such services (though not always in these terms). Our theory of health-care needs should provide a basis for a reasonable set of such distinctions. If we can assume (1) that there is some scarcity of health-care resources, and (2) that we cannot or should not rely just on market mechanisms to allocate these resources, then we need such a theory to guide macro decisions about priorities among health-care needs.

These two assumptions may draw some fire. First, people are quick to point out that scarcity in resources for human services is caused by what they believe are frivolous uses of resources elsewhere in the economy, such as on bubble-gum or MX missiles. A rational economy would not force us to treat health-care resources as scarce. Though I am in sympathy with the feeling behind this complaint, I will ignore it here. Indeed, it rests on distinctions about the importance of different needs a theory of needs should illuminate, and even such a rational economy, unless it were the Garden of Eden, would have to make choices in which needs are weighed against needs. Second, my inquiry does not derive its importance from the fact that medical markets are non-ideal in ways familiar to economists. My analysis has a bearing on the deeper moral issue of whether health care ought to be marketed even in an ideal market.

In short, a theory of health-care needs must come to grips with two widely held judgments: that there is something especially important about health care, and that some kinds of health care are more important than others. The philosophical task is to assess, explain, and justify or modify these distinctions we make about the importance of different wants, interests, or needs. Before turning to this task, it will be useful to consider one further objection to my strategy.

Can we avoid talk about needs?

Many people view the notion of needs as vague and problematic and would prefer we avoid talk about them in favor of talk about preferences and strength of preferences. For example, the latter are the notions given prominence in welfare economics. Consider the following Argument From Fair Shares, which is intended to show that we can avoid talk about health care needs:[1] Suppose we agreed to abide by a particular theory of distributive justice, and we knew that we each had a *fair income share* according to that theory. Suppose further that there was a *competitive medical market* in which a variety of insurance schemes could be bought, much as many US employees have a choice between enrolling in one of several pre-paid group plans (health maintenance organizations) or various traditional insurance schemes (Blue Cross/Blue Shield, Aetna, etc.). Then we could protect ourselves against the risk of needing health care through voluntary purchase of insurance. We would each be responsible for buying insurance at a level of protection we desired. No one, except children or the congenitally handicapped, would have a *claim* on *social* resources to meet health-care needs. Each would be entitled – whatever his needs – only to what he was prudent enough to purchase from his fair income share, though charity might intervene to keep people from dying in the streets. In this market (so the argument assumes), demand, understood as our preferences for different insurance

---

[1] I paraphrase Charles Fried (1978: 126ff.). I here ignore an issue of paternalism which Fried may have wanted to pursue but which is better raised when fair shares are clearly large enough to purchase a reasonable insurance package. Should the premium purchase be compulsory?

packages, will be *efficiently* matched to supply, understood as resources and services.[2]

Such a system would provide protection against expensive but rare needs for health care, for which relatively inexpensive insurance could be bought. Similarly, common but inexpensive services could either be risk-shared through insurance or paid for out-of-pocket without great sacrifice, whichever might be preferred. But expensive and potentially common 'needs' – for example, to be provided with artificial hearts or dialysis – would not become a drain on social resources. Individuals who want protection against facing these 'needs' would have to buy expensive insurance out of their own fair shares. This way of meeting individual preferences for health services would not create a bottomless pit into which we are forced to drain all available social resources. No one could claim a right to have extravagant 'needs' met – unless he had already bought appropriate insurance. Most importantly, in such a system we would need no general theory about which health-care needs we have social obligations to meet. The scheme allows individual preferences to resolve all resource allocation questions through a medical market.

This Argument From Fair Shares fails to show that we can do without a theory of health-care needs. Suppose we define a *reasonable* health-care insurance package as one which meets the health-care needs or risks it is rational for a prudent person to insure against. Though we know little else about 'fair income shares', it seems plausible to insist that an income share is *fair only* if it is adequate to permit the purchase of a reasonable insurance package. If an income share is too small to cover the premium for a reasonable insurance package, then the share is inadequate: it is *unfair* that whoever has it cannot buy reasonable insurance. So, to know whether income shares are fair, we must know that they can buy reasonable coverage. But to know what coverage is reasonable, we need to know what health-care needs it is prudent to insure against. Thus we must talk about health-care needs after all! We cannot reduce the problem of just health care distribution to the problem of just income distribution, for the latter *presupposes income adequate to meet reasonable needs*.

My response to the Argument From Fair Shares is itself open to the following objection: There is no level of insurance which is 'prudent' for all persons. What is prudent for an individual, so the objection goes,

---

[2] Reasons why medical markets are not efficient are given in Arrow's (1963) classic paper, which traces their anomalies to the uncertainties in them.

depends on his resources, needs, and preferences. The rich will not insure against all risks and the poor will prudently accept greater risks. So there is no sense to the notion of a 'reasonable' health-care insurance package since there is no one package any prudent person would want to buy.

The kernel of truth to this objection is that prudent choices will vary with resource constraints, though not as drastically as is claimed. If the objection were the full story, then we would have to treat all cases of people excluded from certain markets – for food, clothing, shelter, and health care, for example – not as instances of 'market failure' calling for income redistribution or aid-in-kind, but as instances of prudent choices made by the poor not to buy these goods. Our notion of prudence has a structure to it which reflects our concern for meeting certain basic needs, and we cannot use the notion in a way that ignores the difference between being able to participate in a market for those needs and being excluded from it. Indeed, we would probably be correct in saying that exclusion from the market for those needs denies people the chance to act prudently. For the purpose of my argument, then, we might acknowledge that the notion of a prudent person is hypothetical or abstract: not just any rational choice, given drastic resource limitations, counts as the choice a prudent person would make. My original conclusion still stands: The notion of a fair income share presupposes income adequate to meet reasonable health-care needs.

A theory of health-care needs is implicit in the insurance scheme approach in yet another way. The approach puts health-care needs on a par with other wants and preferences, allowing them to compete for resources within a medical market. But this stance *is* a view of health-care needs: it treats them as one kind of preference among many, with no special claim on social resources except that which derives from *strength of preference*, measured by willingness to pay for insurance. To be sure, where strength of preference is high, needs may be met, but strength of preference may vary in ways that fail to reflect the importance we ought to (and usually do) ascribe to health care. Such a market view needs justification, and it is not a justification simply to point to the existence of such a market.

Sometimes needs-based theories are criticized because they give us too small a claim on social resources, providing only a floor on deprivation. In contrast, the objection embedded in the Argument From Fair Shares warns against granting precedence to the satisfaction of needs because we then allow too great a claim on social resources. I return later to consider how a needs-based theory can avoid this problem. It is worth noting that needs-based theories cut two ways. Egalitarians use them to criticize the failure of inegalitarian systems to meet basic human needs. Inegalitarians use them to justify providing only minimally for basic needs while allowing significant inequalities above the floor. In what follows I will not try to respond to the inegalitarian by expanding the category of needs to consume such inequalities.

Not all preferences are created equal

The conclusion of the preceding argument is that we must talk about health-care *needs* if we are to explain what is special about health care and thus be in a position to give an account of distributive justice for it. But the concept of needs has been in philosophical disrepute, and with good reason. The concept seems both too weak and too strong to get us very far toward a theory of distributive justice. Too many things become needs, and too few. And finding a middle ground seems to involve many of the issues of distributive justice one might hope to resolve by appeal to a clear notion of needs.

It is easy to see why too many things appear to be needs, for the concept is opportunistic. Without abuse of language, we refer to the means necessary to reach any of our goals as 'needs'. To reawaken memories of Miller's, the neighborhood delicatessen of my childhood, I need only the smell of sour pickles in a barrel. To stay at Cape Cod in August, I need a reservation. For emphasis, we often refer to things we simply desire or want as things we need: my son Noah insists he *needs* the latest space-fantasy action figure. Sometimes we invoke a distinction between noun and verb uses of 'need', so that not everything we say we need counts as *a need*. But any conceptual distinction we might draw between noun and verb uses depends on our purposes and the context, and it would still require an explanation of the kind sought here. Since the concept of needs is so unabashedly expansive, the problem of the importance of needs seems to reduce to the problem of the importance or urgency of preferences or wants in general. (I leave aside the fact that not all the things we need are even expressed as preferences.)

Just as not all preferences are on a par – some are more important than others – so too not all the things we say we need are. It is possible to pick out various things we say we need, including needs for health care, which play a special role and are given special moral weight in a variety of moral contexts. If, in requesting $200, I appeal to my friend's duty to act beneficently, I will most likely get a quite different reaction if I tell him I need the money to get some root-canal work than if I tell him I need the money to go to the Brooklyn neighborhood of my childhood to smell pickles in a barrel. Indeed, it is not likely to matter in his assessment of *obligations* that I strongly *prefer* to go to Brooklyn. Nor is it likely to matter that I insist I feel a great *need* to reawaken memories of my childhood – I am overcome by nostalgia. Of course, he might give me the money for either purpose, but if he gives it so I can smell pickles, we would probably say he is not doing it out of any duty at all, that he feels no obligation, that it is just friendly generosity. Similarly, if my appeal was directed to some (even Utopian) social welfare agency rather than my friend, it would adopt criteria other than my mere preferences in assessing the importance of my request.

Part of what is going on here is that in certain contexts we use an *objective* rather than a *subjective* criterion in assessing well-being (Scanlon 1975). We need *some* such criterion to assess the importance of competing claims on resources in a variety of moral contexts. A *subjective* criterion uses the individual's own assessment of how well-off he is with and without the claimed benefit to determine the importance of his preference or claim. An *objective* criterion invokes a measure of importance independent of an individual's own assessment, i.e., independent of the individual's strength of preference for the benefit. In contexts of distributive justice and other moral contexts, we *in fact* appeal to some *objective* criteria of well-being. But it is important to see that it is not just a question of rejecting subjective criteria in favor of objective ones, say on the grounds that we can have better knowledge of them. The rejection is not epistemological. What counts is the *kind* of objective criteria we invoke.

Suppose we adopted a view central to utilitarian (and egoist) moral theory, that how well-off an individual is depends on the level of satisfaction of *all* his various preferences. In other words, how well-off someone is depends on how much of what he wants in life he gets. This view requires that we be concerned with the *full* or *complete* range of an individual's preferences and their satisfaction. Suppose further that we could agree intersubjectively on how satisfied or happy individuals are: we could agree, that is, on a 'social utility function'. Such a full-range standard would be objective and not merely subjective. But that objectivity would not be sufficient grounds for using the *complete* scale to assess the importance of certain preferences or to measure the relevant notion of well-being in various moral contexts. Indeed, in our actual moral practice, especially where we are concerned with issues of distributive justice, we do not use any such full-range or complete scale of well-being.

What is distinctive about the scale we do use for measuring well-being and assessing the importance of an individual's preference is that it does not include or reflect the full range of kinds of preferences people have. Rather, we use a *truncated* or *selective* scale.[3] The satisfaction of preferences falling into certain categories, e.g., the satisfaction of certain needs, weighs heavily in the truncated scale; the satisfaction of certain other preferences may not be counted or viewed as relevant at all. It is agreement with the use of this truncated scale that would lead me to admit that the root canal, but not the smell of pickles in a barrel, is a more important preference of mine, is something I *really* need (assuming the dentist is right). It is a need and not a 'mere desire'. My admission is an awareness that some of the things we claim to need fall into special categories which give them a weightier moral claim in contexts involving the distribution of resources, depending, of course, on how well off we already are within those categories of need (Scanlon 1975:660).

So far I have not shown that we *ought* to use such a truncated scale. I have only claimed that in our moral practice we use one in favor of a full-range or complete scale of well-being. That is, I have said something about what our moral practice is, not what that practice ought to be. I shall return in Chapter 3 to argue more directly in favor of the appropriateness of a selective scale, but it will be helpful first to continue our examination of the concept of needs already embodied in these moral practices. Our philosophical task will be to characterize the relevant categories of needs in a way that *explains* two central properties they have. First, they are *objectively ascribable*. We can ascribe them to someone even if he does not realize he has them or even if he denies he does because his preferences run contrary to his needs. Second, and of greater interest to us, these needs are *objectively important*: we attach a special weight to claims based on them in a variety of moral contexts. Our

---

[3] The difference might not be in the *extent* but in the *content* of the scale. An objective full-range satisfaction scale might be constructed so that some categories of (key) preferences are lexically primary to others; preferences not included on a truncated scale never enter the full-range scale except to break ties among those equally well-off on key preferences. Such a scale may avoid my worries expressed above, but it needs a rationale for its ranking. The objection raised here to full-range satisfaction measures applies, I believe, with equal force to happiness of enjoyment measures of the sort Richard Brandt (1979: Ch. 14) defends.

task is to characterize the class of things we need which has these properties and to do so in a way that explains their importance.

Needs and species-typical functioning

One plausible suggestion for distinguishing the relevant needs from all the things we can come to need is David Braybrooke's (1968) distinction between 'course-of-life needs' and 'adventitious needs'. *Course-of-life needs* are those needs which people 'have all through their lives or at certain stages of life through which all must pass'. *Adventitious needs* are the things we need because of the particular contingent projects, which may be long-term ones, on which we embark. Human course-of-life needs would include food, shelter, clothing, exercise, rest, companionship, a mate (in one's prime, says Braybrooke), and so on. Such needs are not themselves deficiencies, for example, when they are anticipated. But a deficiency with respect to them 'endangers the normal functioning of the subject of need *considered as a member of a natural species*' (Braybrooke 1968:90, my emphasis).[4] A related suggestion can be found in J. H. McCloskey's discussion of the human and personal needs we appeal to in political argument. He argues that needs 'relate to what it would be detrimental to us to lack, *where the detrimental is explained by reference to our natures as men and specific persons*' (McCloskey 1976:2f., my emphasis).[5] Thus course-of-life needs are important when we abstract from many particular choices and preferences individuals might make or have.

Our hypothesis, then, is that the needs which interest us are necessary to achieve or maintain species-typical normal functioning. Do such needs have the two properties noted earlier? Clearly they are objectively ascribable, assuming we can come up with the appropriate notion of

---

[4] Personal medical services do not count as course-of-life needs on the criterion that we need them all through our lives or at certain (developmental) stages, but they do count as course-of-life needs in that deficiency with respect to them may endanger normal functioning of an individual considered as a member of a natural species.

[5] McCloskey (1976), unlike Braybrooke (1968), is committed to distinguishing a narrower noun use of 'need' from the verb use. McCloskey's proposal is less clear to me than Braybrooke's: presumably our natures include species-typical functioning but something more as well. Moreover, McCloskey is more insistent than Braybrooke in leaving room for *individual natures*, though Braybrooke at least leaves room for something like this when he refers to the needs that we may have by virtue of individual temperament. The hard problem that faces McCloskey is distinguishing between things we need *to develop our individual natures* and things we come to need in the process of what he calls 'self-making', the carrying out of projects one chooses, perhaps in accordance with one's nature, but not just by way of developing it.

species-typical functioning. (So, incidentally, are adventitious needs, assuming we can determine the relevant goals by reference to which the adventitious needs become determinate.) Are these needs objectively important in the appropriate way? In a broad range of contexts we do treat them as such – a claim I shall not trouble to argue. What is of interest is to see *why* being in such a need category gives them their special importance.

A tempting first answer might be this: whatever our specific chosen goals or tasks, our ability to achieve them, and consequently our happiness, will be diminished if we fall short of normal species functioning. So whatever our specific goals, we need them whatever else we need. For example, it is sometimes said that whatever our chosen goals or tasks, we need our health, and so appropriate health care. But this claim is not, strictly speaking, true. For many of us, some of our goals, perhaps even those we feel are most important to us, are not necessarily undermined by failing health or disability. Moreover, we can often adjust our goals, and presumably our levels of satisfaction, to fit better with our dysfunction or disability. Coping in this way does not necessarily diminish happiness or satisfaction in life to a level below that achievable with normal functioning.

Though normal functioning is not in this way a necessary condition for satisfaction or happiness in life, meeting health-care needs may have a definite *tendency* to promote happiness. This tendency may be all the utilitarian needs to guide public policy, and it may give us an explanation of why health care is thought so special. I have no conclusive response to this position: it is a generalized version of the view that health care is special because it reduces pain and suffering, which much of it no doubt does. Of course, the advocate of this view must now be willing to weigh this reduction of pain and suffering against the satisfaction of all other kinds of preferences, if he takes as his goal the promotion of happiness. It is this empirical estimate of the strength of the tendency that makes health care special: the specialness disappears when the estimate changes. In what follows, I sketch an alternative to this account, one that I believe to be more plausible because it better explains the special importance or priority we seem to give to meeting health-care needs.

The alternative account turns on this basic fact: impairments of normal species functioning reduce the range of opportunity open to the individual in which he may construct his 'plan of life' or 'conception of the good'. We may think of a life plan as a long-term plan in which an individual schedules activities so that he can harmoniously satisfy his desires. The good for an individual is defined by reference to this plan and the choice of goals, projects, and means for achieving them it contains (Rawls 1971:92ff.). We can consider a person happy when he is successful in carrying out his plan. The notion of a plan of life thus has some similarity to the utilitarian's notion of a utility function, but it directly implies a plan to satisfy desires over the long term.

Life plans for which we are otherwise suited and which we have a reasonable expectation of finding satisfying or happiness-producing are rendered unreasonable by impairments of normal functioning. Consequently, if persons have a fundamental interest in preserving the opportunity to revise their conceptions of the good through time, then they will have a pressing interest in maintaining normal species functioning (which will be defined more carefully in the next section) by establishing institutions, such as health-care systems, which do just that. So the kinds of needs picked out by reference to normal species functioning are objectively important because they meet this fundamental interest persons have in maintaining a normal range of opportunities. I shall try to refine this admittedly vague answer, but first I want to characterize health-care needs more specifically and show that they fit within this more general framework.

Disease and health

To specify a notion of health-care needs, we need clear notions of health and disease. I shall begin with a narrow, if not uncontroversial, 'biomedical' model: the basic idea is that health is the absence of disease, and diseases (I include deformities and disabilities that result from trauma) are *deviations from the natural functional organization of a typical member of a species*.[6] The task of characterizing this natural functional organization falls to the biomedical sciences. These sciences must be thought of broadly. In some cases, for example, when a scientist makes claims about the natural function of certain features of an organism – when he makes 'functional ascriptions' – he commits himself to other claims about the design of the species and its fitness to meeting biological goals. Thus we must include evolutionary theory among the relevant biomedical sciences. The concept of disease that results is not merely a statistical notion – deviation from the statistical norm. Rather, it draws on a theoretical account of the design of the organism.

---

[6] My account draws on a fine series of articles by Christopher Boorse (1975, 1976a, 1977); see also Macklin (1972).

The task of characterizing species-typical functional organization and departures from it is the same for man and beast with two complications. First, for humans we require an account of the species-typical functional organization that permits us to pursue biological goals as *social* animals. So there must be a way of characterizing the species-typical apparatus underlying such functions as the acquisition of knowledge, linguistic communication, and social cooperation in the broad and changing range of environments in which we live.

Second, adding mental disease and health into the picture, which we must do, complicates the issue further. We have a less well-developed theory of species-typical mental functions and functional organization. The biomedical model clearly presupposes we can eventually develop this missing account and that a reasonable part of what we now take to be psychopathology will show up as diseases within the model (Boorse 1976a:77). The difficulty of so extending the biomedical model to mental disease does not deter me from assuming such an extension here. To anticipate the result of this extension: psychopathology covers an important class of diseases which generate major health care needs, many of which are *unmet* in our health-care system.

The biomedical model has controversial features. First, some insist it too narrowly defines health as the absence of disease, a narrowness which encourages too much focus on acute care. In contrast, some – as in the definition codified by the World Health Organization[7] – view health as an idealized level of well-being. But health is not happiness, and confusing the two over-medicalizes social philosophy. Nor does a 'narrow' bio-medical view of disease mean that we should ignore its social etiology. The bias of our health-care system toward acute care and its neglect of preventive and 'holistic' care derives from many powerful economic and social forces, not an erroneous concept of disease.

Second, some insist that the concept of disease is not descriptive, as in the biomedical model, but strongly normative: a disease is a deviation from a *social norm* (Engelhardt 1974), not merely a deviation from species-typical functional organization. But even if some conditions or behaviors historically have been *viewed* as diseases – for example, 'drapetomania', the disease that made slaves run away, or masturbation – such views do not *make* them diseases. Whales were not fishes merely

---

[7] 'Health is a state of complete physical, mental, and social well-being, and not merely the absence of disease or infirmity.' From the Preamble to the Constitution of the World Health Organization. Adopted by the International Health Conference held in New York, 19 June–22 July 1946, and signed on 22 July 1946. *Official Record of World Health Organization* 2, no. 100. See Callahan (1973).

because people thought they were for centuries. Nor does the fact that many diseases are discovered and treated only when people complain about them make being an object of complaint a necessary feature of diseases. The biomedical model allows us, of course, to make normative judgments *about* diseases, for example, about which ones are undesirable and justify our entering into a 'sick role'. These normative judgments yield the normative notion of *illness*, not the theoretically more basic notion of *disease*; this distinction admittedly departs from looser ordinary usage.[8]

Some pure forms of the biomedical model also involve a deeper claim, namely that species-normal functional organization can itself be characterized without invoking normative or value judgments. Here the debate turns on hard issues in the philosophy of biology. For example, we need an account of functional ascriptions in biology which does not depend on our making normative judgments (Boorse 1976b). More specifically, we need to be able to distinguish genetic variation from disease, and we must specify the range of environments taken as 'natural' for the purpose of revealing dysfunction. The latter is critical to showing that the biomedical model is non-normative: for example, what range of social roles and environments is included in the natural range? If we allow too much of the social environment, then racially discriminatory environments might make being of the wrong race a disease; if we disallow all socially created environments, then we seem not to be able to call dyslexia a disease (remember I include certain disabilities).

Fortunately, these difficult issues need not detain us. My discussion does not turn on this deeper, strong claim about non-normativeness advanced by some advocates of the biomedical model. It is enough for my purposes that the line between disease and the absence of disease is, for the general run of cases, *uncontroversial* and *ascertainable through publicly acceptable methods*, such as those of the biomedical sciences. It will not matter if what counts as a disease category is relative to some features of social roles in a given society, and thus to some normative judgments, provided the core of the notion of species-normal functioning is left intact. The model would still, I presume, count infertility as a disease, even though some or many individuals might prefer to be infertile and seek medical treatment to render themselves so. Similarly, unwanted pregnancy is not a disease. Again, dysfunctional noses count as diseases, since noses have normal species functions and normal functional

---

[8] Boorse's (1975, 1977) critique of strongly normative views of disease is persuasive independently of some problematic features of his own account.

organization (or, simply, normal anatomy). If the dysfunction or deformity is serious, it might warrant treatment as an illness. But deviation of nasal anatomy from individual or social conceptions of beauty does not constitute disease. This is a distinction well-known to cosmetic plastic surgeons. Since most third-party payers will not reimburse for surgery that does not correct disease or deformity, some plastic surgeons conspire to commit fraud in order to obtain reimbursements for their patients by describing the surgery as corrective. In Massachusetts, Blue Cross/Blue Shield recently crossed this line in a different way: it suspended reimbursements for reconstructive plastic surgery following mastectomy. Public outcry reversed the policy, which made it clear that the public understood and wanted to preserve the distinction between restoration of anatomy to the normal range and mammoplasty undertaken for purely cosmetic reasons.[9]

The biomedical model thus allows us to draw a fairly sharp line between uses of health-care services to prevent and treat diseases and uses which meet other social goals. The importance of such other goals may be different and may rest on other bases, for example, in the induced infertility or unwanted pregnancy cases. My intention is to show which principles of justice are relevant to distributing health-care services where we can take as fixed, primarily by nature, a generally uncontroversial baseline of species-normal functional organization. If important moral considerations enter at yet another level, to determine what counts as health and what disease, then the principles I discuss and these others must be reconciled. This is a task which the biomedical model makes unnecessary at this stage, and one which I want to avoid here if possible. Of course, a more comprehensive theory than the one I sketch in Chapter 3 would have to establish priorities among principles governing the meeting of health-care needs and principles for using health-care services to meet other social or individual goals, for example terminating unwanted pregancy or improving the beauty of the population.

There is one minor implication of this account for the present debate about Medicaid-funded abortions in the US. Non-therapeutic abortions do not count as health-care needs, since unwanted pregnancy is not a

---

[9] Anyone who doubts the appropriateness of treating some physiognomic deformities as serious diseases with strong claims on surgical resources should read Frances C. MacGreggor's (1979) study. Even where there is no disease or deformity, there is nothing in the analysis I offer that precludes individuals or society from deciding to use health-care technology to make physiognomy conform to some standard of beauty. But such uses of medical technology will not be justifiable as the meeting of health-care needs, as defined above.

disease. So, *if* Medicaid has as its only legitimate function the meeting of health-care needs of the poor, then we cannot argue for funding the abortions as we do for funding other medical procedures which treat diseases. Their justifications will be different. But if Medicaid should serve other important goals, like ensuring that poor and well-off women can equally well control their bodies, then there is justification for funding these abortions. There is also the worry that not funding them will contribute to other health problems induced by illegal abortions or by the lack of adequate prenatal care for poor, teenaged girls. Indeed, purity about meeting only medical needs seems disingenuous when the system actually fails to meet many such needs and may therefore be unjust.

Though I have deliberately selected a rather narrow model of disease and health, at least by comparison to some fashionable views, *health-care needs* emerge as a broad and diverse set. Health care needs will be those things we need in order to maintain, restore, or provide functional equivalents (where possible) to normal species functioning. They can be divided into:

1 Adequate nutrition, shelter
2 Sanitary, safe, unpolluted living and working conditions
3 Exercise, rest, and some other features of life-style
4 Preventive, curative, and rehabilitative personal medical services
5 Non-medical personal and social support services

Of course, we do not tend to think of all these things as included among health-care needs, partly because we tend to think narrowly about personal medical services when we think about health care. But the list is not constructed to conform to our ordinary notion of health care, but to point out a functional relationship between quite diverse goods and services and the various institutions responsible for delivering them. I will say little explicit about (1) or (3) in the following chapters, but the point about the functional relation still holds.

Disease and opportunity

I have argued that not all preferences are of equal moral importance and that when we judge the importance of meeting someone's preferences we use a selective or truncated measure of well-being. Among the kinds of preferences to which we tend to give special weight are those which meet certain *important* categories of need. I have argued that among the important needs are those necessary for maintaining normal functioning for individuals, viewed as members of a natural species. Health-care needs fit prominently into this characterization of important needs because they are things we need to prevent or cure diseases, which are deviations from normal functional organization.

But we now need to fill an important gap in this argument: What is so important about normal species functioning? Why give such moral importance to health-care needs and to the somewhat broader class of needs within which it falls, merely because they are necessary to preserve normal species functioning? To answer this question, I shall develop the remark made earlier about the relationship between species-typical functioning and opportunity, but this will require the notion of a normal opportunity range.

The *normal opportunity range* for a given society is the array of life plans reasonable persons in it are likely to construct for themselves. The normal range is thus dependent on key features of the society – its stage of historical development, its level of material wealth and technological development, and even important cultural facts about it. This is one way in which the notion of normal opportunity range is socially relative. Facts about social organization, including the conception of justice regulating its basic institutions, will also determine how that total normal range is distributed in the population. Nevertheless, that issue of distribution aside, normal species-typical functioning provides us with one clear parameter affecting the share of the normal range open to a given individual. It is this parameter which the distribution of health care affects.

The share of the normal range open to an individual is also *determined in a fundamental way by his talents and skills*. Fair equality of opportunity does not require opportunity to be equal for all persons. It requires only that it be equal for persons with similar skills and talents. Thus individual shares of the normal range will not in general be *equal*, even when they are *fair* to the individual. The general principle of fair equality of opportunity does not imply levelling individual differences. Within the general theory of justice, unequal chances of success which derive from unequal talents may be compensated for in other ways. For example, in Rawls's (1971) theory, socio-economic inequalities are allowed to work to the advantage of those with more marketable talents only if the inequalities also maximally benefit the worst-off individuals, who, we may suppose, have less marketable talents. I can now state a fact central to my approach: impairment of normal functioning through disease and disability restricts an individual's opportunity *relative to that portion of the normal range his skills and talents would have made available to him were he healthy*. If an individual's fair share of the normal range is the array of life plans he may reasonably choose, given his talents and skills, then disease and disability shrinks his share from what is fair.

Of course, we also know that skills and talents can be undeveloped or misdeveloped because of social conditions, e.g., family background or racist educational practices. So, if we are interested in having individuals enjoy a fair share of the normal opportunity range, we will want to correct for special disadvantages here too, say through compensatory educational or job-training programs. Still, restoring normal functioning through health care has a particular and *limited* effect on an individual's share of the normal range. It lets him enjoy that portion of the range to which his full array of skills and talents would give him access, assuming that these too are not impaired by special social disadvantages. Again, there is no presumption that we should eliminate or level individual differences: *these act as a baseline constraint on the degree to which individuals enjoy the normal range*. Only where differences in talents and skills are the results of disease and disability, not merely normal variation, is some effort required to correct for the effects of the 'natural lottery'. (There will be problem cases: Should we regard mental retardation as a disability? If so, why is it to be regarded as qualitatively different from lack of brilliance or mere dullness, which have their market value. These are matters I cannot pursue here.)

Two points about the normal opportunity range need emphasis. First, some diseases constitute more serious curtailments of opportunity than others relative to a given range. But, because normal ranges are defined by reference to particular societies, the same disease in two societies may impair opportunity differently and so have its importance assessed differently. For example, dyslexia may be less important to treat in an illiterate society than in a literate one (suppose we could cure it with brain surgery). Thus the social importance of particular diseases is a notion which we ought to view as socially relative.

Second, within a society the normal opportunity range abstracts from important individual differences in what I will call *effective opportunity*. From the perspective of an individual who has a particular plan of life and who has developed certain skills accordingly, the effective opportunity range will be only a part of his fair share of the normal range. Suppose a college teacher and a skilled laborer each finds his manual dexterity impaired by disease. The impairment of the effective opportunity range for the skilled laborer may be greater than for the college teacher, but if both originally had comparable dexterity, their shares of the normal range would be equally affected by the disease. By measuring the impact of disease on opportunity by reference to an individual's share of the normal range, and not by reference to its impairment of his effective range, I abstract from special effects that derive from an individual's conception of the 'good' or plan of life. This way of proceeding seems plausible in light of judgments we are inclined to make about access to medical services: we do not want to be in the business, I believe, of deciding who gets what medical services on the basis of occupation or other results of prior individual choices of a similar sort. Thus the level of abstraction in my account seems appropriate given our search for a measure of the social importance, for claims of justice, of impairments of health.[10]

My conclusion is that we should use impairment of the normal opportunity range as a fairly crude measure of the relative importance of health-care needs at the macro level. In general, it will be more important to prevent, cure, or compensate for those disease conditions which involve a greater curtailment of an individual's share of the normal opportunity range. Of course, impairment of normal species functioning has another distinct effect. It can diminish individual happiness or satisfaction, which depends on the individual's conception of the 'good'. Such effects are important at the micro level – for example, to individual decisions about utilizing health care. At this micro level, an individual is deciding which services to use from among those society is obliged to provide – if the society is just. Here individual choices about happiness will be the final determinant of what is done. But this appeal to individual happiness will not solve my central problem, which concerns what society is obliged to provide. I am here seeking the appropriate framework within which to apply principles of justice to health care at the macro level. In the next chapter I shall have to look further at considerations that weigh against appeals to satisfaction at the macro level.

[10] One issue here is to avoid 'hijacking' by past preferences which themselves define the effective range. Of course, impact on the effective range may be important in micro-allocation decisions, including decisions by individuals whether they want to receive certain services.

3 · Toward a distributive theory

Satisfaction and social hijacking

So far my discussion has been primarily descriptive and not normative. I have been describing and explaining certain features of our moral practice, not actually justifying that practice. Specifically, in many moral contexts, including those of justice, we must judge the relative well-being of individuals or groups in order to assess the urgency or importance of claims they make on us. We do not just take their claims at face value. In our moral practice, especially in contexts of justice, we assess well-being by reference to a scale which gives more weight or importance to certain kinds or categories of preferences over others. That is, our scale for assessing well-being is selective or truncated. It discounts many kinds of preferences which would play a role on a complete or full-range scale of satisfaction. The 'important' preferences or needs which play a role on the selective scale seem to be necessary for maintaining normal species functioning. In turn, such normal functioning affects an individual's share of the normal opportunity range. I have suggested that it is this effect on opportunity that allows us to explain why people treat these needs as special and important: people have a fundamental interest in protecting their share of the normal range of opportunities.

This description and explanation of our moral practice falls short of giving us a normative account in two ways. First, there is the question, *Should* we use the objective, truncated scale of well-being we happen to use rather than a more complete measure of satisfaction? Simply having a practice does not justify it. Second, *Ought* we to protect our shares of the normal opportunity range? Is there a social obligation to provide such protection? Simply having an interest in such protection does not mean there are social obligations to provide it.

Unfortunately, both of these normative questions take us deep into the general theory of justice and beyond our focus on just health care. I will not be able to provide adequate answers to them here. Considering the health-care context alone, for example, is not likely to yield a conclusive case for or against either scale of well-being. Thus a utilitarian might argue that any social application of a satisfaction scale would depend on the *general tendencies* of types of health-care needs to improve levels of

36

satisfaction; such an approach might be roughly equivalent to concentrating on the ways in which health-care needs affect opportunity. I will nevertheless try to suggest why I think the answers to both normative questions are positive. As we shall see, the account I offer will be *conditional* on there being positive answers to these questions at the level of the general theory of justice. My intention is to provide foundations for claims about just health care, but there are foundations and there are foundations. My work here must stop short of digging to the deepest levels in the general theory.

With these apologies out of the way, let us consider the question whether we should use the truncated scale we do use to measure well-being, rather than a full-range scale of satisfaction. Consider a special case in which our moral judgment inclines us against using a complete satisfaction scale, namely the case of 'social hijacking' by persons with expensive tastes (Rawls 1982b). Suppose we judge how well off someone is by reference to the full range of individual preferences in a satisfaction scale. Suppose further that *moderate* people adjust their tastes and preferences so that they have a reasonable chance of being satisfied with their share of social goods. *Extravagant* people, however, form exotic and expensive tastes, and they are desperately unhappy when their preferences are not satisfied. Since the extravagants are so unhappy compared to the moderates, should we increase their shares? They seem, after all, to be much less well off. Yet, it seems unjust to deny the moderates equal claims on further distributions just because they have been modest in forming their tastes. Rather, it seems reasonable to hold people responsible for their unhappiness when it results from extravagant preferences which could have been otherwise. The utilitarian might promise us that he could establish institutions which provide disincentives to 'social hijacking', thus allowing us to use the satisfaction scale without actually facing such cases. But in conceding the need to protect us against this possibility, he seems to acknowledge the power of the underlying moral judgment that such hijacking is morally wrong and should be avoided. The selective or truncated scale builds that view into the weighting it gives different kinds of preferences; it does not rely on contingent social arrangements to protect us.

The scope of justice

A more general division of responsibility is suggested by this hijacking case. John Rawls (1982b) urges that we hold *society* responsible for guaranteeing the individual a fair share of basic liberties, opportunity, and the all-purpose means, like income and wealth, needed for pursuing individual conceptions of the 'good'. Together these are called the *primary social goods*. But we should hold *individuals* responsible for choosing their ends in such a way that they have a reasonable chance of satisfying them under just arrangements. This division presupposes that people have the ability and know they have the responsibility to adjust their desires in view of their fair shares of primary social goods (Scanlon 1975:665–6). Consequently, the special features of an individual's own system of preferences do not give rise to special claims of justice on social resources – despite his level of dissatisfaction.

This suggestion about a division of responsibility is really a fundamental claim about the *scope* of theories of justice. That is, it is really a claim about the kinds of goods with which theories of justice are directly concerned. Just arrangements are supposed to guarantee individuals a reasonable share of certain basic or primary social goods – and these primary goods constitute for Rawls the relevant, truncated scale of well-being *for purposes of justice*. (I shall come shortly to the problem of fitting Rawls's scale and my talk about *needs* together.) The immediate object of justice is not, then, happiness or the satisfaction of desires, though just institutions provide individuals with an acceptable framework within which they may pursue happiness. But in this pursuit, individuals remain responsible for the choice of their ends, so there is no injustice in not providing them with means sufficient to reach extravagant ends.

A full defense of this claim about the scope of justice and the social division of responsibility, and thus for the restriction to a truncated scale of well-being, cannot rest on isolated moral intuitions like those appealed to in the hijacking example. Such intuitions cannot be treated like 'crucial tests' of moral theory, and they need justification themselves. In Rawls's full argument for his view, the argument against the satisfaction scale turns on its incompatibility with a plausible view of the nature of persons. The satisfaction scale forces us to view persons as mere 'containers' for satisfaction. It leaves us no basis for not wanting to *be* whatever person, construed as a set of preferences, has a higher level of satisfaction. To borrow a term from Bernard Williams (1973), the satisfaction scale undermines the *integrity* of persons.[1] Thus the satisfaction scale is incompatible with a view of the nature of persons which in turn underlies much of our moral practice. Though this argument of

---

[1] See Rawls (1982b: Section VI–VII). The view that issues here turn in a fundamental way on the nature of persons is pursued in Parfit (1973), Rawls (1974–5), and Daniels 1979a).

Rawls's does not turn on appeals to isolated intuitions, like the hijacking case, it does depend on an appeal to the coherence of one area of our moral beliefs with another, but the circle within which justification takes place is much wider.

I am sympathetic with Rawls's very interesting argument, and it suggests the kind of consideration, deep at the heart of moral theory, which underlies rejection of the full satisfaction scale. But this argument is not uncontroversial, and I am content here to suggest the kinds of difficulty that would face us if we were to abandon our moral practice, with its truncated scale of well-being, in favor of a more complete one. We would have to give up much else in our moral practice, including our concern for the integrity of persons and our ability to offer prudential and moral advice of various kinds. The implausibility of such radical changes is evidence for Rawls's view.

Fair equality of opportunity

I have argued that we can explain the importance we attribute to meeting health-care needs once we observe the effect of disease on an individual's share of the normal opportunity range. But observing that individuals have an interest in protecting their shares of that range does not show that society *ought* to protect normal opportunity range, that there is any social obligation to do so. If we could show that justice required guaranteeing fair equality of opportunity, then we could complete our justification of the importance we attribute to meeting health-care needs. We would then be able to assert that the social obligation to meet health-care needs derives from the more general social obligation to guarantee fair equality of opportunity. As I noted earlier, I cannot offer that more general argument for a principle guaranteeing fair equality of opportunity without digressing too far into the general theory of justice. But I do want to suggest some widely held reasons for supporting such a principle.

Liberal political philosophy has relied on what is essentially a *procedural* notion, equality of opportunity, to justify a system in which unequal outcomes are thought morally acceptable. It is morally acceptable that there are winners and losers, even in races where the prize is a share of important social goods, provided the race is *fair* to all participants. Since major rewards in our society derive from jobs and offices, the competition for securing these positions must be fair. Specifically, certain *morally irrelevant* features of persons – race, religion, ethnic origin, sex – must not be the basis on which people are selected for positions. Rather, their talents and skills, at least those relevant to the positions being sought, should determine who is selected and ultimately rewarded. (I discuss features of this theory in more detail in Chapter 8.) In Rawls's theory of justice as fairness, for example, inequalities in shares of primary social goods are justified on the grounds that it would be irrational – even for the worst-off people – to rule out inequalities which work to their advantage. But a proviso is included: competition for positions must be fair, and a fair equality of opportunity principle is given high priority in Rawls's theory. Specifically, fair equality of opportunity cannot be traded away to provide material gains for individuals: fair equality of opportunity is given *lexical* or *lexicographical priority* over the principle which permits inequalities in other social goods. When a principle has lexical priority in a series of principles, it must be satisfied first, before we can move on to satisfy further principles.

Even this narrow notion of equal opportunity, concerned only with access to jobs and careers, is both problematic and controversial. It is conceptually problematic for several reasons. Thus, some claim equal opportunity is not well defined or is illusory. Irreducible differences in talents and skills between persons will always make opportunity greater for some in competitive situations. We cannot 'level' people down to their 'bare personhood', where all distinguishing traits of individuals – their talents, skills, and other accidental features which might confer advantages – are eliminated. We might try to avoid this complaint, by accepting some irreducible differences in talents and skills as a natural baseline, as I did earlier in defining normal opportunity range (see Chapter 2). But this opens us to another difficulty. Any such baseline of talents and skills may seem to be morally arbitrary: we do not deserve the advantages or disadvantages the baseline confers. These talents and skills are largely the result of genetic accident or the social good fortune of having effective parents – neither of which we in any sense deserve. Rawls (1971) tries to accommodate this point by arranging inequalities in other social goods, such as income and wealth, so that they work to make the worst-off individuals maximally well off, as well off as they could be under all alternative social arrangements with lesser inequalities. In this way, he treats talents and skills, in part at least, as a *social asset* which works to the advantage of the worst-off individuals, those with the least marketable talents and skills. This solution is challenged by many.

A different complaint is that equal opportunity is an unachievable goal. For example, there are ineliminable effects of family upbringing on the development of talents and skills (Fishkin 1983). This suggests that the goal of achieving equal opportunity completely is unrealizable unless we threaten liberty by interfering with parental autonomy in drastic ways. A somewhat pragmatic response would be to suggest that we achieve what equality we can without violating more basic liberties; we must then live with the fuzziness in the theory that results.

This conflict with liberty suggests another reason that equality of opportunity is a controversial notion. Some construe it as a *negative* constraint which requires only that society refrain from imposing certain barriers to equal opportunity, such as anti-black 'Jim Crow' laws or racial or sexual quotas on hiring. This negative view gives us what Rawls (1971) calls *formal* equality of opportunity. Others insist there is a *positive* obligation to correct for all the influences which interfere with equal opportunity. Where competitive disadvantage, such as the under-development of talents and skills, results from racist or sexist practices or as effects of poor family background, then social programs to correct for the disadvantage are required. These might include compensatory education programs, like 'Headstart' in the US, or 'affirmative action' hiring procedures. This positive conception is called *fair* equality of opportunity. General distributive theories differ dramatically in their willingness to move from the negative to the positive conception, and resolving this dispute would take us far afield.

In this investigation we shall have to settle for less than a full justification of the principle of fair equality of opportunity. In particular, we shall settle for a weaker, conditional claim. Health-care institutions should be among those governed by a principle of fair equality of opportunity, provided two conditions obtain: (1) an acceptable general theory of justice includes a principle which requires basic institutions to guarantee fair equality of opportunity, and (2) the fair equality of opportunity principle acts as a constraint on permissible economic inequalities. A theory of just health care can go only this far. In the discussion that follows I will ignore these provisos – though I have not forgotten them. I urge the fair equality of opportunity principle as an appropriate principle to govern macro decisions about the design of our health-care system. Such a principle defines, from the perspective of justice, what the moral *function* of the health-care system must be – to help guarantee fair equality of opportunity. This is the fundamental insight underlying the approach developed here.

It is important to note that this conditional claim does not depend on the acceptability of any particular theory of justice, such as Rawls's contractarian theory. A utilitarian theory might suffice. For example, a principle of fair equality of opportunity might be part of a system of principles, an ideal moral code, general compliance with which produced at least as much utility as any alternative code. For example, the principle might be the most effective way to protect the society against the productivity lost when individuals are not given a fair opportunity to develop their skills and talents (although I have never seen a persuasive utilitarian argument of this sort). That utilitarian theory could then be extended to health care through the analysis provided here. It is far less likely that a libertarian theory would be compatible with any such fair equality of opportunity principle. In fact, the main theory which has incorporated a fair equality of opportunity principle is Rawls's (1971) contractarian theory of justice as fairness, which I have cited in the above explanation of the reasons for the principle. In the Preface, I noted that I once despaired of seeing a plausible way to extend Rawls's theory to health care. In the next section, I shall suggest how Rawls's theory can be so extended through its fair equality of opportunity principle, though there remain some problems. This exercise is intended to clarify how such a general theory can be made to fit with the analysis I have been offering. It is not an endorsement of Rawls's theory of justice as fairness; nor does the weak, conditional claim I make above depend on the acceptability of justice as fairness.

Extending Rawls's theory to health care

Earlier (pp. 37–9), I cited an argument Rawls (1982b) offers to show that a full-range satisfaction scale is an inappropriate measure of well-being in certain moral contexts, especially the general theory of justice. Rawls's argument for a truncated scale is, of course, for a specific one, composed of his primary social goods. But my talk about a truncated scale has focused on the importance of certain basic needs – in particular, things we need to maintain species-typical normal functioning. Health-care needs are paradigmatic among these. A task that remains here is to fit the two scales together. My analysis of the relationship between disease and an individual's share of the normal opportunity range provides the key to doing that.

Rawls's *index of primary social goods* – his truncated scale of well-being used by moral agents seeking a hypothetical social contract – includes five types of social goods:

1 A set of basic liberties
2 Freedom of movement and choice of occupations against a background of diverse opportunities
3 Powers and prerogatives of office
4 Income and wealth
5 The social bases of self-respect

Actually, Rawls uses two simplifying assumptions when using the index to assess how well off (representative) individuals are. First, income and wealth are used as approximations to the whole index. Thus the two principles of justice Rawls defends require basic structures to maximize the long-term expectations of the least advantaged, estimated by their income and wealth, given fixed background institutions that guarantee equal basic liberties and fair equality of opportunity (Rawls 1971:302). Second, the theory is idealized to apply to individuals who are 'normal, active, and fully cooperating members of society over the course of a complete life' (Rawls 1982b:168). Such idealization allows Rawls to construct a theory of justice for the simpler, idealized case, and then to worry about extensions of the theory to contexts in which conditions are more realistic and people are not all normal. In effect, *there is no distributive theory for health care because no one is sick*!

This simplification seems to put Rawls's index at odds with the thrust of my earlier discussion, for the truncated scale of well-being we in fact use includes needs for health care. Rawls's index of primary goods seems to be *too truncated* a scale, once we drop the idealizing assumption that all people are normal. People with equal indices will not be equally well-off once we allow them to differ in health-care needs. Moreover, we cannot simply dismiss these needs as irrelevant to questions of justice, as we did when we said people should be held responsible for their tastes and preferences (I am supposing that individuals are not responsible for the diseases they have, a simplification I return to later). But if we simply build another entry into the index, adding health care to the list of primary goods enumerated above, we raise thorny problems about how to weight items on the index, for now we have to weigh health care against opportunity, income, powers and other social goods on the index. This may force us to make interpersonal comparisons of utility Rawls had hoped to avoid.

Kenneth Arrow (1973) has suggested two problems follow from merely adding health care to the list of primary goods. First, the force of

Rawls's Second Principle of justice, which requires inequalities to work
to the advantage of the worst-off (representative) individuals, would be
to drain excessive resources into the satisfaction of the special needs of
persons with extreme health-care needs, perhaps to the point where the
rest of society is reduced to poverty (Arrow 1973:251). Second, adding
health care to the construction of the index, and allowing its trade-off
against income and wealth, would force Rawls into the interpersonal
comparisons of utility he had hoped his index would avoid (Arrow
1973:254). It is not clear to me that Arrow is right in saying that the
problem of interpersonal comparisons arises simply because there is a
need to rank or weight different primary goods, but I will not argue the
point here, however important it is in assessing Rawls's theory.[2]

[2] Rather, I want to raise a different problem, which is, in any case, already present prior to
the attempt to introduce health care as a distinct primary good. (I am indebted to Joshua
Cohen for discussion of this point.)

As presented, Rawls's theory abstracts from the problem of weighting items on the
index by taking income and wealth as rough indicators of the over-all value of the index.
Consequently, Rawls does not discuss in any detail how to weight acknowledged
primary goods, such as powers and prerogatives of position (including worker control
over the workplace), against income. Yet it is not at all clear how this ranking problem
can be solved from the point of view of the original position, given how little people in it
know about their ends or about their society. It seems likely one would have to know
various things about the particular society in order to arrive at such a ranking or
weighting. For example, democracy in the workplace might be weighted more heavily
than income at one level of industrialization but not at another. Similarly, if health care
were added as a primary good, its rank or weight compared to income and wealth would
also depend on facts about the historical period and society for which the index is to
work. Rawls admits that social conditions may affect the weights, but he thinks we can
arrive at some initial constraints similar to those involved in his argument that shows
basic liberties should be given priority over other index items (see Rawls 1975:97). But
no such constraints are proposed. In their absence, the theory chosen in the original
position is really only a schema for a theory of justice. We have to treat the index, which
is intended to give specificity and content to the distributive theory, as a variable whose
values cannot be filled in without more specific knowledge of the society to which the
theory is to be applied.

To be sure, Rawls already assumes that the principles of justice acquire specificity on
many matters only in the constitutional or legislative stages of designing a just society,
for in these the 'veil of ignorance' is lifted. But if not even the structure of the index can
be determined from within the Original Position, the degree of abstractness is
qualitatively greater. Once the index is relativized in this way to historical period and
context, Rawls's principles of justice turn out to be far more formal and contentless than
they first seemed; we can turn them into determinate substantive principles of justice
only for given societies or historical periods. At a higher level, the formalism of Kant's
theory returns to haunt us. This is not quite true, since the schematic principles do
impose some substantive constraints on the fleshed-out principles of justice, even if the
details of the index are not known: the worst off, however determined by an appropriate
index, must be made maximally well off. But this advances little toward a substantive
theory for health care. All we know is that our fair share of social goods will be weighted
according to some appropriate consideration of our health-care needs, given social
conditions, etc. If this is *all* that emerges from the contract theory then we have not

Similarly, if we treat health-care services as a distinct primary social good, we abandon the useful generality of the notion of a primary social good. We risk generating a long list of such goods, one to meet each important need (for a defense of this approach, see Green 1976). Finally, I argued (pp. 20–3) that we cannot just finesse the question of whether there are special issues of justice in the distribution of health care by assuming that fair shares of primary goods will be used in part to buy reasonable health insurance. A constraint on the adequacy of those shares is that they permit one to buy reasonable protection – so we must already know what justice requires by way of reasonable health care.

The most promising strategy for extending Rawls's theory simply includes health-care institutions and practices among the basic institutions involved in providing for fair equality of opportunity.[3] Because meeting health-care needs has an important effect on the distribution of opportunity, the health-care institutions are regulated by a fair equality of opportunity principle.[4] Once we note the special connection of normal species functioning to the opportunity range open to an individual, this strategy seems the natural way to extend Rawls's view noted earlier, about the *scope* of theories of social justice. Health-care institutions will help provide the framework of liberties and opportunities within which individuals can use their fair income shares to pursue their own conceptions of the good.

Including health-care institutions among those which are to protect fair equality of opportunity is compatible with the central intuitions behind wanting to guarantee such opportunity. Rawls is primarily concerned with the *opportunity to pursue careers* – jobs and offices – that have various benefits attached to them. So equality of opportunity is

---

moved very far toward knowing what our entitlements to health care are likely to be, which was the point of turning to the theory in the first place.

[3] The primary social goods themselves remain general and abstract properties of social arrangements – basic liberties, opportunities, and certain all-purpose, exchangeable means (income and wealth). We can still simplify matters in using the index by looking solely at income and wealth – assuming a background of equal basic liberties and fair equality of opportunity. Health care is not a primary social good – neither are food, clothing, shelter, or other basic needs. The presumption is that the latter will be provided for adequately from fair shares of income and wealth. The special importance and unequal distribution of health-care needs, like educational needs, are acknowledged by their connection to other institutions that provide for fair equality of opportunity. But opportunity, not health care or education, is the primary social good here.

[4] Here I shift emphasis from Rawls (1971:62) when he remarks that health is a *natural* as opposed to *social* primary good because its possession is less influenced by basic institutions. Moreover, it seems to follow that where health care is generally inefficacious, as in earlier centuries, it loses its status as a special concern of justice and the 'caring' it offers may be viewed more properly as a concern of beneficence or charity.

strategically important: a person's well-being will be measured for the most part by the primary goods that accompany placement in such jobs and offices. As noted earlier, Rawls argues it is not enough simply to eliminate formal or legal barriers to persons seeking such jobs – for example, race, class, ethnic, or sex barriers. Rather, positive steps should be taken to enhance the opportunity of those disadvantaged by such social factors as family background. The point, as noted above (p. 40), is that none of us *deserves* the advantages conferred by accidents of birth – either the genetic or social advantages. These advantages from the 'natural lottery' are morally arbitrary, because they are not deserved, and to let them determine individual opportunity – and reward and success in life – is to confer arbitrariness on the outcomes. So positive steps, for example, through the educational system, are to be taken to provide fair equality of opportunity.[5]

But if it is important to use resources to counter the advantages in opportunity some get in the natural lottery, it is equally important to use resources to counter the natural disadvantages induced by disease. (Since social conditions, which differ by class, contribute significantly to the etiology of disease, we are reminded that disease is not just a product of the natural component of the lottery.) But this does not mean that we are committed to the futile goal of eliminating or 'levelling' all natural differences between persons. Health care has normal functioning as its goal: it concentrates on a specific class of obvious disadvantages and tries to eliminate them. That is its limited contribution to guaranteeing fair equality of opportunity.

The approach taken here allows us to draw some interesting parallels between education and health care, for both are strategically important contributors to fair equality of opportunity. *Both address needs which are not equally distributed among individuals.* Various social factors, such as race, class, and family background, may produce special learning needs; so too may natural factors, such as the broad class of learning disabilities. To the extent that education is aimed at providing fair equality of opportunity, provision must be made to meet these special needs. Thus educational needs, like health-care needs, differ from other basic needs, such as the need for food and clothing, which are more equally distributed between persons. The combination of their *unequal distribution* and their *great strategic importance* for opportunity puts these needs in a

---

[5] Fair equality of opportunity does not mean that individual differences no longer confer advantages; rather, the advantages are constrained by the difference principle and work to the advantage of the worst-off. See Daniels (1978).

separate category from those basic needs we can expect people to purchase from their fair income shares, like food and shelter.

There is another point of fit worth noting between my analysis and Rawls's theory. In Rawls's contraction theory, people are charged with the task of choosing principles of justice for their society, but they make their choice in a rigidly defined, hypothetical choice situation. One key feature of that situation is that contractors do not know their abilities, talents, place in society, or historical period. That is, they are behind a thick veil of ignorance which insures that their choice is impartial in certain ways and reflects only their natures as free and equal moral agents. In selecting principles to govern health-care resource-allocation decisions, however, we need a thinner veil of ignorance, for we must know about some features of the society – for example, its resource limitations. Using the normal opportunity range and not just the effective range as the baseline for measuring the importance of health-care needs has the effect of imposing a suitably thinned veil. (Remember that the effective range is the share of the normal range determined by an individual's actual choices about what life plans to pursue and talents and skills to develop; in contrast an individual's share of the normal range is defined relative to his talents and skills, but includes the life plans it would be reasonable for him to select, not the ones he actually does.) The normal range reflects basic facts about the society – since the normal range is socially relative – but it keeps facts about an individual's particular ends from unduly influencing *social* decisions. Ultimately, defense of a veil as a device depends on the theory of the person underlying the account, in particular on Rawls's view that moral agents are essentially free and equal. The intuition here is that persons are not defined by a particular set of interests but are free to revise their life plans. Consequently, they have a fundamental interest in maintaining conditions under which they can revise their life plans as time goes on. This makes the normal range a plausible reference point.

Subsuming health-care institutions under the opportunity principle can be viewed as a way of keeping the system as close as possible to the original idealization under which Rawls's theory was constructed, namely that we are concerned with normal, fully functioning persons with a complete lifespan. Preventive health-care institutions can thus be viewed as a first defense of the idealization: they act to minimize the likelihood of departures from the normality assumption. Included here are institutions which provide for public health, environmental cleanliness, preventive personal medical services, occupational health and safety, food and drug protection, nutrition education, and educational and incentive measures to promote individual responsibility for healthy life styles. We might think of these institutions as keeping us close to the less controversial, simplified core of our theory, for we have not yet had to correct for departures from normality.

Unfortunately, not all departures from normal functioning can be prevented, and we need a second layer of institutions which corrects for departures from the idealization. These institutions deliver personal medical and rehabilitative services that restore normal functioning. Similarly, not all treatments are cures, and some institutions and services are needed to maintain persons in a way that is as close as possible to the idealization. This third layer of institutions is involved with more extended medical and social support services for the (moderately) chronically ill and disabled and the frail elderly. Finally, a fourth layer involves health care and related social services for those who can in no way be brought closer to the idealization. Terminal care and care for the seriously mentally and physically disabled fit here, but they raise serious issues which may not just be issues of justice. Indeed, by the time we get to the fourth layer moral virtues other than justice become prominent.

The picture conveyed by these remarks about four levels or layers of health-care institutions should not be taken to imply that each layer corresponds to a different principle of justice, or that the layers are ranked in moral priority. Each corrects in a particular fashion for a type of departure from the Rawlsian idealization that all people are functionally normal. It is preferable to prevent than to have to cure, and to cure than to have to compensate for lost functioning. But all these institutions and services are needed if fair equality of opportunity is to be guaranteed. It is only where there is no chance of protecting opportunity, as in the fourth level, where we are concerned with the seriously, permanently disabled, that we may be beyond measures that justice requires. Here principles of beneficence may be a more important guide to our obligations.

Some qualifications and clarifications

The fair equality of opportunity account developed here invites several lines of criticism. I would like to clarify the account by anticipating and responding to objections under two main headings. First, I shall examine some difficulties, real and purported, with my effort to base an account of just health care on the notion of fair equality of opportunity. These include complaints that equal opportunity is too vague or expansive for it to be useful in a distributive theory, that it is not strong enough a notion, and that the account is circular. Second, I would like to acknowledge important limitations of the account.

Objections to the fair equality of opportunity account

'Health care is special for other reasons'

When we reflect on the importance of health-care needs, factors other than their effects on opportunity come to mind. Some health care, in a direct and simple way, for example, reduces pain and suffering – and no fancy analysis of opportunity is needed to show why people value reducing them. Similarly, disease reminds us of the fragility of life and the limits of human existence – and the solidarity we show with the ill by caring for them has come to have deep religious and moral significance in many cultures. Also, people want to know what is wrong with them, or what will keep them well, and some medical care has this function. The President's Commission for the Study of Ethical Problems in Medicine and Biomedical and Behavioral Research (1983a) considered the question, 'Why is health care special?', in its report on access to health care. It adopted the eclectic response that health care is special for all of these reasons (see my comments in Chapter 4). Others have tended to emphasize the reduction of pain and suffering, suggesting that the principle of utility remains an appropriate principle for deciding how to distribute health care (see Stern 1983).

I certainly do not want to deny that health care has these varied functions and effects. Indeed, I emphasized the fact that health care is non-homogeneous in its function: it does not just do one thing for us but many. Sometimes it postpones death; sometimes it reduces pain and suffering. Often it merely improves the quality of life in other ways – which shows why the reduction of pain and suffering is not a general enough function to explain the importance of health care. Yet, we do not think all things that improve the quality of life or produce greater happiness are comparable in importance. Having a Bierstadt or Turner on my living-room wall would improve the quality of my life enormously, but I will not get one, alas, when I become eligible for Medicare. The *way* in which quality is improved by health care seems critical to our estimate of its importance. But this is just the distinction which the principle of utility cannot make.

My account abstracts from these varied effects of health care a central *function* – the maintenance of species-typical functional organization – and emphasizes its central effect on opportunity. My contention is that most uses of health-care services which we intuitively find important, such as those in which we seek to reduce pain, will be encompassed by this central effect on opportunity. In this way, while my analysis is not exhaustive, it focuses on that general benefit which is most relevant from the point of view of distributive justice.

My account may be thought too narrow for a related reason. My definition of health-care needs in terms of normal species functioning may, some argue, make it difficult to count certain important health-care services as health-care needs. For example, some have claimed the account may not acknowledge many forms of psychological counselling and therapy as health-care needs. Several points must be made in response. First, how well the account does depends on better articulation of the concept of mental disease, as I noted in Chapter 2. Second, much counselling is also preventive. It may prevent more serious psychopathology both in patients and their families, for it may help people avoid the replication of patterns of social dysfunction which emerge intergenerationally. Still, there is a difficulty we need to be protected against: some of what goes under the name of 'therapy' is of unknown and dubious efficacy; some is pure fad and fashion, or plain quackery. Moreover, many people seek counselling or therapy for reasons that have little to do with real dysfunction. Various dissatisfactions with quality of life prompt them to seek help. Meeting some of these preferences for counselling *might* be important for various reasons, but not for the ones I have been advocating. The practical difficulty is in telling which cases are which. Since the seriousness of undiagnosed, untreated mental disease, and its impact on normal functioning and opportunity range are both so great, I am inclined to err in the direction of permitting ready access to counselling services, at least for diagnostic purposes.

'The fair equality of opportunity account is too vague'

The notion of fair equality of opportunity, as it is used in liberal political theory, including Rawls's theory, is a *narrow* notion: it is focused on producing fairness in the competition for jobs and careers. But in the account developed here, there is a shift to a *broad* – and admittedly vaguer – notion of equal opportunity. On the broad construal, we are concerned with individual shares of the normal opportunity range, the array of life plans it is reasonable for persons to choose in a given society.

Talents and skills determine an individual's share of the normal range – as does normal species functioning. The complaint is that we have a fairly good idea of what things interfere with fair equality of opportunity to compete for jobs, and we can estimate the costs of eliminating them and make social policy accordingly. But it is much more complicated to pick out what constitutes interference with a fair share of the normal opportunity range.

I believe this point has some merit: the broader principle seems more complex than the traditional, narrow one. Moreover, there is a clearer justification for the narrower principle. Access to jobs and careers is of great strategic importance because of the rewards that attach to these positions. It is far less obvious that the broader principle can be justified by reference to the strategic importance of keeping shares of normal opportunity range fair in all the different dimensions the principle seems to require. So the price of modifying Rawls's equal opportunity principle is that we have a less clear idea how to justify the modified principle. A related worry is that the broader principle risks making the principle expansive in a way the narrower one does not.

Consider one way this expansiveness might infect the principle. Suppose that supplying a car to everyone who cannot afford one would do more to remove individual impairments of the normal opportunity range than supplying certain health-care services to those who need them. Does the fair equality of opportunity approach commit us now to supply cars instead of or in addition to treatments?[6] But the difficulty being raised here is not peculiar to the broad interpretation. The example is an instance of a far more general problem – namely, that socioeconomic (and other) inequalities affect opportunity, broadly or narrowly construed, not just the health-care and educational needs that are strategically important to protecting opportunity. My approach does not require me to deny that certain inequalities in wealth and income may conflict with fair equality of opportunity (on either construal) and that guaranteeing fair equality of opportunity may thus constrain acceptable inequalities in these goods.[7] Rather, my approach rests on the calculation that

---

[6] Using medical technology to enhance normal capacities or functions – say strength or vision – makes the problem easier: the burden of proof is on proposals which give priority to altering the normal opportunity range rather than to protecting individuals whose normal range is compromised.

[7] A standard Marxist complaint is that notions like fair equality of opportunity are ideological and deceptive, because there can be no real equality of opportunity without eliminating class inequalities. For example, appeals to equality of opportunity have historically played a conservative, deceptive role, blinding people to the injustice of class and race inequalities in rewards. Historically, appeals to the ideal of equal opportunity

certain institutions meet needs which quite generally have a central impact on individual shares of the normal opportunity range and which should therefore be governed directly by the opportunity principle.

I shall return to further objections that the fair equality of opportunity account is too strong or too expansive. But it is important to note that there are important advantages to using the broad account of opportunity in a theory of just health care. Even on a narrow equal opportunity principle, health care turns out to be an important social good. A *modest* version of my theory would yield the suggestion that *one* important principle governing health-care distribution is that it not interfere with fair equality of opportunity, construed in the narrow, Rawlsian way. But the narrow notion simply does not capture the full importance we do – and I have argued we ought to – attribute to health care, whereas the broader one may. The broader notion gives a more comprehensive theory. More compelling, the narrow construal would yield what many would see as an age-biased and morally objectionable account of health care: job and career opportunities are more important in early and middle stages of life than in later ones, but our health-care needs increase later in life. The broad construal, as I show in Chapter 5, provides us with a way of avoiding age-bias and with plausible suggestions about just health care for the elderly.

'The fair equality of opportunity account is too strong'
One form of this objection is that equalizing opportunity would require eliminating individual differences among persons. I have already responded to this point by showing that the fair equality of opportunity account does not require us to 'level' all differences between persons in their shares of the normal opportunity range. Rather, opportunity is *equal* for purposes of the account when all persons are equally spared certain kinds of impediments to opportunity – most importantly, discriminatory practices in job placement or impairments of normal species functioning, where these can be avoided. But fair shares of the normal opportunity range will still not be equal shares: individual variations in talents and skills determine those shares, assuming these have already been corrected for the effects of social and natural disadvantages, where possible. This correction is what is implied by appealing to 'fair' and not

have implicitly justified strong competitive individual relations. More concretely, we often find institutions, like the US educational system, praised as embodying a commitment to that idea, whereas there is strong evidence the system functions primarily to replicate class inequalities. See Daniels (1976), Cronin *et al.* (1975), and Bowles and Gintis (1976).

just 'formal' equality of opportunity. Health-care institutions have the limited function of maintaining normal species functioning: they eliminate individual differences due only to disease or disability. Thus the broad construal is no more committed to 'leveling' or to a principle of redress against the inequalities handed out by the natural lottery than is the narrow, Rawlsian principle.[8]

The complaint that the fair equality of opportunity account is too strong can be traced to another source as well, namely the fear that health-care needs themselves are so *expansive* and expensive, given the advance of technology, that they create a bottomless pit. Charles Fried (1978:Ch. 5), for example, argues that recognizing individual right claims to the satisfaction of health-care needs would force society to forego realizing other social goals. He cautions that we would end up worshipping opportunity to pursue our goals but having to forego the pursuit. Here we have a different kind of social hijacking argument, hijacking by needs rather than preferences (See also Braybrooke 1968.)

Two points can be offered in response to this worry about expansiveness. First, the narrow model I have given of health-care needs excludes some of the kinds of cases Fried uses to demonstrate the threat of the bottomless pit. Thus Fried's example of retarding the effects of normal aging does not involve correcting a departure from normal species functioning; nor does cryogenic preservation of the dying in order to wait for scientific advance. Such uses of health-care technology may be thought important in a given society. Then, arguments about the relative merits of this use of scarce resources may be advanced. But such arguments would not rest on claims about basic health-care needs and thus may have different justificatory force. Still, technology does expand the ways (and costs) we have of meeting genuine health-care needs. So my account of needs at best reduces but does not eliminate Fried's worry.

Second, there is a difference between Fried's account of individual rights and entitlements and the one I am assuming here (which is quite Rawlsian). Fried is worried that if we posit a fundamental individual right to have needs satisfied, no other social goals will be able to override the right claims to all health-care needs. But no such fundamental right is *directly* posited on the view I have sketched. Rather, the particular rights and entitlements of individuals to have certain needs met are specified

---

[8] I believe this formulation avoids the complaints made by Lawrence Stern (1983); also it makes it clear why neither the *strong* nor the *weak* formulations of the Principle D, which Allen Buchanan (1983, 1984) attributes to me, actually describes my position. I believe I thus avoid their most forceful criticisms.

only *indirectly*, as a result of the basic health-care institutions acting in accord with the general principle governing opportunity. Deciding which needs are to be met and what resources are to be devoted to doing so requires careful moral judgment and a wealth of empirical knowledge about the effects of alternative allocations. The various institutions which affect opportunity must be weighed against each other. Similarly, the resources required to provide for fair equality of opportunity must be weighed against what is needed to provide for other important social institutions. This is true even though guaranteeing fair equality of opportunity has (lexical) priority over principles of justice promoting well-being in other ways. The point is that health-care institutions capable of protecting opportunity can be maintained only in societies whose productive capacities they do not undermine. The bugaboo of the bottomless pit is less threatening in the context of such a theory. The price paid is that we are less clear – in general and abstracting from the application of the theory to a particular society – just what the individual claim comes to.

I believe this price is worth paying, but I note that others seem distressed that no well-defined universal right to health care follows from my general theory. Rights to health care will be derivative, and just how they are to be derived from more general obligations to protect fair equality of opportunity is a very complicated story (see Moskop 1983 and Buchanan 1983). It is also worth noting that my account is stronger than the one embodied in the President's Commission (1983a) Report, *Securing Access to Health Care*. Great care is taken by the Commission to avoid talking about rights to health care. Though there are philosophical grounds for such reservations, I suspect political considerations entered as well. The Commission instead talks about a *social obligation* to provide adequate care without undue burdens, but it is careful to say that such a view involves no commitment to health-care rights. Moreover, the Commission Report remains unclear whether this social obligation is one that follows from considerations of justice, rather than merely benefi-cient public policy. My account is not equivocal on this matter: the social obligation I discuss is rooted in considerations of justice – namely, to protect fair equality of opportunity. Moreover, such obligations will correspond to the rights of individuals. But these are not some prior set of individual rights, but rights and entitlements defined within a set of basic institutions governed by the fair equality of opportunity principle. My account may not be universal enough for some, but it is too strong for others.

'The fair equality of opportunity account is circular'

Some commentators have objected to the fact that the normal opportunity range is defined relative to a given society, and so it is affected by facts about that society. Specifically, if health-care services themselves affect the normal opportunity range, then we cannot use the normal range as a guide to determining what the health-care services should be. Just health care is defined by reference to the normal range, which is affected by existing health care: this verges on a circularity (see Stern 1983 and Buchanan 1983).

Two replies are in order. First, the relativization of the normal range to a society captures an important requirement for a theory of just health care. The importance of illness will vary depending on facts about a society, and a distributive principle must leave room for such variation. As I noted earlier, curing dyslexia might well be more important in some societies than others, though it is a disease in all of them. Secondly, health care will in general affect the *distribution* of shares of the normal opportunity range, not the range itself. The range tends to be an effect of other factors, such as the level of technological development, the social structure, and so on.

This point might be made by reference to an example. Suppose a disease is widespread, even universal, in a society. Say it is a form of anemia which affects all and is debilitating across the board. One might think that impact on the normal opportunity range will not tell us how important it is to treat this disease, since it hurts all individuals equally. But I think the opportunity account still helps us here, for it is not only a principle governing competitive advantage. The anemia in this case is a disease which keeps each individual from adequately carrying out *any* life plan that otherwise would be reasonable in his society. Remember, our reference point is normal species-functional organization and functioning, not functioning in a certain society.

Limits of the account

I have already emphasized some of the limits of my account. A theory of just health care is not a general theory of justice, and I have had to leave unresolved pressing problems in the general theory. Indeed, my account is asserted in a conditional way: it depends on justification of the principle of fair equality of opportunity, suitably broadened and given appropriate priority, which I cannot offer.

It is also worth a reminder that my account is incomplete in other ways. I have not argued that concerns for opportunity are the only ones that should bear on the design of health-care systems. Other important social goals – some protected by right claims or other claims of need – may require the use of health-care technology. I have not considered when, if ever, these needs or rights take precedence over other wants and preferences or over some health-care needs. I noted earlier the implications of my view for the public funding of abortions, which is one example of how the account remains incomplete. Similarly, there is the question whether the demand for equality in health care extends beyond some decent adequate minimum, which we may suppose is defined by reference to fair equality of opportunity. Should those health-care services not considered basic be allowed to operate on a market basis, or should we insist on equality even here? This issue is further discussed in the next chapter.

Finally, my account is incomplete because I have concentrated on social obligations to maintain and restore health and have ignored individual responsibility to do so. But there is substantial evidence that individuals can do much to avoid incurring risks to their health – by avoiding smoking, excessive alcohol, and certain foods, and by getting adequate exercise and rest. Nothing in my approach is incompatible with encouraging people to adopt healthy life styles. The harder issue, however, is deciding how to distribute the burdens that result when people 'voluntarily' incur extra risks and raise the costs of health care (by over 10% on some estimates) by doing so. After all, the consequences of such behavior cannot be easily dismissed as the arbitrary outcome of the natural lottery. Should smokers be forced to pay higher insurance premiums or special health-care taxes? I do not believe my account forces us to ignore the source of health-care risks in assigning such burdens, though it is also not obvious we must take the source into account. In any case, at this point little more be said because much depends on very specific details of social history. In the United States, government subsidies of the tobacco industry, the legality of cigarette advertising, and special subculture pressures on key groups – for example, teenagers – all undermine the view that we have clear-cut cases of informed, individual decision-making for which individuals must be held fully accountable. I return to these issues briefly in Chapter 7.

Summary and applications

My discussion has moved through two main stages. First, I sought to explain why many view health care as a *special* social good. This inquiry was primarily descriptive. It drew on distinctions we actually make about the importance of different prefences in many moral contexts. My explanation of the importance we attribute to health care depended on showing that (1) meeting health-care needs helps us maintain normal species functioning and that (2) normal functioning in turn has a major impact on an individual's share of the normal opportunity range for his society. The suggestion was that individuals have a fundamental interest in protecting that share.

In the second stage, I sought to provide normative foundations for this explanation, to show why we might be justified in thinking society had obligations to protect individual shares of the normal opportunity range. Though I was not able to provide a full justification for a general principle that guaranteed fair equality of opportunity, I did suggest some considerations in its favor. My central claim is that if such a principle can be established, then it provides us with a proper framework for a theory of just health care. Health-care institutions should be governed by a principle that guarantees fair equality of opportunity. I then illustrated how such a principle might work to extend one general theory of justice, Rawls's theory of justice as fairness, to health-care institutions. Doing so required broadening Rawls's principle so that it protected individual shares of the normal opportunity range and not merely access to jobs and offices. I argued that this extension was a natural one, compatible with the reasons for wanting to protect fair equality of opportunity in the first place.

What emerges is the claim that health-care institutions should have the limited – but important – task of protecting people against a serious impediment to opportunity, their failing to enjoy normal species functioning. On this view, shares of the normal range will be *fair* when positive steps have been taken to make sure that individuals maintain normal functioning, where possible, and that there are no other discriminatory impediments to their choice of life plans. Still, fair shares are not equal, since individual talents and skills will still differ, and these form a natural baseline against which individual shares of the normal range are defined. Finally, I tried to defend this account against certain objections.

The task remains now to test the account by examining its implications for health-care institutions. If we recall the discussion of public policy issues in Chapter 1, it will be clear that a central set of implications for a theory of just health care will include what it says about access to personal medical services. In Chapter 4 I try to show that my account brings plausible results to bear on an area of great controversy. In Chapter 5, I demonstrate that my account, using a natural modification of the broad principle of fair equality of opportunity, helps us formulate a plausible account of just health care for the elderly. In this way the account avoids the charge that appeals to opportunity must be age-biased. In the next three chapters, I examine possible conflicts between what just health care requires and the liberties of various groups. In Chapter 6, I note that justice may require us to limit the autonomy of physicians and other providers in ways that are not traditional, at least in the United States: the issue is to determine whether basic liberties are threatened and whether we can retain important features of the doctor–patient relationship. In Chapter 7, I note the implications of the theory for the just distribution of preventive health care and examine possible conflicts between such requirements and the individual liberties of workers governed by the US Occupational Safety and Health Administration, an agency established by the US Congress in 1970 to protect worker health. In Chapter 8, I examine another issue in a preventive context – whether protecting workers with special sensitivities to risks threatens their equality of opportunity.

4 · Equity of access to health care

Sources of disagreement about access

The fair equality of opportunity account has important implications for the public policy debate about access to personal medical services. But to see what is useful and distinctive about the account, it will be necessary to look at the extensive and diverse empirical literature on access. My concern, however, is conceptual and moral, not empirical. I will not try to resolve disputes about numbers.

The literature on equity of access is complex and confusing. Indeed, there is not consensus on what counts as 'equitable access'. There are three central reasons for divergence on this question. First, access is itself a complicated notion, a composite of many factors. Consequently, determining what counts as equality of access, let alone equity of access, is a non-trivial problem; moreover, in some cases considerations about equity already play a role in our judgements about equality. Second, health-care services are non-homogeneous. They have many functions, some more important, more basic, or more urgent than others. So, as I noted in Chapter 1, it is not possible to settle questions about equity of access until we have made it clear what the access is to. Are we worried about access to all the services offered in our health-care system? Or are we worried only about a key set of services, defined by reference to some central or basic function, regardless of their availability within our system? And how can we pick these out in the context of an evolving system and technology? Third, and perhaps most fundamentally, divergence on what counts as equitable access derives from divergence on more basic moral questions, specifically questions of distributive justice. There is moral disagreement about the nature of health care as a social good, about what sort of special importance attaches to it, if any. Moreover, disagreement on this question is tied to other fundamental disagreements about which distributions of social goods are just.

I shall begin by explaining why the problem of defining equality of access is not trivial. This point runs counter to the view that we have a clear, non-controversial notion of equality of access and that our only disagreements are about which departures from such equality are morally acceptable or equitable. I shall then discuss three approaches to the definition of equity of access. These include a utilization and needs-based account (Aday 1975, 1976; Aday and Andersen 1974, 1975, 1978; Aday, Andersen, and Fleming 1980; Andersen 1978a; Andersen, Anderson, and Kravitz 1975; Andersen, Anderson, and Lion 1976), a more 'process' oriented approach (Bentkover and Sloan 1979), and a distinctively different 'market' based account, variants of which abound in the medical economics and planning literature (I shall here include voucher schemes, such as Enthoven 1980). I shall look at the strengths and weaknesses of each of these approaches and suggest ways in which their fundamental differences depend on broader disagreements about the nature of health care as a social good and about other principles of distributive justice. I shall then take up the question, To what must we have access? Specifically, I will look at the presuppositions about equity underlying reform proposals such as those advanced by Enthoven. These are important because they force us to consider the view that equitable access is access to a 'decent basic minimum' of health care. Finally, I shall show how the implications of the fair equality of opportunity account avoid some of the problems facing these other approaches to equity of access, even if the account itself leaves some issues unresolved.

A note on usage: In the literature on access the term 'justice' or 'just distribution' does not appear. Instead, we encounter the term 'equity of access'. I shall use the term 'equity' in a broad sense, roughly equivalent to 'distributively fair or just'. There is a narrower usage in which equity is an 'interstitial' concept, one that raises questions of justice only against a background of institutions whose conformance with principles of justice is not at issue (Barry 1965:152ff.). I use the broader notion, though I might prefer to restrict 'equity' to the narrower one, because the literature on access to health care seems to employ the broader concept.

When is access equal?

It is tempting to think that we can give a completely non-controversial definition of equal access to health care – much as we can do for equality of income – and reserve all controversy for debates about which departures from equality conform to acceptable principles of justice. Suppose I earn $10,000 less than you. The inequality might be thought equitable by some if you work longer or harder than I, by others if your skills have a higher market value than mine, and by others if you need more than I do. Here our moral disagreements about appropriate distributive principles show up as disagreements about just or equitable income distribution, though there is no controversy about whether our incomes are equal. The situation is arguably different for the notion of equal access: to arrive at a notion of equal access, we must already have made various decisions about what considerations ought to count in judging when access is equal. These decisions reflect our purpose or interest in making the judgment about equality, and some of these discriminations are themselves moral. So moral considerations are already embedded in the specification of equality and are not held at bay until we get to decisions about equity.

Consider the problem in a slightly different context. There is a coffee supply in a lounge not far from my office. When is access to the coffee equal among my colleagues? Some cases seem clear: if the lounge is open only to male colleagues, then female colleagues can complain they do not have equal access to the coffee. If the lounge is up a flight of stairs and there is no wheelchair ramp, then my paraplegic colleague may have grounds for claiming unequal access to the coffee. After all, he has to ask someone to fetch it, but none of the rest of us does. (Does his complaint disappear if in fact he drinks as much coffee as we do?) Other factors have a less clear impact. Should we worry about the fact that not all offices are equidistant from the pot? Some are thirty feet away, some only ten. Does it matter how the offices were assigned – randomly, by choice, or by seniority? Does it matter if the distance correlates negatively with coffee use? Should we worry that some colleagues use more calories in walking to the pot than others? Suppose the lounge is painted a brilliant green, a color I so dislike that it takes more psychological effort for me to fetch coffee than it takes my colleagues, who chose the color. Is our access unequal? Suppose that, on a previous job, I had unpleasant coffee-room experiences and their memory hinders me from getting coffee; my colleagues had pleasant coffee-room experiences. Do we have equal access?

I am not suggesting we spend much effort figuring out when access to the coffee is equal, for I do not want to trivialize the problem of access to health care. Still, it is worth seeing what underlies my inclination to say that the access to the coffee is *equal* despite variations in office distance, use of calories, preference for the color of the lounge, or past experiences that influence preferences. Where we have something that is *merely an amenity*, variables that merely impact on preference orderings are properly ignored in judging equality of access. Factors like the 'male only' lounge or the flight of steps have an impact in a way independent of effects on preference orderings. If I felt differently about the importance of coffee, say because I thought it met a basic need (let us ignore habit or addiction), I might be more sensitive to factors that affect preferences and I might want to make finer discriminations, especially where there is an effect on utilization of the coffee pot.

My assessment of the importance of the coffee is connected to other views I have about which variables that affect access or use are relevant to issues of *equity*. That is, I allow my notion of *equality of access* to be determined, in part, by *prior judgments about equity of access*. Lest the case of the coffee pot be suspected because of its triviality, consider the same point in a non-trivial context that we have already encountered in Chapter 3. Thus, one tradition in our society is content to judge that equality of opportunity obtains if there are no formal – for example, legal or quasi-legal – barriers to persons of different races or sexes competing for a job or office. Others argue that positive steps must be taken to compensate for various natural and social variations between people which arguably confer 'unfair' or at least undeserved advantages. On this view, unless the impact of this 'natural lottery' is compensated for, equality of opportunity does not obtain (Rawls 1971: sects. 14, 17). Clearly, this difference in judgment about what counts as equality of opportunity is itself the product of other moral assessments, and so the notion of equal opportunity is itself controversial. Consequently, it cannot serve (without further argument) as a non-controversial baseline which we can use in debating the equity of inequalities in opportunity. The case is the same, I am suggesting, for equal access to health care.

This point may not seem to jibe with the fact that in a broad range of settings individuals and legislators talk as if there is agreement on what counts as equal access. Thus we find the remark in the US Health Planning Act of 1974 (PL 93–641) that it is an important objective of Federal policy to provide 'equal access to quality care at a reasonable cost'. It is probably fair to say that all that most people have in mind when they talk about equal access is a negative criterion, specifically that certain traditional constraints on access, mainly financial and geographical, should play a minimal role in determining whether people who need health care get it. There may be implicit in this negative characterization a positive ideal – for example, 'any two persons of comparable health status who want appropriate care have an equal chance of getting it'. But nothing so schematic may be in anyone's mind at all; there may be only a moral complaint against a particular inequality. Thus there is agreement about what to call equal access only because there is agreement not to accept a particular kind of inequality. My point is confirmed, not disconfirmed by the example.

Three accounts of equitable access

Equity as utilization for need

The Aday and Andersen approach as an analytic framework

I turn now to examine the ethical presuppositions and implications of three accounts of equitable access, a use- (or use per need) based account, a 'process' variable account, and what I shall call a 'market' account. The framework provided by Aday and Andersen (1975), and Aday, Andersen and Fleming (1980) is a useful place to start. Not only is their work seminal, but seeing what motivates their project will allow an economical discussion of the alternative approaches. I stress that my goal here is to point to ethical implications of the work, not to undertake a systematic, empirical assessment of it. Moreover, I must confine myself to the central thrust of each approach and not the subtle ways in which the accounts may be refined, extended, or combined. My central point will be to show the way in which these accounts of equitable access are really disguised ways of talking about principles of distributive justice for health care.

Aday and Andersen's work has both an *analytic* and *normative* importance. To see its analytic function, consider the fact that alternative theories of the behaviors or processes through which people seek health care suggest many factors which could have an effect on the use of health-care services. We need a way of testing which of these factors actually do have a significant effect on access. These *potential access* factors are of two (by some classifications, three) kinds. Some are structural features of the health-care system, such as the availability of physicians or hospitals in different geographical areas, as measured, say, by physician–patient ratios. Other factors reflect predisposing and enabling features of individuals in the population, such as age, health status, and cultural background for the former, and income level or insurance coverage level for the latter. A particularly important subgroup of factors is sometimes viewed separately and called 'process' factors. They play an important role in the process of seeking health care, at least in some theories of the process. The analytic task is to decide which variations in these many factors influencing potential access are important. Which ones count because they really contribute to differences in access to health care?

Aday and Andersen seek to test the importance of potential access variables by determining their effect on measures of actual or *realized access*, the output of the system. Measures of realized access are of two main types: *subjective* measures, which reflect satisfaction with treat-ment; and *objective* measures, which are concerned with various utiliza-tion rates. The over-all strategy is thus to look at variations between population subgroups on some measure of potential access to see if there is an effect on realized access, here utilization rates. Suppose our working theory of the process through which we seek health care suggests that a certain variable, say waiting time for an appointment, will have a big effect on access to health care. Aday and Andersen propose a method for 'testing' such claims: potential access variables are important only if they produce an intergroup effect on realized access (utilization rates). If a process variable, say waiting time for an appointment, does not have an effect on utilization rates for population subgroups, then it is not causally significant according to the criterion being proposed. So the utilization rate test is a way of saying that the proof of the pudding is in the eating; the test of access is use.

Of course, details become important here. A process variable – for example, time spent in a waiting room – may have a significant effect on measures of satisfaction with care, but have relatively little effect on utilization rates. So the choice of objective or subjective measures of realized access may yield different assessments of the importance of a process variable and, ultimately, of the equity of access to health-care services. In contrast to Aday and Andersen's primary emphasis on utilization rates, some critics who are particularly interested in process factors tend to emphasize satisfaction measures (Sloan and Bentkover 1979). Even if we are inclined to use an objective measure, however, it matters which one. For example, utilization rates between income groups in the US have not differed significantly following the introduc-tion of Medicare and Medicaid. But if health status of lower-income groups is lower than that of higher-income groups, there may still be variation in a measure of use per need, say use per disability days or use per bed-disability days.

Aday and Andersen urge us to use a measure of utilization per need. Even here, detail matters. Different measures of need will give different utilization per need rates and may lead to different assessments of which variables are 'important' in the sense so far discussed. For example, if some income or cultural groups report an inflated number of disability days, say because of different attitudes toward adopting a sick role or different absenteeism incentives (Sloan and Bentkover 1979:3), we may find that measure of need to be problematic for the analytic task at hand. Similarly, studies suggest that the choice of bed-disability days as a measure of need can reveal a difference in use per need between high- and low-income groups which is not apparent with the less severe measure of need, disability days (Davis, Gold and Makuc 1981).

It is important to see that the focus on use per need rates stops short of measuring possible differences in the *efficacy* of the services delivered to different population groups. It is at least conceivable that use per need rates could be similar, but the quality – here, efficacy – of the services might vary, so that use per need would not effectively measure impact on health status. This point bears on the relevance of the focus on use per need rates and on the ultimate rationale for the definition of equity based on use.

Normative use of the account

It is crucial to see that the framework Aday and Andersen advocate is advanced primarily for its *normative* implications, not merely for its relevance to understanding or describing the causal relationships among the phenomena involved in access to health care. Indeed, we find the analytic test for the causal importance of a potential access variable reformulated as a definition of equity of access. Aday and Andersen argue that 'The greatest "equity" of access is said to exist when need, rather than structural (for example, availability of physicians), or individual (for example, family income) factors determine who gains entry to the health care system' (Aday *et al.* 1980:26; Andersen, Anderson and Kravitz 1975:10–11). In other words, access is equitable if the *important* potential access variables, as operationally defined, are all related to health status in the proper way. If, however, important potential access variables are not related to health status, then an inequity of access obtains. As Aday *et al.* (1980:43) put it:

Inequity in health service distribution occurs when individuals receive services primarily according to their place in the social structure, their enabling characteristics, or the characteristics of the health system instead of according to their need . . . The inequity may be only 'apparent,' however, if the lower access levels can be explained by varying age structure (demographic or illness levels). For example, lower use rates for an ethnic group consisting of predominantly younger persons in reasonably good health may be only 'apparent inequity.' Excess utilization is indicated if a subgroup has higher utilization rates than the rest of the population. However, like inequity, it may be only 'apparent excess.' One example would be higher utilization rates by the elderly which could be attributed to the larger number of symptoms and disability days they experience.

This normative account of equity of access is extremely influential. Though others point to some 'inequities' between subgroups that Aday and Andersen fail to find (Davis *et al.* 1981), nevertheless they appeal to the underlying Aday and Andersen definition. The differences lie in how the estimate of need is measured or operationalized.

The argument from function (again)

The attempt to recast the utilization rate test for important potential access variables as a normative criterion for equity of access needs justification. Why ought we to look at variations in utilization rates in this way? Here Aday *et al.* (1980:41) draw on a widely held view, namely that an ' "equitable distribution" of health care services is one in which illness (as defined by the patient and his family or by health care professionals) is the major determinant of the allocation of resources'.

One common way to defend this view involves the *argument from function*, introduced in Chapter 1, which can be paraphrased like this: 'The (main) function of health-care services is to prevent and cure illness, i.e., to meet health-care needs. A distribution of health-care services that is not determined by the distribution of health-care needs is therefore unreasonable in some important sense. Specifically, it ignores *similarities* and *differences* – here in health status – between persons which, given the function of health care, ought to be relevant to establishing its reasonable distribution. Ignoring such relevant similarities and differences is what it means for a distribution to be inequitable.' A version of this argument is clearly foreshadowed in Bernard Williams's (1971:27) now classic discussion of equality in which he concluded that, 'leaving aside preventive medicine the proper ground of distribution of medical care is health; this is a necessary truth'. In any case, of course, the argument at most establishes a *necessary* but not a *sufficient* condition for distributions to be equitable. (My remarks on the argument in Chapter 1 show it is not valid as it stands and works, if at all, only for some needs. Still, in chapters 2 and 3, I suggest health-care needs are among those to which a version of the argument may apply.) As we shall see, some people argue that it is not even a necessary condition for equity that health care be distributed according to needs. For example, some object that the argument mistakenly presupposes that health-care services are homogeneous in function and that people will always have preferences that correspond to their presumed health-care 'needs'.

The underlying view about equity is a central and powerful one. It is a view with a long history of advocacy. I shall come later to sketch a position which incorporates what I think is correct about it. Still, we can see it is not the whole of the story if we examine more carefully some objections to the Aday and Andersen approach.

Objections to the utilization for need account

One central objection is that a focus on utilization rates ignores at least one other necessary condition for equity of access. Specifically, variations in certain potential access variables, especially process variables, can have equity implications even if they do not show up as important on the Aday and Andersen criterion, that is, by reference to their effects on utilization rates. Time spent in a waiting room, or out-of-pocket health-care expenditures, if they vary with income group (corrected for health status), are differentially burdensome even if utilization rates (or use per need rates) are not affected. More generally, someone may argue that some inequalities in potential access variables between subgroups raise equity questions even if they do not affect the outcomes of health-care-seeking behavior, as measured by utilization rates. They still affect other outcomes – for example, what else someone has the chance to do with his time or money.

A second objection is that uniformity between subgroups in utilization rates (or use per need rates) is not even a necessary condition for equitable access. Some subgroup variations that correlate with utilization rate differences will reflect differences in attitudes toward health care. Consequently, these variations may not be inequities in the access to health care at all. A standard example might be the deliberate under-utilizer who, for religious, esthetic, or cultural reasons has a principled aversion to some or all traditional (mainstream) health-care services. Another form the problem may take has already been mentioned. Attitudes toward assuming a sick-role may differ between cultural or income groups, so that some might judge themselves to need a 'disability day' more readily than others. But if one group inflates its need in this way relative to another, the equity of the distribution is affected (Sloan and Bentkover 1979:3). Of course, we need to draw finer distinctions, say between those attitudes toward health based on ignorance, which society has a responsibility to correct, and those based on principled, informed choice. But clearly, some modification of the Aday and Andersen account is needed to accommodate these worries. In any case, they clearly leave room for such a modification.

The issue is even more complex, however. *Some* variation in utilization rates, even corrected for health status, may not be importantly related to *health outcomes*, that is health status after treatment. It is at least arguable that only those utilization rate variations are inequitable which reflect significant differences in the preventative, curing, and caring functions of health-care services. Aday and Andersen shy away from looking at health outcomes because so many factors intervene between utilization and outcome; but their simplification here may leave room for a systematic bias. The kind of case of greatest interest is one in which the course of treatment is more intensive than an alternative but for which there is no evidence that the more intensive treatment is more efficacious. The issue arises, for example, in the context of mental health care, where some evidence suggests that more intensive interventions (therapy) are used for upper-middle-class groups and less intensive (more drug-oriented) treatments are more frequently used for low income and minority groups (Mollica and Redlich 1980). If there were no demonstrable difference in efficacy between the two types of treatment, would the inequality in utilization rate by income group constitute an inequity? Finally, one might insist that some differences in utilization rates, even where there are effects on health-status outcomes, reflect informed choices about how risk-free one wants to be. They reflect a choice about how important one thinks health-care services are compared to other things one may want to spend income on. Such choices may well lead to utilization rate differences, but they still do not indicate inequity of access.

It is now possible to explain what I am calling the 'process' and the 'market' accounts of equity of access in terms of the possible objections we have just noted to the utilization rate account. A process account seems committed to the view that the utilization rate account at most captures one necessary condition for equitable access, and, in any case, fails to capture another necessary component of equity, intergroup equality in process variables. Indeed, the process account may even drop intergroup uniformity in use per need rates as a necessary condition for equitable access. In this case, the process account clearly overlaps with what I am calling the 'market' approach, for the latter insists that uniformity of use per need is not even a necessary condition for achieving equitable access. Of course, the market approach parts company with the process account in that it also rejects the view that intergroup variations in process variables constitute inequity of access.

Equity as equality in process variables

Sloan and Bentkover's (1979) account

Consider as an example of the 'process' approach Sloan and Bentkover's fine study of access to ambulatory care. Their view is not so much that one should ignore utilization rates, which they admit are an important measure of realized access. Rather, they object to its selection as the sole or even primary criterion in an account of equitable access (1979:2–3). Their concern for the way in which certain process variables – for example, travel or waiting time – may vary with income group, race, or geographical area is a concern for what they refer to as the 'humaneness' of the care delivered (1979:4). Such variations are likely to be captured more by *subjective* (satisfaction) measures of realized access even when they do not affect *objective* (utilization rate) measures. Process variable differences, even where they do not affect utilization rates, may reflect differences in the difficulty of seeking care – that is, inequalities in the burdens that attend seeking care. As Sloan and Bentkover (1979:24) put it, 'Many, for example, would view the long waits the poor experience in clinics as an injustice, irrespective of the effect patient waiting might have on utilization rates' (see Gutmann 1981). The basic contention is that *access* to health care cannot be considered equitable if it is much more difficult for some people to get care than it is for others, even if people make adjustments to the burdensomeness of the process and get the amount of care they need.

Amenities, quality, and claims to access

There is a certain plausibility to this worry about the burdensomeness of the process of seeking care and the claim that equity of access considerations are raised by such differences. What is missing, however, is the kind of moral argument we saw was immediately forthcoming in support of the utilization rate approach. What we need to know is why ease of access must be roughly equal for population subgroups even when the 'ease' factor does not affect utilization rates. The problem is made more glaring by a formulation of the issue which can be found in Sloan and Bentkover themselves. Specifically, they tend to group the impact of these process variables under the heading of 'quality' factors in health care. Indeed, within an economic model they discuss, the term 'amenities' is used (Sloan and Bentkover 1979:24–5). The picture that emerges is that health care for some population subgroups may have more 'amenities' than for other groups – for example, less travel or waiting time, more physician contact time – though not necessarily higher utilization rates or better health-status outcomes. Do these subgroup differences in 'amenities' constitute inequities of access? If the 'process' account of equitable access can be construed as asking for a more egalitarian distribution of these amenities, and not just of utilization per need rates, what justified the demand?

The problem here is that only some qualitative aspects of health-care services clearly seem relevant to worries about equity of access, but others seem less directly connected. It is worth noting in this connection an important simplifying assumption that underlies the utilization rate account we have looked at. Utilization rates tell us nothing about the *quality* of the services rendered, where quality is some measure of net benefits minus harms (Donabedian 1979). Such a measure of quality is concerned largely with the efficacy of services rendered. The simplifying assumption is that when use per need rates are roughly equal, we are dealing with qualitatively equal sorts of services in the sense that their impact on health outcomes is likely to be roughly equal. But the 'amenities' involved with many of these process variables, when rendered, are *not* clearly linked to health-status outcomes – only to subjective measures of satisfaction with the treatment. So an argument that grants health-care services a very special status because of their primary function of meeting health-care needs does not by itself seem powerful enough to justify the concern, present in the process account, that the equal distribution of amenities is also a necessary condition for equity of access.

A more promising line of argument for the process account might go something like this. In order to be sure that variations in use per need rates are in fact the result of informed choices or preferences about the use of health-care services, we must be sure that decisions to utilize are not made harder for some persons than others because of variations in the process variables. But it is not obvious what the force of this argument is in the face of evidence that use per need rates are equitably distributed, because, as it were, it still must be argued that we have a difference here that makes a difference. Still, variations in process variables are a useful concern to raise when an attempt is made to explain away a variation in use per need rates, for example, by saying they are merely the result of differences in preference. Such an argument puts the process account more in the role of an opponent of the market view than an opponent of the use per need account.

Of course, strongly egalitarian views about distributive justice in general might be invoked to justify a concern about equality among process variables. If, for example, one was prepared to argue that only differences in need or preference should be allowed to explain variations in the services used by different groups, then systematic variations in even 'amenities' would look like inequities, just as unequal distributions of *any* goods that cannot be fully accounted for by need or preference differences constitute inequities in distribution. Or if one were to allow inequalities only if they act to maximize the well-being of the worst off, then some variations in 'amenities' might count as inequities. But I am not concerned to discuss such strongly egalitarian views here, largely because I am interested in the *special* arguments people are inclined to make about equity with regard to health services which they are not inclined to make for many other social goods. Still, more specialized arguments may be invoked here. Dickman (1983) argues that a principle requiring us to show 'equal respect for persons', plus the fact that people in need of health care are especially vulnerable to affronts to their self-respect, requires that we pay special attention to the (roughly) equal distribution of at least some reasonable set of 'amenities'. Interesting though the argument is, I cannot consider it here (see Jonsen 1976a).

Equity as the market availability of a decent basic minimum

Constraints on the market

I should like now to sketch in more detail what I have called the 'market' approach to equity of access. In contrast to the utilization rate and process variable approaches, the market approach is not really a position represented in the empirical literature on access. Rather, it is a composite abstracted from views which are common in economics and health planning literature. It is of interest here because of the quite different limits it places on the notion of equitable access and because of the quite different underlying view of health care and distributive justice. Nevertheless, as with the utilization rate approach in particular, an underlying approach to issues of distributive justice plays a prominent role in defining what counts as an equitable access.

I have already noted that one central line of objection to the utilization rate approach is that similarity in intergroup utilization per need rates is not even a necessary condition for equitable access (or distribution). A view that provides a rationale for such a claim is the view that health-care services are commodities like any others (see Chapter 1, p. 10). On this view, there is nothing so 'special' about these services that cannot be accommodated by allowing a market for them to respond to people's preferences for them. On such a view, equity of access is assured if three main conditions obtain: (1) the commodity must be available at something like 'true social cost'; (2) individuals are capable of making rational (informed) decisions about using the system; (3) income distribution must be (approximately) equitable. The second condition requires that information about alternatives – for example, therapies or insurance schemes – is available and that people are competent and informed enough to make use of the information. Some access inequities arise when this condition is not met and these must be addressed by public policy; but I will say nothing about them here.

Aside from the problem of subsidies to the poor to guarantee equitable income distribution, the central problems of access are those brought about by departures of the medical market from the ideal of a truly competitive market (Arrow 1963). In particular, there may be various distortions on the supply side which amount to the market's not delivering services at their 'true social cost'. For example, some groups – rural populations or inner city minorities – may not be able to get the care they want and can pay for. They may not be able to get it in the desired quantities, or at the desired times with the characteristics they desire. Viewed in this way, the problem is that the market is unresponsive to consumer preferences on the supply side and interventions may be needed to correct the problem, generally by addressing structural problems in capital expenditure policy. A central problem here is the way in which the choice of a health insurance plan is tied to features of employment and the unavailability of an adequate range of plans – for example, ones that cover people between jobs. One structural feature of the insurance market is the relative unavailability of per capita, prospective rather than fee-for-service, schemes; this feature is a central focus of criticisms by a number of planners (Havighurst 1971, 1974, 1977). The central issues of access and equity of access are concerned with these supply malfunctions of the market.

The third condition, about equitable income distribution, usually comes only to this: that sufficient income redistribution take place to insure that no one falls below the officially defined poverty line. The assumption is that income transfers will be available to make sure that everyone can support himself at a subsistence level. Moreover, it is a common requirement that the sum of cash and aid-in-kind benefits to the poor must not produce work disincentives. Where such a ceiling is not argued for just on efficiency grounds, it is also claimed that an inequity would result if employed workers were less well off than the unemployed poor. (Much could be said about the adequacy of these views of equitable income distribution (see Brown, Johnson, and Vernier 1981, and esp. Daniels 1981), but this is not the occasion.) One real issue that concerns us here is how to characterize the cash, voucher, or aid-in-kind transfer schemes that would be needed to meet these assumptions. The position that seems to be held in common – either explicitly or implicitly – by many 'market' proponents is that a transfer must be adequate to buy a 'decent basic minimum' of health care. If the transfer falls short of this, it is agreed we have an inequitable transfer. So the market view I am sketching is not that of the pure libertarian who might reject all such transfers, but rather one in which there is implicit acceptance of some important moral claims that might loosely be characterized as 'welfare rights'. I shall examine the problems involved in characterizing the decent basic minimum shortly, but in any case it seems clear that there are definite limits to the size of the transfer needed in order to assure that equitable financial access to the medical market place is provided.

Implications of the market account

Assuring equitable access in the ways defined by the 'market' approach leaves extensive room for all sorts of departures from equitable access as defined by either of the other two approaches we have considered. Surely, there may be variations in the 'amenities' that accompany health-care services, if that is how we want to look at (some) process variables. Equal *quality* in these dimensions is surely not required, any more than everyone 'prefers' equal quality in, say, automobiles. Similarly, utilization per need rates may vary with 'suspect' variables like income or race and yet not indicate any inequity of access, contrary to the Aday and Andersen formulation. Rather, the unequal distribution of health care – in quantity and quality – can be viewed merely as the expression of different preference curves, just as food budgets might vary among a welfare recipient, a factory worker, and a wealthy industrialist. If we take the underlying income distribution to be morally acceptable, its expression in terms of utilization of health services need indicate no inequity.

Put succinctly, then, the 'market' approach I am considering here comes to this: access to health care is equitable if and only if there are no information barriers, financial barriers, or supply anomalies that prevent access to a 'reasonable' or 'decent basic minimum' of health-care services. How plausible such an account is depends on the characterization of such a decent minimum and the moral arguments maintaining that provision of such a minimum is all that justice or equity demands. The problem facing the 'market' proponent thus appears to be the other side of the coin from the problem facing the utilization rate account. One central problem with that account was its simplifying assumption that health care is relatively homogeneous in function and that the proper basis for its distribution must be the realization of that function. If, however, we want to treat health-care services as non-homogeneous in function, and we are willing to ground equity claims only by reference to some features of some of those services, we owe an account of how to draw the lines.

Decent minimums and the requirements of justice

Problems of characterization

Lists versus criteria

Earlier I noted that there is a basic question which must be answered before we can understand disagreements about access: access is always access *to something*, but to what? There is a tendency in the utilization and process variable accounts to assume that the answer must be 'access to whatever range of services is available in the system'. This answer ignores the non-homogeneity in function of health-care services and systems. In contrast, the market approach circumscribes the demands of equity with regard to access in a way which may avoid this objection. It insists we are concerned only with access to a 'decent basic minimum' of care. I want here to examine some of the problems with this notion.

What is meant by a 'decent basic minimum'? There are three ways to elucidate the notion: (1) the provision of a general *criterion* by reference to which we can tell if services are within the minimum or are above it; (2) the description of a fair *procedure* for determining the minimum; or (3) the simple *listing* the types of services included. In the market literature – indeed in much of the literature – there is little attempt to give a general criterion or describe an appropriate, fair procedure. What attempts we get are far too vague. Charles Fried (1976:32), for example, suggests that the 'decent minimum should reflect some conception of what constitutes tolerable life prospects in general. It should speak quite strongly to things like maternal and child health which set the terms under which individuals will compete and develop.' There may be the nucleus for a helpful idea here, but it is not developed enough to tell when 'prospects' are 'tolerable'. As John Arras (1981:32) asks, tolerable to whom?

More specific is the characterization that emerges from Enthoven's discussion of what he calls a Consumer Choice Health Plan. To qualify for tax credits, vouchers, or Medicare payments, an insurance plan would have to meet certain requirements (Enthoven 1980:128). 'A qualified plan would be required to cover, at a minimum, the list of services called "basic health services" in the Health Maintenance Organization (HMO) Act of 1973 (as amended). This list includes physician services, inpatient and outpatient hospital services, emergency health services, short term outpatient mental health services (up to twenty visits), treatment and referral for drug and alcohol abuse, laboratory, and X-ray, home health services, and certain preventive health services.' Enthoven adds, however, that 'it might make sense to start the program with a less costly list', which, unfortunately, leaves the specification by list indeterminate, a point to which I shall return shortly. Qualified plans would be required to offer a low-option plan, consisting of just the basic services (or an acceptable subset of them), in addition to any higher-option plans they might market.

Equity of access is guaranteed on the market approach if there are no important information, financial, or structural obstacles to buying into a low-option plan. Enthoven suggests that structural barriers will be reduced if qualified plans are required to have 'open enrollment' to all eligible in its service area and 'community rating', to avoid division of qualified plans into high- and low-risk groups. Furthermore, breaking the connection between employment and type of insurance plan available will remove another anomaly of the insurance market and close an important gap in access. Enthoven assumes that using vouchers to enhance the purchasing power of rural areas, which have relatively poor populations, will improve the availability of services. One must ask, however, whether or not open enrollment is sufficient to guarantee that plans are available to all in an area, or whether there should be requirements specifying the mix of population subgroups served and the options offered them (see Havighurst 1971). Similarly, we must know how well manpower and facilities will disseminate geographically, simply because vouchers increase purchasing power in under-served areas. Whether Enthoven's measures are adequate to eliminate structural problems affecting access I leave to a more empirically focused discussion. Instead, I return to the question about what equitable access is access to.

Low- and high-option plans

Consider again Enthoven's effort to specify the decent minimum by reference to a list. The list is open to emendation – not everything on the

1973 HMO Act list is mandatory. By virtue of what are things put on the list in the first place? By virtue of what can we leave them off? Dental care, for example, is not included; can we also leave off mental health services? It should be remembered that we cannot determine *the list* just by reference to average costs for actual categories: these costs are themselves the costs for types of service – for example, doctors or hospital care. When Enthoven (1980) suggests that $1,350 per year would be the voucher appropriate for a family of four which has a maximum total annual income of $4,200, he bases the figure only on actuarial costs for physicians and hospitalization, and does not include mental health services. So we have to know what is to be on the 'decent basic minimum' list before we calculate the voucher. Unfortunately, we have neither a principle offered us nor a fair procedure for arriving at the list.

Consider now some ways in which low-option plans might differ from high-option plans. The indeterminacy in what must be included in the low-option plan will of course show up as an equity of access question if more comprehensive plans include broad categories not included in basic plans – for example, mental or dental coverage. But comprehensiveness can vary even within categories: What surgical procedures are covered? What mental health therapies? What dental care?

There are other important ways in which low- and high-option plans may vary. Suppose the extensiveness of diagnostic services is allowed to vary between lower- and higher-budget plans. Then we might imagine persons with similar health status being given less or more extensive diagnostic services. One way to conceptualize this variation is as a variation in quality, here taken to be a measure of the net health benefits minus burdens (Donabedian 1979; I return in Chapter 6 to this issue). If we imagine that, under different budget ceilings, quality can be optimized in different ways, we return to our fundamental problem. Suppose, for example, one quality optimization, available under a high-option plan, allows some greater degree of freedom from risk, say of risk of undiscovered cancer, than is available under the low-option plan. We can imagine people thus 'buying' a degree of freedom from risk, so that people who like to be relatively risk-free would buy the high-option plan, and those who want to tolerate a greater risk would buy the low-option plan.

Do we now have an equity of access problem? The decent basic minimum approach would (at least implicitly) be setting a degree of freedom from risk against which it is 'decent' to be protected. Anything higher must be viewed as a matter of preference – a commodity to be floated in the market. But it is not clear we have any such clear idea of a decent minimum. No doubt some of the variation here would be curtailed by malpractice litigation, but it is also not obvious that this litigation is the proper forum in which to decide these matters of health policy. Nor is it obvious that we can appeal to 'standards of practice' to resolve this question. Where such standards are based on good studies of efficacy and cost-effectiveness, we may resolve some issues. But where the standards are derived from a clinical practice setting in which reimbursement is generally on a fee-for-service basis, the issue of what standard is acceptable under different budget ceilings has not been squarely faced. Of course, where the differences in 'quality' are primarily of the sort Sloan, Bentkover and others worry about under the heading 'amenities', we expect the 'decent minimum' standard to allow some care to be considerably less decent than others.

My criticisms of Enthoven's characterization of the decent basic minimum do not respond to one defense he might make. He might say that the decent basic minimum must be defined relative to existing practices within the society, specifically those that lead to the average actuarial costs for the items on his list. The decent minimum is defined by reference to the average. How can the worst-off complain if they end up doing as well as the average? Of course, this response ignores the flexibility of the list itself; still, it rests on a healthy pragmatism.

Unfortunately, the healthy pragmatism may mislead us. The suggestion is that we take *average use* or, more plausibly, *average use by people in the upper-middle income levels*, as a guide to defining the decent basic minimum. But such a criterion risks incorporating into the decent basic minimum all that is already *askew* in our health-care system. The medical market which operates at the heart of that system may have induced significant distortions in patterns of consumption of health care. The distortions may be the result of basic features of medical markets, such as the uncertainty in it. This uncertainty includes lack of patient expertise, which implies dependency on physicians, who act as agents. It also includes provider uncertainty about the outcomes of utilizations, which encourages 'defensive medicine' under the threat of malpractice litigation. There may also be biases built into the system in terms of the kinds of needs that the system is designed to meet – perhaps the needs of upper-income users more than the needs of the poor. Constructing the decent basic minimum out of an 'average use' criterion risks replicating all of these distortions. (It is worth noting that the President's Commission

Report on *Securing Access to Health Care* (1983a) is sensitive to these problems about appealing to 'average use' to define the decent basic minimum, which it calls 'adequate care'. I will return shortly to comment on the notion of *adequate care without excessive burdens*, which is central to the Commission Report.)

These distortions might not seem so serious if all we were seeking was a characterization of *equity* that was completely system relative. We might then not seek an account of equity which told which *needs* a system must meet. Rather, we may be concerned only that a system treat all groups within it equitably, whatever needs it happens to meet. The 'average use' criterion for characterizing the decent basic minimum might be construed in this way: it tells how equally we must treat different groups served by the system, whose basic structure is taken as fixed. I believe this view treats *equity* as a purely 'interstitial' notion, taking the over-all system as morally acceptable in its basic design. I have throughout this account been looking for a more fundamental characterization of just health care and of 'equity' as well.

One way some commentators have tried to convert the 'average use' criterion into a more theory-based account is to suggest that the system as a whole, despite certain market peculiarities, gives a rough measure of the utility of different services. More specifically, survival in the medical market is an indicator, albeit rough, of the utility of a service, an indicator that it is cost-beneficial to use it. But if, for example, rhinoplasty survives, indeed thrives, in our medical market because it is strongly desired by many well-off people, but personal-care services for the partially disabled elderly do not, I do not believe we have a real measure of the relative utility of these services, let alone of their relative importance (see Stern 1983).

My suggestion that the notion of a 'decent basic minimum' is inadequate to support the moral weight it bears in the 'market' approach is best supported by the proposal of an alternative account. We must look for a more principled way of characterizing what justice requires if access to health care is to be equitable. I would like to put the fair equality of opportunity account to work in this direction.

Access and the fair equality of opportunity account

The fair equality of opportunity account of just health care has several important implications for the issue of equitable access we have been discussing. The account says that health care is special because meeting health-care needs has an important effect on the opportunity open to individuals to choose reasonable plans of life. Moreover, if there is a social obligation to protect fair equality of opportunity, construed in this broad way, then health-care institutions should be designed to meet that obligation. Consider the implications of this view for access to care.

First, the account is compatible with, though it *does not imply*, a multi-tiered health-care system. In contrast, the 'market' approach *requires* at least a two-tier system – the lower tier provides the decent basic minimum, and upper tiers provide what the market will bear. Thus the fair equality of opportunity account shares with the market approach the view that health-care services have a variety of functions, only *some* of which may give rise to social obligations to provide them. As I noted earlier, the market approach does not explain the basis for obligations it recognizes, whereas my account is clear on that point. The basic tier on my account would include *health-care services that meet health-care needs, or at least important health-care needs – as judged by their impact on the normal opportunity range.* Other tiers, if they are allowed, might involve uses of health care services to meet less important health-care needs or to meet other needs and wants. My account leaves open the possibility that other tiers of the system might also be important enough to be given special precedence over other uses of social resources – but, if they were, it would be for reasons different from those which give such precedence to the basic tier. That is, there may be social obligations to provide access to services which fall in a tier above the basic one: this issue is not addressed by my account, incomplete as it is, though I return to it shortly.

Second, the fair equality of opportunity account provides a principled way of characterizing the health-care services that fall in the socially guaranteed tier. They are the services needed to maintain, restore, or compensate for the loss of normal species-typical functioning. In turn, normal functioning contributes substantially to defining the share of the normal opportunity range open to individuals. This 'principled' way of characterizing the basic tier is, to be sure, abstract. It requires moral judgment in its application, as well as a considerable amount of information about health care and the resources available in the society. Still, it provides a basis for argument about what should be included in the basic tier, a basis which is lacking in the notion of a decent basic minimum or in glosses on the notion, such as Fried's (1976) remark about 'tolerable life prospects'.

Third, however the upper tiers of the health-care system are to be financed, there should be no obstacles – financial, racial, geographical, and so on – to access to the basic tier. The importance of such equality of access to the basic tier follows from two main lines of argument. First, the basic tier is defined by reference to the impact of health-care services on opportunity, and inequalities of opportunity are not to be tolerated for the sorts of economic reasons that might make the preservation of these obstacles appealing. Second, the importance of equality of access follows I think from basic facts about the sociology and epistemology of the determination of health-care needs. The 'felt needs' of patients are at best only initial indicators of the presence of real health-care needs. Structural and other process barriers to initial access, for example, to primary care, compel people to make their own determination of the importance of the symptoms they experience. Of course, every system requires some such assessment, but financial, geographical, and other process barriers (waiting time, for example) impose the burden for such assessment on particular groups of persons. Indeed, where it is felt that sociological and cultural barriers exist to people utilizing services, positive steps are needed (in the schools or through relevant community organizations) to make sure decisions are informed.

The Aday and Andersen approach may be helpful here. Their 'utilization per need' criterion – or a refinement of it – gives us a way of telling when a potential access factor is likely to affect opportunity through its impact on utilization rates. Moreover, whereas their unqualified assumption about the homogeneity of health care was found to be problematic for the health-care system as a whole, it is not problematic in this context, where we are discussing the basic tier. The basic tier has the central, uniform function of protecting fair equality of opportunity. Indeed, my account characterizes that function in a perspicuous way, so we can see why it has special moral importance. In addition, my account permits 'suspect' variations in utilization per need rates to be explained away as informed choice where this is plausible. (Aday and Andersen also leave room for such modifying explanations.) In short, I think the account I offer takes what is reasonable from the argument from function which underlies the utilization per need account and provides a clearer moral rationale for it.

Fourth, the fair equality of opportunity account remains silent on what to make of demands for strict equality in process variables ('amenities'), that is, independently of their effect on utilization per need rates. Where amenities have no effect on *health status*, they have no effect on *fair equality of opportunity*. Thus my account does not insist on equality of amenities that do not affect health status. It also remains silent on equity of access requirements for the upper tiers, if there turn out to be any. It also needs to be carefully applied if it is to answer the kinds of problems I raised for the market approach with regard to variations in quality – that is, efficacy and protection from risk. These are not issues I am prepared to take a direct stand on here. Still, it is worth characterizing in general terms the kinds of argument that might be brought to bear. The crude taxonomy of arguments I will suggest in the next section will at least tell us what kinds of consideration we should avoid conflating.

Before considering these other kinds of arguments that bear on access to higher tiers, I would like to comment on the President's Commission proposal regarding access, which has a rough similarity to mine on certain points.[1] In the President's Commission Report on *Securing Access to Health Care* (1983a:4), the claim is made that there is a social obligation to provide 'adequate care for all persons without excessive burdens in securing care'. This social obligation derives, the Commission argues, from an analysis of what is special or important about health care. But, in addition to noting the impact on opportunity, the Commission adds the effect of health care on the well-being of people (the reduction of pain and suffering), the information it provides people about their own bodies and prospects, and the symbolic centrality issues of life and death have in many religious and cultural settings. I noted in chapters 2 and 3 that my account of what makes health care special is not intended to be exhaustive or exclusive: the Commission is certainly right to note these other functions and effects of health care. But my account singles out what I take to be the central effect from the point of view of the theory of distributive justice. The result of this narrowing of the answer to the question, Why is health care special?, is that we get a fairly well-defined account of just health care – namely, the fair equality of opportunity account. In contrast, though the President's Commission says health care is special for four main reasons, and then infers a social obligation to provide adequate care from that special importance, it does so without a clear theory of distributive justice to ground its inference. The

---

[1] Some of the similarity is not accidental. Earlier versions of the material in chapters 1–3 influenced the thinking of the President's Commission staff, especially the succession of staff philosophers Dan Wikler, Dan Brock, and Allan Buchanan, even though there remain important differences in our views. Material for this chapter and Chapter 5 originally was written for the President's Commission. Differences between the positions taken by the Commission Report and my own also reflect strong political pressures on the drafting of the report by some of the Commissioners, especially the late Reagan appointees, who had not been party to much of the discussion that went on early in the process (though it might not have made any difference).

Commission Report, which has many merits, remains vague at a crucial point, one for which I have tried to provide foundations.

Having said that there is a social obligation to provide adequate care, the Commission Report then acknowledges that there is no easy formula or algorithm for determining what counts as adequate care. Here the report shares abstractness, that sanctuary for philosophers and den of iniquity for policy planners, with my own account. Determining what counts as 'adequate care without excessive burdens' requires moral judgment and extensive empirical knowledge about health care and the resources in a particular society. The Commission Report also shares with my account the view that what justice requires will vary with other facts about the society, and thus is society-relative. Similarly, the President's Commission Report, like my account, does not define the 'decent basic minimum' merely by reference to the basic features of the existing health-care system: it is intended as a way of making more fundamental criticisms of the existing system and not merely making sure different groups are treated equally within it.

My main complaint is that the Commission Report has taken the wrong side of a tradeoff from the one I have adopted. I have chosen not to be exhaustive or eclectic in my account of why health care is special. The narrowness of my account then makes it much easier to specify foundations in the theory of justice for an account of just health care. The Commission chose not to leave anything out of its account of why health care is special, but the price paid is that we have no very clear view of the underlying principles of justice which should govern health care. The Commission conclusion, that there is a *social obligation* to provide adequate care, may be right: my account shows why it is for at least that part of the notion of adequate care that bears on opportunity. But the more diverse notion of adequate care is less clearly an obligation of *justice*: some of the obligation may simply be the result of general duties of government to provide for the well-being of its citizens, a special case of duties of beneficence, perhaps. I also believe there is a further consequence of the tradeoff accepted by the Commission. In a sense, their view is more pragmatic: it appeals to all the reasons people might have for thinking health care is special and thus for thinking society ought to provide access to adequate care. But the pragmatism invites the risk that we lose sight of principle and slip toward a definition of adequacy based on central features of the existing system. This is not the intention of the Commission's report, but it is a risk. In contrast, by concentrating on fair equality of opportunity as the underlying, *principled* characterization of the function of the basic system, there is less risk of losing our critical footing.

A taxonomy of arguments about equality

I return now to provide a taxonomy for arguments which raise issues of equity going beyond the implications of my account. Arguments about equity concerning 'suspect' variations in 'amenities' or in health-care quality (protection against risk, for example) fall into three main kinds. The first kind of argument rejects the inequality on grounds deriving from general theories of distributive justice, which work independently of our specific concern with health care. Such a *general distributive* argument, for example, might suggest that income inequalities of the sort the market approach tolerates, which do not allow some people to buy extensive amenities or superior quality, are themselves not justifiable. One need not be a strict egalitarian here. Even a principle that constrained inequalities in the way Rawls's (1971) Difference Principle does, by allowing inequalities only if they act to make the worst-off groups best-off, might not allow the kinds of inequality tolerable on the market approach. Though I am inclined to take a rather egalitarian stand on income distribution, for our purposes here such general distributive arguments are not as interesting as arguments which more specifically address problems about health care.

Arguments that are directly concerned with health care divide into two kinds. A *primary* health-care argument is one that asserts that all health-care services are special in some way and that this specialness forces us to be egalitarian in ways we need not be with regard to many other social goods. For example, as I noted when I discussed possible rationales for the 'process' account of equity, someone (see, for example, Dickman 1983) might argue that there is a special connection between health care and self-esteem. Consequently, a society fails to show equal respect for persons if it allows inequality of access to even nonbasic health-care services. Or someone might argue that virtually all of our health-care manpower, facilities, and technology at one point or another have been heavily subsidized by public funds; consequently all citizens deserve equal access to what society has so extensively funded. The latter argument, it should be pointed out, is inadequate to justify equal access to health care in societies that have not subsidized their health-care systems. My own suspicion is that primary arguments about equal access to all health-care service are not likely to succeed. For example, they may assume a homogeneity of function for health-care services which is contrary to fact; or the property they pick out, for example, public funding, also characterizes many things or institutions where no comparable argument about equal access is plausibly advanced.

A *secondary* health-care argument urges egalitarian distribution, not because of the 'specialness' of all health-care services, but because of the causal relationships between basic and nonbasic services in the system. Secondary health-care arguments may hold more promise, but they are likely to rest on far more complicated and disputed empirical claims. For example, a secondary argument might grant a distinction between basic and nonbasic categories of health-care services, or between adequate and above-adequate levels of quality. Still, because the tiers or sectors that deliver both kinds or qualities of service are causally connected, allowing a market for the nonbasic level might threaten the possibility of delivering the basic level equitably. For example, a market approach to nonbasic services might undermine the quality or raise the cost of the basic tier by draining manpower and competing for resources (see McCreadie 1976). Of course, counter-arguments of the secondary type are possible too. For example, it has been argued that a market tier above the decent minimum promotes innovation, or that prohibiting such a tier will generate a black market (see Fried 1976).

My sketch of a fair equality approach thus leaves some important issues unresolved. Still, it points the way toward taking the best from various approaches which it is otherwise difficult to reconcile.

Other issues of access

Most of the discussion in this chapter has concentrated on access to personal medical services, but such services, though the focus of most public policy dispute about access, are only a part of what I have been referring to as *health care*. Health-care services are also preventive: I will discuss what justice or equity requires of preventive services in chapters 7 and 8. But another important function of health-care services deserves special mention here, for serious issues of equal access arise concerning it.

Personal medical services have as one of their tasks the restoration of handicapping dysfunctions, for example of vision, mobility, and so on. The medical goal is to cure the diseased organ or limb where possible. Where cure is impossible, medical care has the task of making function as normal as feasible, through corrective lenses or prostheses and rehabilitative therapy. But where restoration of function is beyond the ability of medicine per se, we begin to enter another area of services: non-medical social supports. Such social support services provide the blind person with the closest he can get to the functional equivalent to vision – for example, he is taught how to navigate, provided with a seeing-eye dog, taught braille, and so on.

From the point of view of their impact on opportunity, medical services and social support services that meet health-care needs have *the same rationale and are equally important*. Yet for various reasons, probably having to do with the profitability and glamour of personal medical service and careers in them as compared to services for the handicapped, our society has taken only slow and halting steps to meet the health-care needs of those with permanent disabilities. These are matters of justice, not charity. We are not facing conditions of scarcity so severe that these steps to provide equality of opportunity must be foregone in favor of more pressing needs. The commitment of my account to such social support services is not without serious budget implications. Costs are high, though not all these services need be in addition to existing ones; some may be alternatives. The point also has implications for the problem of long-term care for the frail elderly, but I address these implications in Chapter 5.

5 · Am I my parents' keeper?

> Must no one at all, then, be called happy while he lives;
> must we, as Solon says, see the end?
>
> Aristotle, *Nichomachaen Ethics*

Opportunity, age-bias, and competition for resources

If an acceptable general theory of distributive justice requires us to guarantee fair equality of opportunity, then a principle for the distribution of health care seems to follow. Institutions delivering health-care services, both preventive and curative, should be governed by the fair equality of opportunity principle. On this view, health care is 'special' because of its connection to the special social good, opportunity. Health-care needs are things we need to maintain, restore, or compensate for the loss of normal species functioning. Impairment of normal functioning means that an individual might not enjoy his fair share of the range of opportunities normal for his society. Thus meeting health-care needs is as important as guaranteeing individuals that their opportunity is within the normal range for their society.

The fact that we age raises an important objection to the approach I have been developing. Any distributive theory for health care, we may suppose, should account for the importance of meeting the health-care needs of young and old alike. In the US system, people over the age of 65 use health-care services at roughly 3.5 times the rate (in dollars) of those below that age. In 1977, per capita expenditures for those over 65 in the US were $1,745; they were $661 for those age 16–64 and $253 for those under 19 (Gibson and Fisher 1979: 3–16). But, so goes the objection, if fair equality of opportunity were the relevant principle of distributive justice, we could not justify such extensive use of services for the elderly. Their opportunities lie in the past and are no longer a matter of pressing social concern, especially if we concentrate on opportunities to enter jobs and careers (which I do not; see Chapter 3). Consequently the opportunity principle cannot possibly provide a justification for our current distribution of health-care services. Like the discounted 'future earnings approach' to the problem of valuing lives, the fair equality of opportunity approach seems age-biased; it would discriminate against the elderly in a morally unacceptable way.

Of course, it might be possible to counter this accusation of age-bias by arguing that it is our current practice, not the opportunity principle, which is age-biased. Some urge that we spend too much on health care for the elderly, for example in a last ditch effort to extend life marginally or to prolong dying. One study shows that 50% of all hospital charges are to some 13% of the patients, the seriously chronically ill. About 40% of these 'high-cost' patients are over 65, whereas only 15% of the low-cost patients are (Zook and Moore 1980: 996–1002). In recent years, the elderly have become users of dialysis and intensive care.[1] We seem compelled to employ life-prolonging technologies whenever we can, which is more frequently among the elderly. Yet we are blind to the impact of such a policy on the health prospects of the young. For example, in a context of rising costs and scarce resources, and, in any case, of tightened public budgets, we are more willing to impose stricter eligibility requirements and budget ceilings in Medicaid, most of whose recipients are young women and children, than to alter our practices with regard to the dying elderly. As a result, infant mortality rates have soared between 1980 and 1983 in Boston, Massachusetts (Knox 1984). Such rationing, so the reply goes, is age-biased against the young.

I believe both the objection and the reply are too crudely drawn to help us assess the status of the fair equality of opportunity approach to health-care distribution. But they do serve to raise a prior, indeed, more interesting and general question: *When is a distributive system, such as a health-care system, age-biased?* Moreover, they highlight the importance of the question by raising the specter of age groups competing for scarce resources, pitting father and son and mother and daughter against grandfather and grandmother. After all, we believe 'honor thy father and thy mother'! But how much? And for how long? Once raised, the specter of age-group competition for scarce resources threatens traditional values, like duties to the elderly, by eroding our confidence that we understand their limits. Similarly, the view that the elderly are entitled to

---

[1] 44% of all intensive care patients at Massachusetts General Hospital were over 65, and 25% were over 75, yet only 17% of people in the hospital catchment area are over 65. Similarly, patients over 70 years old, a group excluded from some coronary care units in the past, were 32% of all admissions in another study. See Campion, Mulley, *et al.* (1981), and Thibault, Mulley, *et al.* (1980).

support and deserve it, because of their past contributions to cooperative, productive schemes, also gives little guidance in answering the question, How much? (Morgan 1976: 67–9). And other moral notions, like the injunction to respect persons equally, seem to give less guidance than we might hope (Jonsen 1976a: 97–105). Yet, these questions about competition for resources must be answered, and they will be answered, *either by principle or by default*. So we must look for a principled way to tell when distributive schemes are age-biased or fair.

Before answering the objection to my fair equality of opportunity account, I will formulate more clearly the general question about age-bias and compare it to other distribution problems it may seem to resemble. What makes the age problem distinctive is that people born at the same time (birth cohorts) age, and they are transformed successively into different age groups. Moreover, as they age, they pass first as youth, later as adults, and then as elderly through social institutions which distribute resources to them. Under resource constraints, what these institutions distribute to them at one stage of life will not be available at another. What is expended on youth is not saved for old age. As we age, our needs change, and prudent individuals want institutions to be responsive to these changes.

I propose that we solve the age-group distribution problem by considering how prudent planners would design these institutions. The allocations prudent planners would approve for each early stage of life and the 'savings' they would make available for later ones should be our guide to morally acceptable distributions among age groups. Of course, I will have to describe more fully how we are to think of these 'prudent planners' if this model is to be a reasonable solution to the moral problem of determining what distributions are just. I argue that the notion of an *age-relative opportunity range* should play an important part in the deliberations of such prudent planners, and this suggests how my opportunity approach to just health care can be spared the charge of age-bias. Indeed, when this modification is properly understood, we gain an edge on important resource allocation issues that underlie many criticisms of the US health-care system and its treatment of the elderly.

There is a further problem facing 'savings' institutions, whether health care or income support, and this problem of equity between birth cohorts has received much attention in the popular press. Differences in size between birth cohorts – which may lead to higher ratios of retired elderly to employed workers than in previous periods – and shifts in economic growth rates can lead to greater burdens on some cohorts than others. I comment on this problem with reference to the US Social Security System.

When are acts, policies, or institutions age-biased?

It is tempting to think about age-bias, or agism, on the model of race and sex bias. Although philosophers have not written much about aging or age-bias, the gerontological literature has drawn some clear parallels. The elderly are portrayed as a minority that is treated in unfavorable, even discriminatory, ways by the more powerful majority. Some, using methods standardly employed to measure the effects of racism, e.g., measures of economic inequality, have suggested that agism induces even greater inequality than racism or sexism (Palmore and Manton 1973). Others have pointed out ideological similarities. Crude age-related stereotypes are generated. These may have a psychological appeal, based on fear of aging and death, and a rationalizing function, 'justifying' policies, like compulsory retirement, that favor younger cohorts. These stereotypes notoriously interfere with the delivery of considerate, quality medical care and are reflected in derogatory hospital and nursing home jargon (and practices). Others see age-bias at the root of the problems in our long-term-care system, which prematurely and inappropriately institutionalizes the elderly, denying them support unless they accept a 'sick role'. Here the stereotype, that to be old is to be ill, at once leads to a misestimate of the needs of the elderly and rationalizes the economic incentives for institutionalization which are built into Medicare and Medicaid reimbursement policies. Similarly, special problems arise from agist attitudes in mental-health-care contexts (Butler 1969:243–6; Butler and Lewis 1977: 141–3; Callahan and Wallack 1981).

It is easy to think of cases in which appeals to age are morally wrong in much the way that certain appeals to race or sex are morally objectionable. A policy that cut off voting privileges for the elderly, or required them to take a competency test (on the model of driver recertification tests), would be morally objectionable, though, of course, we *do* allow age to play a role in assigning voting rights to the young. A practice that excluded the elderly from certain kinds of housing would be similarly objectionable. Job discrimination against the elderly – or against a protected age group (say those over 40) – has received attention, though not to my knowledge any sustained philosophical examination. Specifically, hiring practices or other job assignment and wage practices that appeal to age criteria and not competence seem morally objectionable in the way sex or race criteria do.[2] Of course, there is an asymmetry here: we do exclude the young (say those under 16) from job eligibility, presumably because there is an overriding social concern that there are better things than working which the young should be doing for themselves. But this exception points us to the general issue: age, like race or sex, seems to be a *morally irrelevant* criterion for a broad range of contexts.

To be sure, we have to unpack the notion of *moral relevance* if we are to get a useful explanation, and this difficult task is not one I can undertake here (see Chapter 8 for more discussion). Still, many cases are clear. Race is not an indicator of competency to perform a job, and so it is morally objectionable to use it as a guide to hiring practices (except, possibly, in the context of certain compensatory practices, like affirmative action). Age is not an index of the likelihood of being a good tenant, and so is morally irrelevant to rental practices. And where some associate a relevant trait (industriousness, intelligence, crankiness) with a generally irrelevant one (race, age), the associations usually are, in the important cases, false; that is, they are part of a racist, agist, or sexist myth.[3] At best they are crude, statistical generalizations which will clearly be unfair (by denying fair opportunity) to individuals, about whom the generalization is quite wrong.

Although these cases and considerations explain the temptation to draw parallels between the use of age, sex, and race criteria, other cases challenge the analogy. Consider the question in a rationing context that has been criticized as age-biased by many, namely the policy that has existed (at least implicitly) in the British National Health Service of not giving renal dialysis to those over age 65 (Caplan 1980, Aaron and Schwartz 1984). Let us suppose that dialysis is medically effective for elderly patients, permitting relatively normal functioning, so that the age criterion is not merely a guide to medical suitability. Does the appeal to such an age criterion in rationing constitute an *age-bias*, by which I mean

---

[2] A qualification may be needed here: age criteria may not function exactly like race or sex criteria in such contexts. It might not seem imprudent for age-related practices, like the seniority system, to be given weight. Indeed, from the perspective of a prudent person allocating job opportunity over a lifetime, it might seem worth trading greater training options in one's youth for greater job security in his later years. No such reference to race or sex criteria is plausible, largely because the prudential saver model allows greater freedom here than where distributions more clearly cross the boundaries between persons. See pp. 96ff.

[3] Daniels 1976. It is important to remember that the elderly are a non-homogeneous group; see Pegels 1980.

a *morally unacceptable discrimination?* Our earlier considerations suggest it does. If the sole difference between two persons, one age 64 and the other age 66, is their age, and *that* is the basis for deciding who gets dialysis, then it surely *looks* like the rationing scheme is age-biased in a morally objectionable way.

But the rationing case is more complicated; contrary considerations come to mind. Consider two rationing schemes. Scheme A involves a direct appeal to an age criterion: no one over age 70 is eligible to receive any of several high-cost, life-extending technologies, e.g., dialysis, bypass operations, or major organ transplants. Because age rationing greatly reduces the utilization of each technology, there are resources available for developing all of them. Scheme B rejects age rationing and allocates life-extending technology solely by medical need. As a result, it can either develop just one such technology, say dialysis, making it available to anyone who needs it, or it can develop several and ration them by lottery. Given our earlier discussion, Scheme A seems age-biased in a way that B is not. The effect of B, however, because many young would not win the lottery, is to reduce the likelihood of people under 65 reaching a normal lifespan (say, 'three score and ten'). Some would contend that Scheme B, though it lacks reference to an explicit age criterion, has a systematic negative effect on younger age groups and is in that sense age-biased in a morally objectionable way.[4] Of course, the contention depends on showing that maximizing the likelihood of reaching a normal lifespan is morally preferable to merely extending life wherever we can (without any reference to age). Considered moral judgments differ on this and related issues (and in ways that may reflect our interests, given our ages); moreover, there are strong considerations and arguments inclining us in opposing directions. The problem is made to seem even more intractable because these moral disagreements are set in the context of a distributive framework that makes one group's gains look like another group's losses.

I would like suggest a different distributive framework for conceiving the problem, one that permits a fresh theoretical perspective. The key idea is the prudent 'saving' and allocation of resources over a lifetime, through which we transfer resources from one period in our lives to another. The perspective can be introduced by observing an important fact about certain health-care insurance schemes. Suppose we have a

---

[4] The allocation issues here are numerous. For example, the young might prefer investing in preventive efforts, like health hazard regulation, whereas the (current) elderly may not benefit from such long-term investments.

health-care financing scheme that guarantees substantial access to medically needed health-care services for the elderly. The details of the scheme do not much matter here. It could be a universal national health insurance scheme with subsidization for those who cannot afford premiums,[5] or it could be a composite financing system that included private as well as publicly subsidized programs. But even a scheme that does not redistribute income raises the same issues, provided that it is 'community rated' and incorporates all ages into one 'riskpool'. The central fact is that health-care needs vary with age, so that the elderly will use certain health resources at a higher per capita rate than the working-age population. In 1977, the 10.8% of the US population over 65 incurred 29% of the total personal medical services bill. Consequently, *any such insurance scheme involves a transfer of wealth from later birth cohorts to earlier ones, from younger age groups to older ones.* But if the insurance scheme continues over a long period of time, birth cohorts that are now transferring wealth – or aid-in-kind – to their elders will eventually be the beneficiaries of such transfers from later birth cohorts. Consequently, *any such health-insurance scheme can be viewed over time as a savings scheme*: participation in the scheme transfers resources, in the form of contingent claims on health-care services, from one's youth to one's old age. Of course, such savings are not 'vested' assets, like money in the bank; but we are deferring resources from one point in our lives to another, and so have a kind of savings scheme.

Notice how focusing on an institution – the insurance scheme – that operates through time forces a shift in our perspective on the rationing problem. We are driven to converting the *synchronic* or *time-slice* distribution problem we first raised – namely, how to ration health-care resources between competing groups while avoiding age-bias – into a *diachronic* perspective in which we are concerned with the treatment of the *same* people through the various stages of *their* lives. From this perspective – from my perspective – three questions about the design of the institution, here the insurance scheme, arise in a quite natural way:

1   At what rate of savings should I defer the use of health-care resources within my life?

2   What do I most need and want by way of health-care benefits at each stage of my life?

[5] Partly because of retirement policy and partly because of inequalities in income distribution throughout earning years, about 25% of the elderly are below or near the poverty line in the US. The average older couple receives less than half the income of younger couples (Pegels 1980: Ch. 4).

3   How can I be sure that my participation in the scheme involves equitable transfers between my birth cohort and both earlier and later ones, given the fact that economic and population growth rates vary through time?

The last question is familiar, of course, because of current worries about inter-cohort inequities in the US Social Security system, and I shall return to these matters later. The answer to question (1) will have a bearing on the answer to (2). I have raised these questions in the first person. But, because we are concerned with cooperative social schemes, it may be necessary to answer the questions from a more general perspective, that of a prudent saver, or even some more hypothetical construction in which the saver operates behind a 'veil of ignorance' of appropriate thickness. I return to this issue shortly, but first I want to return to the rationing problem I posed earlier, using the perspective suggested here.

Suppose I know I have available to me a lifetime health-care allocation, say in the form of an insurance benefit package. However, it is up to me to budget, once and for all, that allocation or benefit package so that it is used to meet my needs and preferences over my lifetime. How would it be rational for me to budget it – given all the uncertainties about my future health, wealth, and family situation? One plausible proposal might be for me to reserve certain life-extending technologies for my younger years, reasoning that my doing so maximizes the chances of my living a normal lifespan. I then might use the 'savings' embodied in that restriction to provide myself with more social support services in my old age. I might reason that such services could vastly improve the quality of my years in old age and that such an improvement is worth the increased risk of a slightly shortened old age. I might then instruct – through my benefit package – providers to treat me accordingly, that is, to appeal to an age criterion in their utilization decisions concerning me. This package is intended to resemble the age-rationing scheme the British NHS apparently uses for renal dialysis, and a rationale for the NHS scheme *could* be modelled on my reasoning about my package (but see pp. 111 ff.).

In this scenario, although age is used as a criterion in the utilization decisions involving me and everyone else who joins the same insurance scheme, there is a minimal basis for suggesting my treatment is age-biased in a morally objectionable way. It might be thought that there is no 'bias' here merely because I consent to – buy into – the scheme. But the fact of my *actual consent* to the scheme is not the main issue here. Consent does not quite count for everything: blacks or women might consent to race- and sex-biased treatments without thereby overriding all claims that the treatments are morally objectionable.[6] As I suggest in the next section, there is an important difference between the age and the race or sex distribution problems, and it is *this* difference, not consent, that explains why age-rationing in such schemes is not morally objectionable in the way rationing on the basis of age or sex would be.

We are not in a position to answer the question, When are acts, policies, or institutions age-biased? But we have seen strong reason to think that not every appeal to an age criterion for rationing is as morally unacceptable as comparable appeals to sex or race would be. We must explore further why the cases are different.

Does aging pose a distinct distribution problem?

The distribution problem between age groups is usefully contrasted with two distribution problems it somewhat resembles. Consider first whether the age-group problem is just a special case of the problem of obligations to future generations. After all, age cohorts are commonly referred to as 'generations'. And both seem to raise the issue of competition for resources: present and future generations – just like age groups – compete with each other. The problem of obligations to future generations is also sometimes formulated as the problem of finding a *just savings principle*. So too the issue of a just savings principle arises in the age-group problem, at least if we view schemes that transfer income or health-care benefits from younger cohorts to older ones as a kind of 'savings institutions'. What rate of transfer, what savings rate, is just? Moreover, there is another point of similarity: transfer schemes operating through extended periods must be concerned that different birth cohorts enjoy equitable 'replacement ratios' (ratios of benefits to contributions). This problem of equity does strongly resemble the just savings problem between generations.[7] Nevertheless, I think the dif-

---

[6] The issue is quite complicated and arises often in making moral judgments about race, caste, or sex practices in other cultures. Often we try to avoid the issue by discounting consent, say by labeling it 'false consciousness'. But what if the consent seems genuine? Do such problems make the appeal to Kantian views of the person and hypothetical contracts all the more problematic, or all the more attractive?

[7] It is worth noting a point of contrast between the aging problem posed here and the just savings problem as it is discussed by John Rawls (1971: secs. 44, 45). Rawls is primarily concerned with *preserving* adequate capital and non-renewable resources so that successive generations are in a position to maintain institutions of justice. In contrast, we are

ferences between the aging and the future generations problems are greater than their similarities.

The major difference is that young birth cohorts are transformed in time into elderly cohorts: they age. But no current generation becomes a future generation. It follows that certain special features of the future generations problem do not arise in the aging problem. We do not have to consider the great uncertainties about conditions of life in the very distant future; we do not have to worry about the puzzling conceptual problems that may attend positing obligations by existing people to nonexistent ones. But the most important consequences of this difference between the problems is that *some form of prudential reasoning* is naturally appropriate to solving the age-group distribution problem. I know I will grow old, or at least that I must prepare for the eventuality of growing old. So, I have a concern for the structure of institutions that will help me defer the use of resources in a prudent way. In no such direct way does prudence make me concerned about saving resources for future generations. (Of course this contrast will have to be qualified somewhat in the next section, since we will ultimately be talking about prudence in a more hypothetical context.)

A further difference between the aging and future generations problems is that different age groups coexist and compete politically for social goods distributed in cooperative arrangements. Future generations are not here to fight for their interests. This difference may be an important psychological and political fact; it is less clear how relevant it is to the problem of deciding what arrangements are in principle just. It does, however, introduce some issues about the implementation of cooperative

concerned with institutions that transfer income or aid-in-kind between age groups so that their consumption will yield just income-support and health-care distributions through our lifetimes. Rawls's approach to the just savings problem involves his device of a thick veil of ignorance: we do not know which generation we will be in when we are choosing our principles of justice. Moreover, he imposes a motivational constraint on parties making the hypothetical contract: they are concerned about the well-being of a generation or two in each direction (from their grandparents to their grandchildren). Contractors operating under such constraints would prudently grant each generation an equal claim on resources necessary to maintain institutions of justice. In this way the just savings rate acts as a constraint on other principles of justice, such as the difference principle: no society can maximize the well-being of the worst-off unless it has set aside the resources required by the just savings principle. The question (3) posed in the last section, about equity in replacement ratios between birth cohorts participating in the scheme, may need for its resolution arguments based on such a hypothetical contractual apparatus. But I think that answers to questions (1) and (2), about the rate of savings and the content of the benefits 'saved', may be approached more directly, with a less 'veiled' form of prudence. Still, the answer to (3) will constrain answers to (1) and (2), much as the savings principle constrains the difference principle.

schemes and the contrast between ideal and nonideal arrangements, to which I return below (pp. 110ff).

The fact that different age groups coexist and share in a distribution scheme contemporaneously may make the age-group problem resemble more closely the distribution problem among other demographic groups (races, sexes, classes) than it does the future generations problem. The similarity enhances the sense that we are concerned with a synchronic distribution problem, a time-slice in which competition rages. Moreover, many of the same issues arise in all these demographic competitions. The moral arbitrariness of certain appeals to age resembles the arbitrariness of appeals to race or sex. Similarly, we are concerned that our treatment in cooperative schemes should reflect the fact that we are all equally to be considered as persons, regardless of age, sex, race, class, and so on.

But the very same fact that makes the aging problem different from the future generations problem also makes it different from the distribution problem involving other demographic groups. Young birth cohorts age and are transformed into older age groups. We become old, but we do not change generation, race, sex, or (usually) class. As Zeckhauser and Viscusi (1978: 54) put it, 'the elderly comprise a minority group we can all hope to join'.[8] This basic fact points to the naturalness of the suggestion that we think about cooperative social schemes that bear on aging in prudential terms, even though we may have to abstract somewhat from the perspective of a real individual, that is, from the economist's 'prudent saver'.

It is now possible to explain why the appeal to an age criterion in some rationing schemes works differently from appeals to race or sex criteria. From the perspective of institutions operating over time, the age criterion operates *within* a life and not *between* lives. One important criticism of utilitarianism, advanced by Rawls (1971: Sect. 3), is that it extends a principle of individual rational choice appropriate to distribution within a life into a social principle of rational choice that crosses personal boundaries.[9] Thus it is rational and prudent that I take from one stage of my life to give to another, in order to make my life as a whole better. But it is *morally problematic* just when society can take from one person to give to another in order to maximize, say, total happiness.

---

[8] Paul Samuelson (1958) offers the classic treatment of this perspective on inter-cohort transfers.
[9] See Parfit 1973; Rawls 1974–5; Daniels 1979a.

Rawls's point would explain the deep problem facing any attempt to ration life-extending resources by race or sex: in this case, taking from some to make society as a whole better off would fail to respect the difference between persons. But now we see the difference between the race and aging cases. Rationing by age criteria *looks like* a case of crossing personal boundaries *only if we take a 'time-slice' perspective*. Once we take the perspective of institutions operating through time, the appearance of crossing boundaries between persons fades and we are concerned primarily with distribution through the stages of a life. No comparable point is true for rationing by race or sex over time.

This general point is not to deny there are some irreducible interpersonal aspects of the cohort issue. For example, the question of equity in replacement ratios between birth cohorts raises an issue of equity between persons in the face of changing economic growth rates or birth rates. This issue aside, however, the core of the age-group problem has a different philosophical texture from either of the other distribution problems we have considered.

The distribution problem between age groups must, of course, be set within a framework that takes more general issues of distributive justice into account. This might suggest there *is* no special problem of distribution between age groups. One might, for example, think Rawls proceeds as if there is no special problem of *justice*. His Difference Principle requires that the worst-off groups are to be made maximally well-off as measured by an index of primary social goods, which includes basic liberties, opportunity, income, wealth, powers, and self-respect. But the value of the index for a representative individual is determined by his share of primary goods *over his lifetime*; thus it is to include what social or economic mobility the individual will enjoy. This lifetime index assignment might suggest that Rawls ignores the problem of distribution between age groups, perhaps dismissing it as a problem for individual savings. But Rawls's simplifying assumption involving the index is not a sleight of hand that makes the problem of distribution between age groups disappear.

The problem we are concerned with reemerges as soon as one tries to arrange basic social institutions that embody the more general principles of justice over time. For then, the problem of rationing income or health-care benefits throughout the stages of a life arises again, and this problem requires the establishment of cooperative schemes or institutions of a rather basic sort. The Difference Principle, to continue with the Rawlsian example, maximizes the index level of representative, worst-off individuals over their lifetimes. But several cooperative 'savings' schemes might be compatible with satisfying the Difference Principle. That is, the more general theory of distributive justice is silent on the age-group distribution problem except where inter-cohort transfer or savings schemes interfere with the Difference Principle. Moreover, if I am right that health-care institutions should be governed by the fair equality of opportunity principle, as I later extend it, then at least this 'savings institution' constrains the Difference Principle.

Prudence and aging

I have been suggesting that we approach the problem of competition – or distribution – between age groups from the perspective of institutions that operate through time to defer resources from one stage of life to another. But in converting what began as an *interpersonal* distribution problem, with all its attendant worries about age-bias, into an *intrapersonal* problem of rational or prudent savings, my approach encounters an objection, one with a paradoxical air about it. The objection is that the shift to talk about prudential allocations of resources within a life, far from telling us when distributions between age groups are just or age-biased, prohibits us from raising the question about age-bias at all. For, when a person favors one stage of his life – or, in a cooperative scheme, favors an age group – it is not viewed as immoral or unjust. It is merely imprudent, at worst.

Consider some examples. Olga is a figure skater who has invested very heavily in the development of certain talents and skills while neglecting others. She has ignored the development of critical social skills, acquired only the narrowest education, and led an austere, even grim, childhood and youth. If she achieves wealth and fame in her career – becomes an international skating star – she may feel the gamble has paid off. Later stages of her life will then reap benefits from the sacrifices she experiences in her childhood. They might be *imprudent* (even if the gamble pays off), but it seems merely metaphorical to say she was 'unfair' to her childhood. So, if the intra-life model precludes saying that the plan is *unfair* to a life-stage or biased against it, it looks as if we are not solving the problem we thought existed. Of course, it does make a difference whether the plan for Olga is *hers* or is imposed by ambitious parents and skating instructors, perhaps even with 'false consciousness' on Olga's part. But here the *unfairness* to Olga is that she was denied both autonomy and the chance to design her own life plan.

Consider a case in which Olga's plan is writ large into a social policy, a kind of initiation rite. From age 20 to 30, people are given just a living stipend for the work they do. They accumulate no property and lead austere lives. After the initiation or 'social indenture' period, they are presented with an annuity policy that enhances their income at a later stage of life, or they are given some other award, perhaps just acceptance as full-fledged citizens who benefit from the labor of the next birth cohort going through the process. Is such a scheme age-biased? Depending on details, a central complaint might be that the system too severely restricts certain liberties, which we may see as a social good that should not be rationed or 'saved' in this way. But, liberties aside, suppose the system were stable, seemed to reflect a shared conception of a rational plan of life, and appeared to be as voluntary as any well-entrenched social custom involving initiation rites. *We* might be inclined to say it is imprudent for the indentured cohort to 'save' in this fashion; *they* might disagree. Of course, we might not be able to say even that, if the 'return on investment' for participation is higher than in alternative schemes. In any case, does our ability to complain about age-bias disappear?

The examples really raise two issues. The first is primarily terminological. Ordinarily, we do not import notions, like fairness and justice, into prudential contexts, namely allocations within a lifetime. But the proposal here is that our *proper standard* for judging the fairness of distributions between age groups – which do exist as distinct groups of people, in contrast to stages within a life – is prudential. We are to view the different age groups *as if* they were but stages of one life, for, from the perspective of cooperative 'savings' schemes operating through time, each person is treated at the different stages of his life in just the same way the different groups are. Accepting the proposal would be grounds for ignoring the suggestion that the language of prudence bars us from raising issues of justice.

But the examples also point out that what is prudent from the perspective of one rational person or group of persons may not be from that of another. The appeal to a prudential or rational savings model usually carries with it the notion of an individual with a given set of preferences or 'conception of the good'. What is prudent is so from the individual's conception of the good. How, then, can we use the suggestion that prudential reasoning is the key to solving the distribution problem for different age groups? The social institutions that bear on saving encompass people with different conceptions of the good.

There are two main strategies. One is the proposal that we rely on market mechanisms to allow people every chance to express their own prudent preferences. The social task, then, is to make sure such markets function properly and that income distribution is initially just. Specifically, with regard to health care, one might look to a market for insurance schemes that differed from one another in their 'rate of savings' for later stages of life. That is, some might have lower premiums and offer less coverage in later years; others might defer more resources, in the form of contingent benefits. People would then buy the packages it is prudent for them to buy, given many facts about their situations, including their conceptions of the good, risk averseness, and so on. This approach converts with a vengeance the problem of age-group distribution into an *individual* savings problem: the social concern is to provide a setting in which individual rationing within lives can take place. But there is little room for social institutions to *guarantee* that prudent allocation takes place. The second strategy is to modify the appeal to prudential reasoning by using a *hypothetical* agent, one which abstracts from certain features of individuals. Such an agent then seeks principles for the design for the relevant social institutions. I shall suggest a version of the second strategy which is appropriate to the 'savings' problem for health care. In its general form the strategy is familiar as the hypothetical contractarian approach used by Rawls and others. But it is worth considering some limitations of the first strategy first.

The strengths and limits of the first strategy are revealed if we consider the way in which a rational consumer might think about the problem of chronic illness or disability. The long-term care such conditions require is a focal point of criticism of the treatment of the elderly. In the US system, chronically disabled or enfeebled persons tend to be institutionalized much more frequently and earlier than comparable persons in other systems, e.g., the British or Swedish. Moreover, they are often institutionalized at inappropriate levels of care, and possibly at higher cost than alternative forms of treatment or service would involve. The incentives for such institutionalization are built into Medicare and Medicaid reimbursement schemes. The effects of such 'overmedicalization' on both the mental and the physical health of the elderly are serious (Morris and Youket 1981). Yet, as Christine Bishop (1981) points out, the uncertainty facing the onset and costs of disability make it an obvious candidate for insurance schemes.[10] The rational consumer would presumably try to buy a package that avoided the features of our current long-term care system.

[10] I draw on Christine Bishop's (1981) excellent discussion in the next five paragraphs.

Any individual faces a significant, actuarially calculable chance of chronic illness or disability over his lifetime; the chance increases with age (let us leave aside those disabled from birth or facing a known genetic disposition to disability). Although only one in twenty persons over 65 is in a nursing home in a given year in the US, one in four will at some time enter one (Palmore 1976). Chronic illness or disability may require large expenditures for medical, personal care, or social support services. Moreover, the size of the expenditures for a given disability will vary with other contingencies, such as family situation and preferences for living conditions. The uncertainty surrounding each of these contingencies and their joint risk suggests that rational consumers will enhance their well-being over their lifetime if they pay a modest insurance premium rather than keep the money and risk a large loss. Specifically, we might expect rational consumers to want insurance schemes that offered them benefits flexible enough to meet their real needs. They would want alternatives to nursing-home institutionalization if they needed lower levels of care, or some family help, or modifiable living quarters. Thus they would buy contingency claims on the *joint risks of disability and other factors*, such as the absence of family support or the unsuitability of living arrangements.

The connection between disability as an insurance problem and as a problem of 'savings' becomes clear when we see, as Bishop notes, that short-term coverage faces special problems. If coverage is actuarially fair and we pool risks by age, high premiums will face the elderly, those most in need of the insurance, and those least likely to be able to pay for it because of declining incomes. The prudent consumer, anticipating such higher premiums, would have to save, perhaps by buying an annuity to cover his later premiums. But since no one knows how long he will live, to 100 or to 66, it is hard to predict how much to save. Notice, however, that plans offering lifetime coverage with a fixed premium are equivalent to such savings: a community-rated lifetime plan has a built-in savings feature because of the distribution of needs by age.

Although these considerations suggest there should be a demand for such insurance, we find no market offering it. Bishop points to several reasons for market-failure: (1) uncertainty about inflation adds to the insurer's risk, where real benefits and not fixed money amounts are involved, so private coverage would be discouraged; (2) administration costs are high and coverage of the population is not extensive; (3) some current public programs would partially undercut the market for such insurance; (4) 'adverse selection', which means too many high-risk people buy, driving premiums up and low-risk people out, and 'moral hazard', say in the form of overstating disability, are especially likely for these forms of insurance. From these facts, Bishop concludes that private marketing of such insurance is not likely to develop and that some form of universal, compulsory insurance should be instituted, different proposals for which she considers.

Bishop's proposal for a unified national insurance scheme for long-term care, encompassing medical, personal care, and social support services, is surely a step in the right direction. Moreover, her discussion of the scope and content of the lifetime coverage scheme is informed by prudential considerations, which I earlier suggested were necessary to undercut the issue of age-group competition. The scheme continues through time so that the young who pay higher premiums (or taxes) now in due time will be beneficiaries of such 'savings', through the similarly higher payments of later birth cohorts.

Still, there is a gap in her argument: the social obligation to provide such compulsory coverage does not follow from the fact of private market failure alone. Nor does it follow from the fact that net well-being might be greater if the public scheme were instituted, for there are many public schemes that might enhance net well-being. We need some argument that the social good protected by such a cooperative social scheme is especially important, say because it is a social good that gives rise to claims of justice. (My argument in chapters 2 and 3 could fill the gap.) Schemes such as the one Bishop discusses involve a significant income redistribution: entitlements to benefits, presumably at an 'adequate' level, will be subsidized for those who cannot buy them. But what determines that level? And why should those who are better off be willing to provide it? Moreover, as long as we are considering such insurance schemes from the perspective of the prudent agent who knows his full situation, we might find much reluctance on the part of some to enter community-rated schemes whose premiums involve subsidization of those with the worst risks. If I know I have several children whom I am likely to be able to prepare for lucrative careers, I might not want to be in a riskpool with childless people. My commitments to a community-rated scheme that is not actuarially fair to me would have to be based on considerations other than prudence alone. My knowledge of particular facts about me allows my individual interests to influence choice. Any bargains struck in the light of full knowledge then risk allowing the *accidents of current age-group competition* to influence unduly the arrangements governing long-term cooperative schemes. These considerations suggest that distributive principles which we need to embody in such cooperative social schemes are not likely to be derived from the prudential perspective of fully informed rational agents.

These limits of the first strategy, and other issues in moral methodology which cannot be discussed here, incline me to the second strategy. That is, for the design of cooperative social schemes, we need a perspective that abstracts in a reasonable way from the full-blown rational consumer used by the economist, but which still permits some form of prudential reasoning about the 'savings' problem for health care. At this point it is tempting to employ some version of Rawls's veil of ignorance.[11] Thus the prudent agents deliberating about principles to govern their cooperative scheme should know nothing of their age, family situation, health status and genetic history, socioeconomic status, or their particular conception of the good. Such a device might be defended on the grounds that the constraints are procedurally 'fair': they reflect the deliberators' status as 'free, equal moral agents'. Of course, the agents would have to have some 'thin theory of the good', like Rawls's primary social goods, or they would have nothing to be prudent about. Any justification for such a hypothetical contractor model would carry me much too far afield.[12] Clearly it is enough to suggest that the constraints on knowledge seem to be but exaggerations of the considerable uncertainty we face outside the veil in planning health, family, and economic eventualities over a lifetime. But since I am not prepared to offer such a defense, I shall have to restrict myself to a suggestion. *Prudent deliberators, appropriately constrained, would seek a health-care and long-term-care system that protected their normal opportunity range at each stage of their lives.* The notion of an age-relative opportunity range needs explanation.

Equal opportunity and health care for the elderly

I have argued that meeting health-care needs is of special moral importance because it promotes fair equality of opportunity. It helps guarantee individuals a fair chance to enjoy the normal opportunity range for their society. Specifically, restoring normal functioning has the particular and limited effect of allowing an individual to enjoy that portion of the normal range to which his skills and talents would ordinarily give him access, assuming that these too are not impaired by special social

[11] For an alternative strategy, see Allan Gibbard 1982.
[12] For a discussion of the presuppositions in such an account, see Daniels 1979c, 1980.

disadvantages. The notion of a normal opportunity range discussed in chapters 2 and 3 must be refined for its special application to our problem about distribution between age groups. Life plans, we might note, clearly have stages, which reflect important divisions in the life cycle. Without meaning to suggest a particular set of divisions as a framework, it is easy to observe that lives have phases in which different general tasks are central: nurturing and training in childhood and youth, pursuit of career and family in adult years, and the completion of life projects in later years. Of course, what it is reasonable to include in a life plan for a stage of one's life not only reflects facts about one's own talents and skills, tastes and preferences, but also depends in part on social policy and other important facts about society. These qualifications already are present in the notion of normal opportunity range itself.

The suggestion I want to explore is that prudent design of the institutions that affect us over the different stages of our lives requires reference to the notion of age-relative opportunity range. Specifically, prudent deliberation about the design of such institutions, carried out with the degree of abstraction from individual perspective appropriate to the task, would attempt to assure individuals a fair chance at enjoyment of the normal opportunity range for each life-stage. With this refinement, the fair equality of opportunity account I am proposing for health care will avoid the pitfall of age-bias. Notice that this refinement is possible only if we adopt the *broad* interpretation of the fair equality of opportunity principle, the one using the notion of normal opportunity range. The *narrow* interpretation restricts the principle to career opportunities and clearly risks importing an age-bias into my account.

Consider now the perspective of designers of a health-care system who are under an appropriate veil of ignorance. It keeps them from knowing their individual health status, conception of the good, age, income, and other important facts about themselves as individuals. At the same time it lets them know important facts about the disease/age profile for their society, its technological level, and even that lifespan has been increasing, largely as a result of other features of social policy. One feature of their problem emerges as critical: in choosing principles for institutions that defer the use of resources, *they must assume lifespan is normal*. Since they cannot appeal to any very special conception of the good, which might lead them to discount the importance of their projections or plans at a certain stage of their lives, they must treat these stages as of comparable importance. Here they are simply in compliance with Sidgwick's (1907) account of rationality: each moment of life is equally valuable and must not be discounted merely because it comes at one point in our lives rather than another.

Of course, there are standard problems facing the Sidgwickian view. Even though it disallows 'pure time preferences', it does not block some 'impure' reasons for discounting the value of certain moments. Nevertheless, given our problem of design from behind a veil of ignorance, some special views people might hold are not available to them. Still, there are other problems. The concept of rationality itself does not determine which moments are to count as 'ours'. If I refuse to plan for 'my' care when 'I' have advanced senility, am I being imprudent? Am I being irrational if I insist that *that* senile person (if he is one) is not really *me* and that I do not care what happens to *him*? I ignore these worries here.

From their perspectives, prudent deliberators will not know just what their situation is, what preferences or projects they might have at a given stage of their lives. Still, they do know that they will have a conception of the good and that it will determine what is meaningful for them in their lives. But then it is especially important for them to make sure social arrangements give them a fair chance to enjoy the normal range of opportunities open to them at any stage. This protection of the range of opportunities they enjoy is doubly important because they know they may want to revise their life plans; consequently they have a high-order interest in guaranteeing themselves the opportunity to pursue such revisions. But impairments of normal species functioning clearly *restrict the portion of the normal opportunity range open to an individual at any stage of his life*. Consequently, health-care services should be rationed throughout a life in a way that respects the importance of the age-relative opportunity range.

Let us consider two implications of this view for the design of health-care systems, keeping in mind that these systems operate through time on all stages of one's life. The first implication is the suggestion that personal medical services have the same underlying rationale for their importance as various personal care and social support services for the disabled. Medical services are intended to preserve or restore normal functioning; in turn, normal functioning is important because of its impact on individual opportunity range. But the same rationale makes personal care and support services for the disabled elderly person important: they compensate for losses of normal functioning in ways that enhance individual opportunity.

A major criticism of the US health-care system, that it encourages premature and overinstitutionalization of the elderly, should be assessed in this light. The issue becomes not just one of costs, not simply of whether institutionalization is more or less cost-effective compared with home-care and social support services. Rather, the point is that the opportunity range for many disabled persons might well be enhanced if they are helped to function normally outside institutions. They would have more opportunity to complete projects and pursue relationships of great importance to them, or even to modify the remaining stage of their life plans within a greater range of options. Often the issue is discussed in terms of the loss of dignity and self-respect that accompanies premature institutionalization or institutionalization at inappropriate levels of care. My suggestion here is that the underlying issue is loss of opportunity range, which obviously has its effect on autonomy, dignity, and self-respect. Viewed in this light, the British system, in which extensive home-care services exist, far more respects the importance of normal opportunity range for the elderly than does the US system.

The second implication is more controversial, and I am less sure of it. I believe that prudence would dictate giving greater emphasis to enhancing individual chances of reaching a normal lifespan than to extending the normal life-span. It might at first seem that such a contention runs counter to the earlier appeal to Sidgwick's principle, that it is irrational to entertain pure time preferences. But I am not urging that a given moment of life for a person older than the normal lifespan is worth less than a comparable moment for a younger person. About that, the prudent deliberator can make no judgment. But he must acknowledge several important considerations. Assume, for the moment, that a society's productivity and birth rate are held constant. Then, increasing lifespan – here beyond the normal range – must compel us to save resources at a greater rate in earlier stages of our lives. Where policies lead to greater longevity primarily because they reduce infant and childhood mortality rates, we are likely to have some increase in productivity, which may not necessitate greater rates of saving. But where the extension is due primarily to extending marginally the lives of elderly people, we clearly are required to save at an increased rate. To the extent that such increased savings undermine the ability to protect normal function in younger age groups, or even in the late stages of a normal span, we face an increased likelihood of not reaching a normal lifespan. Prudence would thus urge us to pursue a different policy. Under the conditions imposed here on institutional design, we can abstract from what might merely be thought a matter of 'personal taste', whether to live a longer life with fewer resources or enjoy a better chance of living a normal lifespan.

Consider the rationing schemes discussed earlier. Recall that Scheme A permitted no one over age 70 to get certain high-technology, high-cost services. Such rationing by age permitted the development and use of more such services for younger people. Scheme B developed fewer such services and rationed them solely by criteria involving medical suitability and lotteries. I am suggesting that prudential considerations would incline our modified prudent deliberators choosing between such schemes to prefer (1) an enhanced chance of reaching a normal life-span over (2) a reduced chance of reaching a normal span but, for those reaching it, an increased chance of living a life somewhat longer than the normal span. If this conclusion is correct about where prudential considerations incline us, then my strategy of using prudence to guide justice in distributions between age groups should lead us to think Scheme A is morally preferable. The whole point here is that the scheme works through time: *each* of us, not just a particular group of people, will enjoy the increased chance of reaching a normal lifespan under A. And *our* gain in this regard is not made at the expense of another group, but at the expense of *our* reduced chance of living to a longer than normal lifespan.

The point brings to mind a rationing practice ascribed to the Aleuts: the elderly, or perhaps only the enfeebled elderly (I believe those without teeth, who can no longer soften skins by chewing), are sent off to die, sparing the rest of the community from the burden of sustaining them. From descriptions of the practice, the elderly quite willingly accept this fate: and it is *fair* that they should. They were the beneficiaries of comparable sacrifices by their parents and grandparents. If prudence demands such a harsh rationing scheme *in the conditions* the Aleuts face, then we are blocked from any suggestion that the practice is age-biased in a morally unacceptable way. Yet this example should remind us that such rationing schemes are prudent only under certain explicit conditions. So the prudence of selecting Scheme A over B in the preceding deliberation is quite sensitive to assumptions about the scarcity of resources and the way in which policies involve explicit trade-offs. *The argument is not a general defense of all schemes for rationing by age.*

It is worth noting one last implication of these considerations and this strategy for approaching the age-group distribution problem. Where prudential considerations do not decide between alternative schemes – and some might reject my argument leading to the selection of A over B –

we may not be dealing with a consideration of justice at all. More generally, several schemes may all appear prudent, and then we have no basis in considerations of justice for distinguishing among them. Where there are honest differences about what is prudent, we may be dealing with cases whose resolution call for a democratic political process, not transcendent principles of justice.

Equity, errors, and the stability of 'savings institutions'

Thus far I have been ignoring an important question facing cooperative schemes in which saving is accomplished through a compact between birth cohorts. In such schemes, one birth cohort transfers resources for the use of earlier birth cohorts and receives similar transfers from its successors. (We support our parents and expect our children's support in return.) How can a given cohort be assured that its benefits from the scheme will be equitable when compared with the benefits enjoyed by other cohorts? If we call the ratio of benefits received to contributions made the 'replacement ratio', our problem is to determine when replacement ratios are equitable (Parsons and Munro 1978: 65–86).

The problem arises because we must operate such a savings scheme under conditions of considerable uncertainty. Most important, there is uncertainty about population growth rates, economic growth rates, and technological change, with its impact on productivity. Consequently, *any such scheme must derive its stability from an underlying commitment to equity in replacement ratios enjoyed by successive birth cohorts.* Errors are likely to abound, and inequities will arise, but the presumption must be that these errors will be corrected. Still this presumption in favor of correcting errors does not mean that everything is up for renegotiation all the time. The basic institution must be stable.

Clearly we need some theory about what equity involves here. I think this problem of equitable treatment between birth cohorts resembles the problem of a just savings rate between present and future generations, but I cannot say more about the connection here (see n. 7). Instead, I shall rely on the point just made about the higher-order interest parties have in ensuring the stability of the savings institution. Stability requires a belief in equity. If one cohort seeks terms too much in its favor, say when it is young, it will very likely pay the price when it is old; similarly, if it seeks too much when it is old, it will risk rebellion from the young. My guess is that there is a tendency to view equity as requiring approximate equality in replacement ratios. In any case, I shall make such an assumption, primarily for the sake of illustrating a slightly different point.

Suppose, then, that 'mature' savings schemes, those in which beneficiaries have been long-time contributors, should treat different birth cohorts equally. They should aim for equal replacement ratios. In the 'steady state' condition, where there is no economic growth and no population increase, the assumption is unproblematic. In favorable conditions, of positive economic growth and increasing population, we can in fact do better in the following sense: benefits can steadily increase, even if rates of contribution do not. Of course, equity considerations between cohorts might incline us to temper this 'chain letter' or Ponzi scheme effect: if we could project the economic and demographic trends, we might raise the replacement ratio of earlier cohorts somewhat to offset anticipated increasing rates of later cohorts. Unfortunately, in the social security and health-care contexts of the US today, we face the opposite conditions: declining birth rates and poor economic growth. What this means in the US Social Security system, for example, is that the current 3:1 ratio of contributors to beneficiaries will decline to about 2:1 by the year 2030 (in the immature system of the 1950s, ratios were even more favorable than 3:1). To maintain current benefit levels, contributors have to be taxed at very high rates. (The same point applies to health-care 'savings' schemes.) What is worse, much of recent American planning, including the major benefit increases of 1972, seemed to ignore these shifts. To have planned for equity in replacement ratios, many critics argue, would have required (1) taxing earlier generations at a yet higher rate than they were taxed, (2) stunning increases in real wages through rapid economic growth, (3) reducing benefits substantially in the interim, or (4) some combination of these steps.

One problem is that the presumption in favor of equitable treatment between cohorts encounters strong resistance in the political arena. Some cohorts are in a better position to protect their interests than others, undermining long-term stability of the scheme. A second problem is that not everyone believes or understands the problem, and there is often reason to think some factors are exaggerated, perhaps for ideological reasons. Thus many people point with alarm to the shifting ratios of contributors to beneficiaries. But there is a countervailing point: the total ratio of employed to nonemployed (lumping retirees with children) is not changing in such an alarming way. The ratio of total labor to nonlabor was lower in 1975 than for any year including projections through 2040 (Schultz 1980: 11). The implication is that the smaller number of children will require fewer resources, which can then be diverted for use by the then elderly baby-boom cohort. What follows, then, is that we must not look too much at one distributive institution in isolation from others.

Nevertheless, the general point remains. We operate an income or savings scheme in a non-ideal context. It will always encounter various sorts of 'interstitial' equity considerations which are generated by both great uncertainty and political expediency (Barry 1965: Ch. 9). A good example is the tremendous replacement ratio advantage offered the early entrants into the US Social Security system: attempting to lower that ratio might have undermined political support for the Social Security system as a whole. Similarly, in the United States, no fund was ever generated which was significant enough to cushion the effects of our current decline in real wages and declining population growth rate. Politicians were afraid to raise tax rates without pairing the increases with benefit increases. And conservative politicians feared that socialism would follow if large capital funds were controlled by the government. More interesting details of this history are available and constitute an important case study of the contrast between ideal and non-ideal contexts (Derthick 1979).

It is interesting to note that health-care savings schemes face comparable – or even more serious – problems of birth cohort equity. First, as with income support schemes, there will be a bias in favor of early entrants. Such a bias is hard to avoid in immature schemes. But there also is an opposite bias in the case of health care. Consider a scheme in which some form of age rationing of new technology is involved. Our Scheme A will do as an example. An elderly person might complain about A by saying it is not really fair to his cohort: his cohort never had the benefit of increasing its chances of reaching a normal life-span because the technology (say dialysis) now being denied it was also not available in its youth.

Two points might be made in response to this complaint. First, it might be argued that each birth cohort is treated equally in the following way. At some point in its life, each cohort will be denied the best available life-extending technologies, but at all other points in its life it will have a better chance of receiving them. To be sure, the particular technology (say dialysis) it is denied may not be the very one it had a better chance of receiving, but there is a fairness in the exchange. Still, if technology improves very rapidly, the bargain is not quite as favorable from a prudential perspective as it might have seemed when we ignored the fact or rate of technological advance. A second point is more general: some such changes, e.g., in technology, are at least as difficult to project as the other factors that lead to error (replacement ratio differences) in saving schemes. Indeed, it seems in general the case that we might be even more prone to error in the health-care setting than in the income support setting. In such a context, given the overriding importance of stability in such schemes, considerable tolerance for error must obtain.

Some qualifications

It is easy to misconstrue, at least to misapply, my argument. It does not in general sanction rationing by age. Such justification is possible only under very special circumstances. First, it is crucial that the appeal to age criteria is part of the design of a basic institution that distributes resources over the lifetime of the individuals it affects. Nothing in the argument offered here justifies piecemeal use of age criteria in various individual or group settings – e.g., by some hospitals or physicians or in any way that is not part of an over-all prudential allocation. Second, despite the setting in which I raised the argument, it should not be taken as a hasty endorsement of age rationing as a convenient 'cost-constraining' device in the context of current debates. Not only is such an application not likely to be part of the design of our basic health-care institutions, construed as a savings scheme, but many of the assumptions about resource scarcity which might make rationing by age prudent in some circumstances are controversial in the context of this public policy debate. Finally it is important to see that my argument is part of an 'ideal' theory of justice, in which we can assume general compliance with principles of justice which govern other aspects of our basic social institutions. The argument does not readily or easily extend to 'non-ideal' contexts, in which no such compliance with general principles of justice obtains. Thus, it would be wrong to say that my argument actually justifies the British system of rationing dialysis by age (see Aaron and Schwartz 1984). At most, my argument shows that such rationing *can* under some circumstances be part of a just institution, that it is not always morally objectionable in the way that sex or race 'rationing' would be. The argument shows the conditions that would have to obtain for such rationing to be just.

The point about ideal and non-ideal contexts needs some explanation (I return to it in Chapter 9), for it underlies much of my reticence here. It is important to see that many of the problems facing large numbers of the elderly in our society are consequences not of 'age-bias' but of *other* inequalities – and, I would argue, injustices. The worst off among the elderly are usually the same people who were worst-off in earlier stages of their lives. The poor old have generally 'saved' their poverty, which is all they had to save. Problems with social and individual savings schemes may exacerbate their plight, but their ultimate situation is largely determined by their earliest position in society. This is not, of course, to say they are getting what they deserve. It is to raise the more basic question about the justice of the underlying distributive institutions. In the context of such injustice – and of our hard-hearted willingness to reduce benefits to the poor of any age, it is just 'blaming the victim' to talk about the 'inadequacy' or even the 'imprudence' of their savings. No one could reasonably be expected to save prudently for old age from inadequate income and wealth shares in their working years. Of course, we can rectify or adjust for underlying inequities by income and health-care support in the later years, which we to some extent do (although the poor elderly – just like their poor younger selves, earlier in their lives – are most at risk when budgets are cut). But this adjustment should not primarily be seen as an issue of 'justice between age groups'; it is really a more basic issue of distributive justice which forces the correction.

Nevertheless, I have been claiming that there is a distinct problem of distributive justice between age groups. The residual problem is to select principles of distributive justice that will govern the basic institutions responsible for distributing social goods through the various stages of life. My proposal has been that some form of prudential reasoning should guide the design of such institutions. From the perspective of such institutions, goods are distributed through the stages of a life, not between different persons in distinct age groups. In the case of health-care institutions, justice requires we allocate health care in a manner that assures individuals a fair chance at enjoying the normal opportunity range, and prudence suggests that it is equally important to protect individual opportunity range for each stage of life. Under certain assumptions, prudence would urge some forms of rationing by age. Similarly, prudence might suggest that some forms of non-medical services which meet the health-care needs of the elderly are more important than certain medical services, because they better protect the normal opportunity range for that stage of life. But suggesting that prudence is our guide to the design of 'savings institutions' does not, of course, mean that these matters of design are not matters of justice. Here prudence guides justice; it does not prevent us from talking about it.

Some qualifications

In proposing that we use prudential considerations to determine the justice of distributions between age groups, I take for granted a background involving other just institutions. It is in this sense that I have been concerned with a problem in what is known as 'ideal' moral theory: we are looking at principles and institutions operating in a society that is in general just. Remarks about the permissibility of rationing by age must thus be taken in this context. If the basic institutions of a given society do not comply with acceptable principles of distributive justice, rationing by age could make things even worse. Indeed, prudential considerations that might endorse rationing by age depend on what sort of resource scarcity exists. Moreover, it is important what the *source* of the scarcity is. If the scarcity is the result of unjust arrangements operating elsewhere in the system, the argument from prudence may well be undermined.

6 · *Doing justice to providers*

Four issues

A just health-care system will protect the fair equality of opportunity of the members of a society. One implication of this view is that there is a social obligation to guarantee equitable access to a broad array of medical and other health-care services. Specifically, this means that various kinds of primary and other acute care must be available to people who need it, regardless of geographical location or ability to pay. The services we are obliged to provide may not just be more of what is already available in our system. Rather, new or different preventive and acute services may be what is needed to maintain and restore a person's normal functioning and thus satisfy the fair equality of opportunity principle. So too, certain social support services will count as health-care needs we are obliged to provide. These are, generally speaking, what just health care demands, and a careful examination of health-care systems in different countries would reveal what specific reforms are required.

But social obligations do not deliver health care: institutions and, ultimately, people do. These people must be adequately trained and equipped in the appropriate specialties, they must be where they are needed, and they must be willing to serve those who need them. If inner-city or rural residents lack adequate access, people must be moved to deliver appropriate care. If the elderly lack adequate primary care or social support services, people must be trained to provide it. Such providers do not come out of a vacuum and are not created *de novo* by the declaration of a theory of just health care. The providers we are discussing have a certain history: they are used to delivering care in an institutional setting which grants them various rights, privileges, and autonomy. Thus they have certain vested interests, and seeking just health-care institutions may well threaten some of those interests. This threat is usually resisted as an infringement of rights, an undue restriction on professional autonomy, and a threat to the quality of care.

In this chapter, I would like to address four issues raised by the fact that providing just health care threatens the interests of some providers of that care. First, I want to clarify the relationship between the claim

114

that there is a *social* obligation to guarantee fair equality of opportunity through health-care institutions and the suggestion, which is often made, that unjust health care is the result of providers – physicians or the medical profession as a whole – not meeting their obligations. What are the obligations of providers to deliver just health care? Second, many perceive the demands of justice as a threat to provider liberties, e.g., the liberty to practice *what* and *where* and *on whom* the provider chooses. Does just health care, as I have characterized it, infringe on fundamental individual liberties of providers? Third, just health care may threaten the economic interests of certain providers. Does just health care do an economic injustice to them? Finally, a just health-care system may impose constraints on what services may be delivered by a physician or other provider to a patient. Such constraints might seem to interfere with the autonomy we ordinarily grant physicians and patients in the choice of treatments. Indeed, they may appear to threaten the 'agency' relationship in which the physician sees himself as an agent who is morally bound to pursue the best interests of his patient. Does just health care threaten traditional ethical obligations of physicians to their patients?

Taken together, these issues pose a challenge to my account. Is my account of just health care compatible with other considerations of justice? We might think of the concerns about provider liberties or economic entitlements – both matters of justice – as possible limits or constraints on the extent to which we may pursue the egalitarian distribution of health care required by the fair equality of opportunity account. This is the classic conflict of equality and liberty: equal opportunity is fine, provided that securing it violates no other rights or liberties. In this chapter I examine this conflict in the acute care setting by seeing what limits provider rights impose on my account. In the next two chapters, I switch to an important preventive context, the work-place, but I continue to explore the limits on my account imposed, this time, by concerns about worker autonomy and job opportunity.

What are the obligations of providers to deliver just health care?

Consider five questions about the distributive obligations of providers:

(1) Does a physician in private practice have an *obligation* to treat (some of) the people who cannot afford care without charge, or to charge them only what they can afford to pay? Does he have an obligation to accept Medicaid or Medicare patients, whose reimbursement rates may be lower than those for privately insured patients? (We may also ask

these questions of other providers: Do proprietary hospitals have such obligations?) Notice that this asks more than whether it would be morally praiseworthy to do so; we want to know if it is obligatory. If it is, then is the obligation one that derives from strict requirements of justice or from more general (imperfect) obligations to be beneficent or charitable? Are anyone's rights violated *by the doctor* if he fails to treat them?

(2) Does a physician practicing in an area more than adequately served have an obligation to move his practice? He might decide to move because it is in his interest to do so, or because he thinks it is a good thing to do, but does he have an *obligation* to do so? Does he have an obligation to contribute a portion of his time to a neighborhood health center in an underserved area? That is, it might be noble to do so, but is it morally wrong not to do so?

(3) Does a 'resident' or 'junior doctor' contemplating entering practice have an *obligation* to pick – and not just an interest in picking – a place that is definitely underserved? Suppose he has no contractual obligations to do so, perhaps deriving from conditions on his educational loans. Is there still an obligation?

(4) Does a resident have an *obligation* to pick a specialty area on the grounds that there are not enough specialists of that type? Again, is there an obligation and not just an interest in doing so? From what does such an obligation derive?

(5) If it is not the obligation of individual professionals to base patient mix, location, and specialization decisions on such considerations, is it instead the *collective obligation of the profession* to make sure that institutions and their incentive structures are arranged so that individuals are distributed in ways that best meet such needs? Or is it the obligation, if there is one, of *society* to so structure its institutions?

These questions all harbor a certain ambiguity: they may be asking about obligations which we *now* recognize are relevant to guiding our behavior, or they may be asking about obligations we *ought* to recognize if we want to make our delivery system more just. I will concern myself with what I think ought to be the case and not just with what a moral anthropologist surveying our practice might discover is the case. It is important to note, however, that in the US at least, an individual provider, and the profession as a whole, have *no legal obligation* to distribute services except to patients to whom they already have contractual obligations.

The central thesis I shall urge is that the primary obligations in the distribution of health care are social rather than the individual or professional obligations of physicians (and other health-care providers). One might be tempted to the opposite view – a view which may seem implicit in the questions listed earlier – by the following consideration. Suppose we find that health-care distribution is inequitable, downright unjust. A causal factor contributing to the inequitable distribution, we might plausibly conclude, is that many physicians' decisions are made with an eye toward physician interests – especially many of the decisions that bear on distribution. We might then think that injustice is the result of physicians failing to recognize that justice calls for a different distribution. This suggests we could rectify the situation if we made physicians aware of *their obligations* to distribute health care justly. 'If they weren't so greedy!'

In this book I have argued that, *if* it is a requirement of justice that basic social institutions guarantee fair equality of opportunity, then health-care institutions should be among those regulated by the equal opportunity principle. It follows from this view that there are strong *social obligations* to distribute health care in a particular way. But should we try to recast these social obligations as obligations on individual professionals and the medical profession taken collectively?

Such an approach is misguided. It seems unlikely that these social obligations could be met by framing as a starting point a set of principles which are intended to guide the decisions and behavior of medical personnel. For one thing, too many social, economic, and technological factors about a society affect the distribution of health-care needs for it to be possible for the individual professional, or even the profession as a whole, to guarantee just health-care distribution. The individual cannot know enough, nor has the profession power enough, to carry out such obligations (whatever power it has exercised in thwarting social obligations). Moreover, since society's interest in securing a just distribution and professionals' interests are not likely to coincide, a system that *depended* on professionals complying with principles of justice would most likely be unstable. Similarly, even if doctors have obligations to do some charity work – obligations which derive from general duties of beneficence and the fact that physicians are uniquely positioned to help the ill – the system cannot depend on this system of obligations. Far more plausible is the view that professionals who enter the health-care system in different roles acquire specifically defined obligations concerning distribution, but their obligations operate at the *micro* and not the *macro* level. That is, social obligations determine the shape of the system at the macro level, and individual obligations derive from one's positions within that system. In effect, there is a division here in responsibility between society and the professional.

Does this mean that individuals and the profession have no obligations that bear on distributive justice? No, it does not mean that. What I am suggesting is that health-care providers acquire obligations in the distribution of health care through specific contractual arrangements when they enter into roles within the social system of health-care institutions. An example will help. Consider a scheme which goes some way toward meeting social obligations to distribute health care more equitably, perhaps in accord with fair equality of opportunity. The scheme is not a proposal, only an example. Suppose a basic tier of a health-care system, defined by reference to a set of basic health-care needs, is to be financed through a national health insurance scheme that eliminates financial barriers. We might suppose further that no alternative insurance is allowed for the basic tier. Suppose further that in order to guarantee that certain important needs are met, such a system employs central planning of resource allocation. To achieve a more equitable distribution of physicians geographically and in specialties, the planners license those eligible for reimbursement in a given health planning region according to some reasonable formula governing physician–patient ratios. (Let us set aside the problem of 'grandfathering-in' – that is, the recognition of entitlements held by physicians in practice before the new arrangement begins.) Additional providers (say physicians) might try to practice in an area, but they would have to do without benefit of third-party payments for all services involved in the basic tier (and for other tiers if these two were included in the national insurance scheme).

On such a scheme, physicians would acquire obligations to distribute health-care services to specific populations upon making their specialty and location decisions and 'contracting' to obtain a license for reimbursement in a specific area. Such agreements involve patient groups, hospitals, educational institutions, etc. The complex array of such specific agreements constitutes a mechanism through which individuals take on their particular obligations, which act together to meet the social obligations. But no one could 'derive' an obligation of a physician to treat a particular group of underserved patients from the general social obligation to provide services to such patients. Where a system of such agreements fails to meet the social obligations that are of ultimate importance, the institutional arrangements must be adjusted, leading to new specific agreements, so that just distribution is achieved. Thus, the individual physician or resident does not have an obligation to treat the underserved patients unless he has undertaken such an obligation through prior agreements and decisions. But if such patients exist, then institutional structures, such as incentives which work through reimbursement schedules, have to be altered so that some physicians are drawn into undertaking the appropriate obligations. The serious case might arise if no system of incentives ends up being adequate to produce the required distributions – but I do not believe this case need ever arise, so I will ignore it.

I have not here argued for any one set of institutional arrangements as the preferred ones for accomplishing social obligations. A number of alternatives are possible. My example involving a national health insurance scheme with limited licensing for reimbursement might be contrasted with a scheme that made it a condition of a license to *practice* that physicians use a sliding scale of fees, including some compulsory *pro bono publico* services. The effect would be to force internal subsidies from one part of the patient pool to another. Such an arrangement might accomplish distribution goals effectively, but it is arguably less fair than the insurance scheme. I mention these alternatives here to show that the structure of specific obligations undertaken by individual providers will differ depending on features of the institutional structures.

One final point: physicians and the health profession do have obligations to seek just social arrangements and not to obstruct their institution. But this is not a *special* obligation of physicians; it is one binding everyone. Unfortunately, many physicians and their professional organizations can be faulted for failing to meet even *these* obligations of justice (see Starr 1982).

Does just health care violate provider liberty?

Do programs that aim at more centralized planning of physician distribution than occurs in our system infringe on any basic liberties of providers? Does restricting or promoting physician entry into certain geographical or specialty areas thwart professional autonomy in a way that infringes important liberties? Do constraints on provider autonomy to determine the *mix* of the patients that providers include in their practices – e.g., the proportion of publicly subsidized patients on Medicaid or Medicare – and the *fees* they charge, interfere with fundamental provider liberties?

Consider how the complaint that liberty is threatened may be raised.

The 'libertarian' physician might argue that all persons should be at liberty to use their skills and talents and to enter into contractual arrangements intended to advance their interests, provided no fundamental liberties of others are violated in doing so. For the physician, this means his being 'free' to enter the specialty he prefers and to practice where and on whom he chooses and for fees mutually agreed upon with his patients. Of course, the physician may, on this model, make special contractual arrangements – e.g., in order to secure loans to pay for his medical education – which bind him to some acceptable constraints on subsequent choices. In advancing this view, the physician argues as if he is really making no special pleading on his own behalf. He suggests that the liberty he seeks to protect for himself is one already enjoyed by everyone else. He may insist that constraining the choices he now has open to him amounts to 'socializing' his individual assets, his talents and skills.

The notion of liberty underlying this view is problematic. There have been recent efforts to provide it with some foundations, for example in Nozick's (1974) defense of strong individual property rights which are immune to being overridden in the name of other social goals. Nozick argues that we cannot treat people merely as means to achieve our social goals: doing so would violate the Kantian view that we should be governed by moral maxims appropriate to people who live in a 'kingdom of ends'. Specifically, we cannot do things to them or take things from them without their consent. We treat someone as an end, and not merely as a means, when we do nothing to him without his consent. This justification, if successful, would give great scope and power to the property rights Nozick posits. The individual can use his natural talents and assets to enhance his interests and not be constrained by appeals to any social goals – including the protection of liberty – unless he consents. From this view, Nozick derives justification for a 'minimal state' which provides various protections to individuals; no such state can act in the name of justice to take from some to give to others.

I cannot here attempt to refute the general theory underlying this view; it remains a central problem in the theory of justice, and, as with other such problems, I have had to sidestep them. It is worth giving, however, some reasons I and others have for rejecting the view. Some critics argue that such a system of unfettered liberty will tend over time to accumulate concentrations of power and wealth which undermine the possibility of there being fair and truly free exchanges between economic and political unequals. Thus, even in the name of liberty, it is important to constrain liberty. Other philosophers (e.g., Scanlon 1977, Scheffler 1976) have noted that the theory gives undue prominence to some liberties at the expense of others – that a more balanced theory of justice would have to constrain property rights in the name of other basic liberties, such as rights to citizen participation and due process. Still others (Rawls 1971) challenge the implicit assumption that our natural talents and skills are our *property* in the sense that we deserve, and are entitled to benefit from, their use in any way that we can through free exchanges. They argue that such endowments are themselves 'undeserved' and should work to the advantage of everyone, not just their possessors.

Most contemporary social philosophers believe the kind of individual liberty advocated by the libertarian lacks adequate foundations – though votes by philosophers do not resolve these issues. The dominant view is that not every constraint on physician choices would count as an infringement of *a basic liberty*, one we are obliged to protect despite calculations of social welfare to the contrary. Rather, there is probably only a fairly narrow or specific set of liberties which we ought to treat as basic in this way (see Hart 1975 and Rawls 1982a). Specifically, such rights as the freedom of thought and expression, certain citizenship liberties, and certain protections of the person would be on any plausible list of basic liberties. But the liberty being claimed by the physician described above should not be on such a list.

I would like to take a somewhat different and less ambitious tack here. I want to show that the kind of liberty or autonomy being insisted on for health-care providers is *inconsistent* with the comparable autonomy allowed other workers and professionals. Consequently, those who demand such strong liberties for health providers are engaged in a kind of special pleading. To extend their pleas to cover all similar cases would transform social relations in ways these defenders of provider liberties would never accept. In fact, the constraints on provider liberties needed to establish just health care are not different *in kind* from those imposed by other competitive markets.

To see the point, consider the 'license for reimbursement' scheme introduced in the last section. It goes some way toward meeting social obligations to distribute health care more equitably than the US system, or at least we may suppose it does. To achieve a more equitable distribution of physicians geographically and in specialties, the planners license those eligible for reimbursement by the national insurance scheme in each health-planning region according to some reasonable formula governing physician–patient ratios. Additional providers might try to practice in an area, but they must do so without benefit of third-party payments for all services involved in the basic tier.

No doubt many physicians would perceive such 'constraints on trade' as a severe infringement of their fundamental liberties. But in fact, the scheme ends up putting physicians in the same relation to market constraints on the availability of jobs that face most other workers and many other professionals. A college professor cannot simply decide there are people to be taught in his favorite, wealthy suburb. He must accept what jobs are available within universities, wherever they are. Of course, he is 'free' not to follow the market – much of which is a product of public decisions about where educational institutions will be located and who will be able to attend them. But then our professor would not be able to teach. Similarly, middle- and high-level managers often are moved around the country by the corporations they work for. Refusing such moves is usually coupled with dead-ending a career and possibly with financial penalty or even dismissal. Or, a worker or manager may not even be hired if he indicates unwillingness to meet the geographical needs of the corporation. Similarly, many workers at all social levels face the need to locate themselves where there is some industry that is willing to employ them.

So the physicians' sacrifice of 'liberty' under my proposal is merely the imposition of a burden already faced by the great majority of the working population at all levels of skill and professionalism. Indeed, the proposal does not change in principle the forces that already motivate physicians. Now they locate where they can establish the most profitable practices and meet their other preferences about where to live. Under the proposed scheme, they would still locate where they can establish the most profitable practices and still meet, presumably weaker, preferences about where to live. The scheme merely shifts, in a socially useful way, where it is profitable for some physicians to practice. Society structures the market in a rather drastic way, but it appeals to the same sorts of interest that operate in a less doctored market.

It might be objected that it is one thing for markets to impose a structure of choices on people as a result of natural market forces, but a quite different thing for the markets to be structured by social policy. The former might be thought to be natural or unavoidable effects on individual liberty, but the latter a clear intervention. This objection is not persuasive. Many markets which affect workers' choices in other work contexts are also structured for various social purposes. Indeed, if justice requires that we view health-care services as a different kind of social good from goods usually distributed through unregulated markets, then we may indeed have to modify the normal market. The point of the argument is that some schemes for meeting the requirements of justice affect provider choices in ways we find unproblematic in other contexts – so the plea for physician liberties looks like special pleading.

It might be helpful to inject a note of political sociology here. The appearance to some that a scheme such as the one in my example violates an enshrined or basic liberty is something of an historical accident. It is the legacy of the fact, more visible in the US than elsewhere, that physicians have been more independent of institutional settings for the delivery of their skills than many other workers and even than physicians in other countries. Had US physicians always operated out of clinics or hospitals, which is the history in many other places, then it might never have seemed that there was a basic liberty – 'to practice whatever and wherever one wanted' – which is now being sacrificed. Of course, the history of the effectiveness of medical professionals in protecting their interests and autonomy is a far more complicated one than this remark suggests, as Paul Starr (1982) shows in his recent treatise (see Daniels 1984). Nor is this just the claim that where a liberty has always been violated, there is nothing to protect. We do not hear the physician bemoaning the lost liberty of other workers. I am suggesting that the talk about a basic liberty here is an attempt to enshrine features of a particular institutional arrangement, a temporary, entrepreneurial one, with the garb of basic moral rights. That is why I earlier said that the appeal to liberty was ideological.

These remarks are hardly a conclusive refutation of the libertarian objection. But they do go some way toward showing that appeals to physician liberty are not adequate to dissuade us from meeting the social obligations to provide equitable access to health care. They suggest we are not concerned with any liberty so fundamental that its violation would be morally worse than failing to provide for equity of access to health care.

A more plausible concern is the effect different schemes may have on long-standing expectations held by current and would-be medical professionals. It is often felt that where such expectations have been encouraged by long-standing social institutions, they are frustrated only at the expense of violating an 'implicit contract' with those who hold them. This argument has some merit, but how much depends on the case. Where a system is altered for some social advantage, but not because it was fundamentally unjust, the expectations that have been developed should be taken seriously. But where the system is altered because it is fundamentally unjust, the expectations that it generated should be taken less seriously. For example, the racist expectations generated by Jim Crow or other caste-enforcing laws should be given no moral weight in arguments about social policy. How much weight such expectations have to be given for tactical, political reasons in achieving social change is a different and more complex issue. Where the expectations of physicians fall on this spectrum of 'legitimate' to 'illegitimate' I will not resolve here.

Does just health care deny physicians just economic rewards or incentives?

Just health-care institutions may constrain in various ways the economic opportunities enjoyed by providers. For example, decisions about capital investment in hospitals could be made subject to public scrutiny and approval in ways which are more effective and comprehensive than the limited effort in the US in this direction, such as the recent 'certificate of need' regulations. A just arrangement that guaranteed equitable access might involve constraints on 'fee for service', retrospective reimbursement schemes, or on tax breaks for the wealthy who seek purely elective procedures, such as cosmetic surgery.

On a very small scale, a recent Massachusetts effort to adjust reimbursement schedules for Medicaid providers raises the issue sharply. Economic analysis of the time and intensity of services showed that existing rates are much too high, relative to true costs, for various procedures, including many surgical ones. Rates are much too low relative to costs for many primary care services. Thus the system has a disincentive to provide needed primary care and an incentive to over-supply high technology interventions. Establishing a rate schedule more in line with actual costs would give incentives to provide more primary care to the eligible population. The proposal is under sharp attack by surgeons (Knox 1983). Suppose, for the sake of argument, that such a scheme would be a feature of a just health-care system. How are we to view the threat it poses to the economic interests of some providers? Does it do them an economic injustice? After all, we are tampering with the existing market rates.

I would like to approach this question from what may seem an odd direction, by considering issues raised during the 1970s when physicians began organizing unions to protect their own interests and their conception of medical practice. Of course, physicians have long organized collectively in powerful professional associations, which have helped them consolidate their power and economic advantages (Starr 1982). I will focus on the small but vocal union movement of the 1970s, not because I think it an important movement, but because the debate about it crystallizes issues which are in any case present in other forms of professional organization by physicians. The focus on unionization is intended to let me address more general points. Specifically, it raises the issues underlying the complaint that justice in health-care delivery threatens the just economic interests of providers. For example, what is the connection between collective bargaining – or professional lobbying – and the pursuit of just distributions in social goods, including wages? Is there a conflict between unionism and the moral demands of professionalism? What is the relationship between physician interests and more general questions about justice in compensation and health-care delivery? Are physicians' economic demands just?

Collective bargaining and social justice

First, let me establish a rather general and important point. Collective bargaining does not constitute a form of procedural justice, not even a very imperfect one. The fact that a union or an employer wins a certain demand through collective bargaining does not show anything about the justice or fairness of the demand or of the over-all settlement. This point needs some explanation. (I draw here on Rawls 1971: 85ff.)

Consider the case of unrigged or 'fair' gambling. Every outcome of a series of bets will be a fair or just redistribution of the players' original stakes. Gambling is often called a case of *pure* procedural justice precisely because there is no criterion of a fair or just outcome distinct from an actual outcome of fair gambling. Of course, just this feature distinguishes gambling from collective bargaining. Most of us have some notion (however vague) of a 'fair wage' or 'just compensation for services rendered' or even of a 'just return on investment'. And we call 'unfair' those cases of collective bargaining in which the outcomes fail to live up to these notions, however imprecise they are. If grape growers collude to share losses in order to weather a farmworkers' strike, then in view of the farmworkers' low wages many will feel that justice is not done if the strike is lost and workers make no gains.

Consider a different case – dividing a cake at a child's birthday party. Unlike the gambling case, here we have a *prior* notion of a fair division.

Assume that equal slices constitute a fair division. But how to get it? The classic solution consists of asking the birthday girl to slice the cake, knowing that she will receive the last piece after each child picks one. Because the procedure almost certainly guarantees our *independently determined* fair outcome, we call this *perfect* procedural justice.

However, consider the case of a criminal trial. There is an independent criterion of a just outcome: conviction of all, but only, those who have committed crimes. And procedures can be devised which bring fairly good, though by no means perfect, assurance of arriving at just outcomes. Many miscarriages of justice occur. This kind of procedure is called *imperfect* procedural justice.

On the surface, collective bargaining appears to have some resemblance to this last case: there is an independent criterion of just outcomes and the procedure sometimes falls short of producing just outcomes. But I think there is considerable difference in the two cases. Criminal trials, with their elaborate theories of evidence, protection of the rights of the accused, and protections in the election of a jury, constitute procedures consciously designed to produce correct decisions (though they can be systematically abused as well). In contrast, the tactics and practices of collective bargaining are not consciously designed, with the exception of certain attempts at fact-finding and arbitration hearings, to show how the evidence in the case points to the rightness of a particular outcome. Historically, and even today, collective bargaining is regulated class struggle or conflict, a test of strength. Might is most tenuously connected to right, even – and some would say especially – with the National Labor Relations Board looking over the contestants' shoulders.

Have I overstated the point about a test of strength? It might be argued that since voluntary agreement results from collective bargaining, it is just as acceptable a procedure for producing just distributions as the free market is in general. After all, what could be more just than the distributions resulting from freely made exchanges? Though there has been some effort recently to make this position respectable again, particularly in Robert Nozick's (1974) work, the 'free' market has proved a very poor procedure in general for arriving at just distributions of social goods. Moreover, the health-care market deviates in such crucial ways from an ideal free, competitive market, that even if one could, in theory, treat other markets as a procedurally just distribution device, in medical practice no such case can be made (Arrow 1963).

Do not mistake my point. I am not arguing that collective bargaining, because it is not a form of procedural justice, is a bad practice. Far from it. Historically, unionization and collective bargaining have been the main way in which various groups of workers have protected themselves against the greater power of owners and employers. To the extent that some greater fairness or justice may now exist in the distribution of income and benefits to certain groups of workers, it is primarily because they fought hard, using collective bargaining, for demands that were just and were able to win some of what they demanded. But the greater justice of the outcomes of such struggles stems from the justice of the demands, not the nature of the process, collective bargaining, which was only a test of the ability of workers to fight for those demands.

What does my argument show? If a person is convicted in a criminal trial judged to be fair, we have ample reason to view the conviction as just. We might be wrong, of course, but we have good reason to believe the outcomes of such trial procedures will in general be just. But we have, in contrast, no reason to think that the outcome of a collective bargaining process brings us closer to just distributions of social goods, even if people agree, in some sense of 'agree', to those distributions. Winning through collective bargaining is not evidence justice is done. This point should be extended: I would argue that 'winning' through effective legislative lobbying is also not evidence justice is done. It shows only that one has effectively exercised one's strength in that political market.

Therefore it is most important for us to assess, as honestly and carefully as we can, the justice of the demands we make on entering into collective bargaining. It is not enough for a doctor, or anyone else, to say: I won a $150,000 income through the process of collective bargaining; therefore, my having such an income is part of a just distribution of social goods. Similarly, one cannot argue: I have a right to protect my interests through collective bargaining, and if I succeed in securing certain interests through that process, then that fact shows the result is part of a just redistribution of social goods. For example, suppose physicians were so powerful that they could hold the health care of the population hostage through strikes or other work actions and force society to grant them far greater income and power than they now enjoy. Would the fact that such an outcome was the result of 'collective bargaining' count in any way toward establishing the justice of the outcome? Or, suppose doctors were so weak – perhaps everyone else united to oppose them – that collective bargaining resulted in reducing the level of benefits enjoyed by doctors to that of an unskilled orderly. Would the fact that the outcome was the result of the collective bargaining process by itself prove anything about the justice of the outcome? Clearly not. From a moral point of view it is far more important to worry from the start about the justice of the goals doctors seek than it is to worry about their 'right' to bargain collectively for their goals. The same point holds for the results of lobbying efforts undertaken by the American Medical Association (AMA).

Professionalism and unionization: a conflict?

Is there a conflict between a physician's professional status and unionization? I think not. As I understand it, the contrast goes something like this. Physicians are professionals. Professionals have a commitment to enhancing the standards of their profession, to preserving and expanding the legacy of knowledge and experience at the heart of their professional activity, and to holding their colleagues to high standards of performance. Moreover, physicians have a special professional relationship to patients, a relationship that places special obligations on them to provide their patients with the best service they can provide and which involves (for physicians) a certain confidentiality, trust, and autonomy. The theory is that this relationship is threatened if patients feel that doctors are significantly motivated by pecuniary interests rather than professional duty. But, so the argument goes, trade unions are primarily instruments for advancing the self-interest of their members, and the physician who becomes a unionist will undermine the doctor–patient relationship at the heart of professional performance. (Presumably, it is far better to pursue physician interests in a less visible fashion, through quiet legislative lobbying.)

The contrast is, I think, overdrawn on both sides. Trade unions have historically been fairly narrow vehicles, fighting for bread-and-butter issues of their members. But where is it written that unions are restricted to such concerns? My own feeling is that unions have seriously failed to serve the real interests of their members because they have had too narrow a view of the interests of their members and of the relationship between the interests of different groups of workers. But introducing broader social concerns into the goals of unionizing, however difficult, does not contradict the purpose and function of unionism. It only strengthens it. To the extent, for example, that health workers' unions fail to make a concern for patient care a central concern, they only divide themselves from the interests of other workers and ultimately weaken their ability to improve their situation and educate people about the connection between their interests in good working conditions, for example, and patients' interests in good health care.

But the contrast is overdrawn on the professional side as well. Built into the professional ideal, as it is often expressed, is the view that health care is provided by the free contract between the doctor and the patient. The doctor, on this view, must be autonomous. He must have the right to decide, free from interference by non-physicians, about what course of treatment is to be followed, provided the patient consents. But the notion of autonomy plays another role in the professional model. It also means that the doctor is autonomous in setting his fees in a fee-for-service system of health-care delivery. There is an unfortunate sliding back and forth between these two notions of physician autonomy. Indeed, the 1934 AMA code of ethics was explicit in viewing these economic forms of autonomy as a requirement of professional ethics (Starr 1982). In general, I think the ideal of professionalism has certain inherent, crucial assumptions about how health care should be delivered and organized and what powers should be reserved for physicians. These assumptions have amounted to a defense of the highly rewarded economic and social position doctors have come to enjoy in this country (Stroman 1976). In Saskatchewan in 1962 and in Chile in 1973 physicians withdrew their services on a large scale – they went on strike. In both cases, the doctors were *not* unionized but rather were organized into professional associations. And in both cases, the issues involved doctors appealing to the ideal of medical professionalism – a defense of physician autonomy and a particular form of the doctor–patient relationship – in opposition to health-care delivery reforms that had been initiated with the support of the majority of the public. To claim that the ideal of professionalism is 'neutral' with regard to the socio-economic interests of the physician is to put one's head in the sand. So, just as it is incorrect to paint unions as necessarily bereft of the social concerns that make for good medicine, so too is it incorrect to paint professional organizations or 'the profession' as standing above the socio-economic concerns of doctors.

Physicians' goals and just demands

But what have physicians involved in organizing physicians' unions said about their goals or the justice of their cause? When some doctors have argued about the advantages of unionizing, they have paid woefully little attention to the relationship between physician goals and justice. Specifically, where doctors have proposed that physicians' unions ought to fight for very high incomes, they have appealed only to vague and rather dubious social theory to establish the fairness or justice of the demands.

Consider the views of one strong proponent of doctors' unions – Sanford A. Marcus, a San Francisco surgeon who was president of the

Union of American Physicians in the mid 1970s. Marcus (1975a) argues, quite plausibly, that recent developments in medicine – the growing strength and presence of third-party forces, the increased dependence of doctors on hospitals for the delivery of their technologically more sophisticated services, the growing efforts by consumers to hold doctors accountable in the courts for the quality of medical practice – all weaken doctors' ability to protect their socio-economic interests. Marcus contends (1975a: 40), 'With the forces that are arrayed against him [in what he calls the "Brave New World of Medicine"], it becomes certain that without vigorous representation of his rights by forces (unions) that have been conspicuously lacking in the past, the physician must certainly be reduced to the level of a public functionary, accorded no more respect or status than the poor postal employees or public-school teachers in *their* preunion days.' Though Marcus (1975a: 40) assures us that 'At the present time the traditional union demand for more probably does not really apply to dollars and cents considerations for physicians', in another article (Marcus 1975b: 204), titled 'The time has come to bargain for higher incomes', he says, 'We must bargain collectively for what we believe our services are really worth.' And he actually does get down to dollars and cents:

All right. So let's say we've reached the point where collective bargaining begins. We've been offered a salary range of $30,000 to $50,000 – a typical opening ploy of setting a low pay level. We should counter with a demand for a scale ranging up to $150,000, on the ground that this isn't too much to pay the professionals who guard the health of the nation. In the bargaining, the figure would probably come down to the norm that I favor – the $100,000 achieved by senior pilots of Delta Air Lines. Marcus 1975b: 204

I am not going to argue here against the justice or fairness of doctors' salaries in the range Marcus discusses. Rather, I want to show the flimsy basis on which he tries to establish the legitimacy of such demands. His argument shows (at most) that doctors ought to be paid about the same as airline pilots. But he establishes nothing about the fairness or justice of salaries in that range. For the reasons I have already discussed, the fact that senior pilots have won such salaries through collective bargaining does not constitute evidence that those salaries are part of a just distribution of social goods; it only shows that these pilots were strong enough to win such demands. Yet Marcus argues as if the fact of winning such a salary proves that that is what one is 'worth' to society. But by this test, no doctors are worth as much to society as top athletes and entertainers.

The view that the superior incomes doctors in the US have been enjoying – and which are now under some threat – are a reflection of doctors' worth to society is widely held in the medical profession. For example, Michael Halberstam (1973) has argued that doctors have been so generously rewarded by society because the medical profession has contributed so 'selflessly' to the health of the nation and has never stooped to bargaining about economic rewards. He argues that unions constitute a trap for doctors and that if doctors stoop to unionizing, losing the economic leverage of their professional idealism, then 'The public's attitude will be, "If they act like garbage collectors, let's pay them like garbage collectors." And they will' (Halberstam 1973: 78). This meritocratic view of society is, in my view, completely unfounded (Daniels 1978). A better explanation of doctors' success in securing superior incomes is the degree to which they have been able to retain the role of private entrepreneurs selling a necessary service, at the same time keeping relatively tight controls on the supply of physicians (Starr 1982). My point is not that there is no great social worth to the services doctors provide, but that our society does not distribute rewards in accordance with such a criterion, and so the relative success of doctors in the past is not by itself evidence for their continuing to merit superior remuneration.

But there is an even more questionable component of Marcus's position than his assessment of the monetary worth of physicians' services. He seems to adopt the view that what is good for doctors is good for patient care. As Marcus puts it:

I'm sure the public will side with us. After all, no one wants to fly with an airplane pilot who's disgruntled because he isn't getting paid enough. Similarly, we can demonstrate that a fair compensation for doctors' services will help to increase the chances of high quality patient care. A dissatisfied corps of doctors cannot reasonably be expected to remain highly motivated in the face of an actual lowering of their standard of living. Marcus 1975: 214

Incidentally, just what does Marcus suppose the pilot would do – crash his plane in frustration? Is he telling us that a doctor has to earn about $100,000 a year before he is adequately motivated to provide good quality health care? Why should this view reassure the public? Why should they put up with doctors who feel that way? Notice too the shift in grounds for justifying the high income demand. First we are told that doctors merit such salaries because of their *social worth*. Next we are told that such salaries are a necessary *incentive* if doctors are to be motivated to provide us with services. In any case, both the merit argument and the incentive argument would probably not fare well on a systematic examination from a sound theory of distributive justice.

But the argument is not always made in so bald a fashion that doctor contentment is a necessary condition for good medical care. Usually, a somewhat more palatable connection between doctor interests and patient interests is alluded to. Thus Marcus says, 'Collectively, however, a union can at least have input through negotiation in defending the professional integrity of its members. Paradoxically, as this is always in the direction of broadening the scope of medical care, the physicians' unions find themselves in the unique position of being perhaps the most effective consumer advocates in the interests of their patients, the American people' (Marcus 1975a: 50). Similarly, Stanley Peterson, a physician, has argued that physicians' unions are in the interests of patients: 'The important message we have to get to the public, is that doctors' unions are being formed to protect the rights of patients as well as physicians; the union's strategy is to make known its opposition to governmental and other third-party programs that affect patient care before a point of no return occurs' (Ferber 1973: 53).

I am in favor of physicians' unions fighting for the improvement of health care. But we must distinguish demands which have a clear connection to the quality of patient care from those which do not. The vaguely stated goal of protecting physician prerogatives or physician autonomy may have only a questionable connection to real issues of patient care, a connection made plausible to doctors only because physicians have trouble accepting any model of health-care delivery that challenges the ideal of the sacred doctor–patient relationship. If other models of health-care delivery promise, and perhaps are proved elsewhere, to provide better health care, then traditional views of the role of the doctor will have to be changed. This change may well involve a reduction in the doctors' ability to achieve superior income and status. If I am right, then the easy optimism of an editorial in the *Western Journal of Medicine* (1975: 138) should be questioned. It asserted, 'The test for every action of every physician, of every group of physicians and of the profession itself is whether or not that action is best for patients and, therefore, for the public generally.' So far, so good. But it concluded, 'It will always be true that what is best for the patients is in the long run best for the medical profession.' This claim is by no means self-evident. And if the satisfaction of physicians' socio-economic demands and the provision of improved patient care are not clearly the same thing, then the need for a theory of justice explaining how to resolve the conflict is obvious. Without the guidance of such a theory, we have no convincing way to resolve such conflicts of interest.

Physicians might well worry, as Halberstam does, that public negotiations built around demands for very high physician incomes are not likely to gather much mass support, especially among patients who directly or indirectly pay the bills. Popularity aside, however, what can be said about the justice of demanding physician incomes in the very high ranges suggested by Marcus? I cannot answer this question here, but I can try to indicate some of the things that might play a role in trying to answer it.

Of course, it is rather fruitless to look at a particular salary level and ask whether it is a just one. Recent philosophical treatments of distributive justice, notably Rawls's (1971), have emphasized the importance of applying principles of justice to basic social structures, including the structures that determine allowable economic inequalities. If one could determine that a given physician salary derives from a basic structure adhering to acceptable principles of justice, then one would be in a position to determine the justice of the particular distribution. Does a physician income of $100–150,000 derive from such a just basic structure? My considered guess is that existing inequalities in the United States, including physician salaries in that range, are not justifiable by any of the plausible candidates for a distributive principle to govern basic structures. I doubt, for example, that physicians' incomes ranging up to 150 times those of the poorest workers are likely to be justifiable on any of these grounds:

1 They are part of a system of inequalities that maximizes average well-being (or 'utility') for members of society.
2 They are part of a system of inequalities that maximizes the well-being of the worst-off members of society.
3 They are part of a system of inequalities that happens to result from the working of free exchanges in a free market among agents all entitled to their holdings at the time of exchange.

But I refrain from arguing for this assertion in any of its specifics and am content merely to show what kind of general claim about the system needs to be established to determine the justice of a given distribution.

Let us step back from the overwhelming question of judging the justice of the system of inequalities as a whole, including physician salaries, and look briefly at defenses one often hears for such high salaries. Sometimes we are told the salaries compensate for the deferred income of the physician during his long, expensive training period. Of course, today large portions of the expense of that training are subsidized by public monies, and interns and residents usually work for salaries as high as, or higher than, average in the United States. In any case, even if we average the high incomes over all training years, physicians are still at or near the top of the (earned) income scale. Sometimes we are told the salaries reflect the burdens of high responsibility, high-risk work. But many workers who have other peoples' lives in their hands and whose work exposes them to greater physical or mental health risks are paid nowhere near as much. Sometimes we are told that such incomes are needed incentives to get physicians to enter the field. But what is the evidence that the quality of health care would decrease if physicians earned less or if selection for entry into the field were determined more directly by the candidates' concern for delivering good health care rather than their concern for the economic status of the physician? Evidence from other countries does not support the view that high incomes are necessary for high-quality care. Sometimes we are told that the salary simply reflects the relative contribution to the social good that doctors make compared to other kinds of workers. But we have a right to ask for the details of this calculation.

I do not mean to single out physicians and to insist that their salaries be subjected to a scrutiny we do not give to other very highly paid professionals and businessmen. My guess is that no one else at the top of the income range would survive such scrutiny either because forces other than a concern for justice or principle determine these economic distributions. But I do want to indicate my skepticism about the type of justification usually offered to rationalize extremely high physician – and other – incomes. The justifications usually appeal to principles which no one, even those who cite them in this context, seriously argues either should or actually do govern distributions in our system. But a real justification of such incomes would have to be based on real appeals to principle.

The demands of justice in health care may pose a threat to the economic interests and power of physicians. If it could be shown that these economic interests and powers of physicians were themselves the requirements of just economic arrangements, we would face a conflict in the requirements of justice. I have argued, largely by examining the generally unimportant movement for physicians' unions and its views about the economic entitlements of physicians, that victories won by such a movement do not in general show the justice of the results. The very same point can be made about the results of the actual mechanisms – lobbying by professional organizations, not unions – which have led physicians in the US to enjoy the unique positions of power and wealth they have achieved. The very peculiarity of that history, so ably documented by Paul Starr (1982), suggests that the arrangements physicians enjoy cannot be justified as the results of a fair procedural process. They too are results of the adroit exercise of power in a uniquely favorable context. Where just health care threatens physician's economic interests, we have little likelihood justice is in conflict with itself, only with vested power and illegitimate expectations.

Does just health care threaten traditional ethical obligations of physicians to their patients?

My examples of how justice in health-care distribution may affect physician autonomy have so far involved issues of access and financing. But the demands of justice may also affect resource allocation in ways that have a bearing on physician decision-making about treatment. The point is that justice may require that we give priority to meeting some needs over others when not all needs can be met. One form such constraints may take is the request for more cost-effective treatment decisions or the 'budget-capping' of some insurance schemes. I would like to examine briefly the implications of such cost-constraining measures on physician autonomy. Usually, the physician insisting on his autonomy argues in a rather different way about the importance of these constraints than he does about constraints which affect his career choices and income. These constraints are attacked for their effect on the quality of care and not on physician 'liberty'.

I shall begin by sketching what I think is a fairly widely held – though not uncontroversial – view of the role of the physician (and certain other providers). On this view the physician is seen as having entered into a relationship with a specific patient which binds him to acting in the best interests of the patient, with the patient's consent, of course. One important product the physician delivers to the patient is reassurance and what is somewhat romantically called 'caring'. No doubt this is an important part of the notion of 'quality' of care. But I here want to leave it out of the picture, at the risk of oversimplifying my discussion. Instead, I want to focus on another feature of the product the physician delivers, namely a package of services – diagnostic and therapeutic – which carries with it various benefits, harms, and risks. Suppose we consider a simplified conception of this package and assume it can be expressed as a sum of benefits and burdens (including risks). And let us for the moment not consider monetary costs among the burdens to anyone – patients or society. We are focusing on the medical impact of the 'benefits-minus-burdens' package. We might try to express this whole package in monetary terms – which of course raises questions about just how to do so. But let me leave this conversion problem aside. The notion I have characterized here corresponds, I believe, to what Donabedian (1979: 279–82) has called 'absolute' quality.

The 'benefits-minus-burdens' package clearly varies with the total quantity, as well as the selection, of services. Since adding services does not always increase the sum of benefits and burdens – we run into unnecessary, iatrogenic services – we can imagine that 'absolute' quality may have a maximum point when benefits-minus-burdens is plotted against quantity of services, i.e., total monetary cost of services. Clearly, absolute quality is a function of the state of medical science, but, as Donabedian (1979: 280) points out, it also critically reflects 'how well the science and technology are used'. Moreover, for any ceiling on the volume of services, stated, say, in monetary terms, the absolute quality of care will be maximal when the sum of benefits-minus-burdens is greatest.

Using this idealized notion of absolute quality, we can now restate the task of the physician according to the traditional view. He is to act in the patient's best interest, by making the patient aware of what treatment package maximizes absolute quality, and, if the patient agrees to such treatment, to pursue it. Of course, from the patient's perspective, the benefits-minus-burdens calculation may come out differently. This is clearly the case if the patient includes in the calculation his cost-sharing of the monetary cost of the treatment package; but we might also find that patients evaluate the costs of lost time, pain, fear, and so on according to their own utility functions or preferences. In any case, the patient may be seen as trying to maximize what Donabedian calls 'individual quality', which includes monetary cost to the patient. The task of the physician then is to help the patient pursue this goal, informing him as fully as possible of the relevant facts about absolute quality so that the patient can make his own adjustments. (This view of the patient as decision-maker is clearly less tenable for very ill patients who want no such burden.) Let us assume, for the sake of simplicity, that absolute and individual quality will differ primarily because of patient cost-sharing. So if patient cost-sharing is eliminated, as it is on some insurance schemes, we can imagine a coincidence of physician and patient goals with regard to the quality of care.

Now we can restate our question in this section. Absolute quality will vary with the over-all quantity of services available. If resource constraints keep the level of available services below the level that leads to an over-all maximal absolute quality, then physicians and patients will have to settle for next-best solutions. One way to put our initial question would be to ask, Is limiting the search for absolute or individual quality to next-best solutions a morally permissible constraint on physician autonomy? I would like to eliminate from this discussion, at least for the moment, the question of who pays for the treatment, for I think the central issue arises regardless of how the financing burden is distributed. The question, again, is whether society is obliged to permit health-care resources to be allocated purely in response to physician–patient intentions to maximize absolute care?

The obvious worry here is that resources are limited and that considerations of justice and efficiency may lead us to question the correctness of allocations made in response to the unrestrained pursuit of absolute quality. Indeed, it is safe to conclude that resources will not be adequate to maximize absolute quality for all patients. Such constraints can be viewed as 'budget ceilings' imposed at a macro-allocation level. These reflect the relative importance of different diseases and the health-care needs they generate. What this amounts to, then, is the claim that what Donabedian (1979: 283–4) calls 'social costs' (assuming minimal cost-sharing) must play a role in at least macro-allocation decisions.

How does this argument affect the view I just sketched about the role of the physician in the pursuit of absolute quality, a role it should be noted which seems to be endorsed by medical codes of ethics? I think it does not force us to abandon that model, but only to qualify it. It suggests that the physician has the task of advising the patient about the best treatment package, the one with the greatest absolute quality, available under the resource constraints imposed by considerations of justice. The physician remains in this way primarily the agent of the patient, though he operates under some social constraints. Still, he does not have to import into his own case-by-case decision-making inferences from general social principles that, at another level, determine macro allocations. Such an arrangement need not jeopardize patient confidence in the physician. Moreover, the patient's entitlements to health-care services are constrained by considerations of justice. But the constraints are not ones he should see the physician as having imposed. It is not the physician who here implicitly puts a price on the patient's life.

Notice that physician autonomy to pursue the patient's interests is defended, not by appeal to 'fundamental' physician liberties, but by appeal to the consequence of permitting such autonomy – namely, better-quality care. But if the importance of that consequence must be weighed against the importance of equity in health-care delivery, then physician autonomy may be compromised accordingly. Once again, traditional degrees of autonomy are not written in stone.

It may seem to some that a system which permits the pursuit of maximal absolute quality in the micro situation is less intrusive than the one I sketch. More to the point, by refusing to put a price on life, it may seem to be morally preferable and to respect 'freedom of choice' to a greater degree. But I think this is an illusion. Such a system would still require rationing in some other way – e.g., by ability to pay for health care – assuming resources are not infinite. For those who cannot gain access to health-care services because they cannot afford them, the implicit price on life is quite low. This point aside, I think a rationing system based on ability to pay violates fundamental requirements of justice bearing on the fair distribution of health-care resources. It thus constitutes a greater moral evil than either the need to place a price on life or the need to restrict the autonomy of the physician in his pursuit of absolute quality.

It should be obvious given my theory of distributive justice for health care that I do not accept 'efficiency' considerations alone as the basis for macro-allocation decisions. What may be called equity considerations play the key role. But there is plenty of room, within the approach I develop, to insert cost-effectiveness methodology, for within the constraints justice imposes on our allocations, we want to be cost-effective. Still, and this is an important point, it is not just the demands of efficiency that lead us to 'put a price on life' in conditions of moderate scarcity; *it is the demands of justice itself*. Pricing life is not simply the result of worshipping the almighty dollar but is something forced on us if we aspire to be just in distributing limited resources.

Conclusion

I have argued that the kinds of constraints on physician autonomy forced on us by requirements of justice in health care do not involve the violation of any fundamental or basic provider liberties, nor do they necessarily do economic injustice to physicians. The restrictions on traditional provider autonomy in matters that affect access to care need involve constraints on choice no worse than those faced by many other classes of professionals and workers. The restrictions on autonomy in treatment decisions imposed by just resource allocation policies also violate no basic liberty of physicians or rights of patients. Moreover, these restrictions need not interfere with valuable features of the doctor–patient relationship, provided there is a division of responsibility between society and the physician, so that rationing decisions are not the responsibility of the physician. In short, in acute-care contexts, pursuit of fair equality of opportunity does no injustice to providers. In the next chapter I consider the conflict between just health-care institutions and liberty in a preventive setting.

7 · Doth OSHA protect too much?

Fair equality of opportunity and preventive health care

A health-care system can protect an individual's share of the normal opportunity range both by curing disease when it arises and by reducing the risks of disease and disability. If we are obliged to protect opportunity, we may neglect neither curative nor preventive measures. The fair equality of opportunity account thus has a bearing on the debate about whether the health-care systems of the United States and other western countries overemphasize acute therapeutic services as opposed to preventive and public-health measures. There are two general implications of the account for preventive health care: protecting opportunity will require (1) reducing the risk of disease and (2) seeking an equitable distribution of the risk of disease.

The first implication is fairly obvious. It is often more effective to prevent disease and disability than it is to cure them when they occur (or to compensate individuals for loss of function, where cure is not possible). Cost-effectiveness arguments will have some bearing on claims about the appropriate distribution of acute vs preventive measures. But the general point emphasized by the equal opportunity account is that the burdens of disease – even where the disease can be treated, and leaving aside financial burdens – have effects on fair equality of opportunity. This suggests that many types of preventive service and practice which reduce the risk of disease will be given prominence in a system governed by the fair equality of opportunity principle.

The second implication of the account, the importance of equalizing the risk of disease, needs some explanation. Suppose a health-care system is heavily weighted toward acute care and that it provides equal access to its services. Thus anyone with severe respiratory ailments – black lung, brown lung, asbestosis, emphysema, and so on – is given adequate comprehensive services as needed. Does the system meet the demands of justice?

The fair equality of opportunity account implies the system is incomplete. If some groups in the population are differentially at risk of getting ill, it is not sufficient merely to attend to their illnesses. Where risk of illness differs systematically in ways that are avoidable, guaranteeing equal opportunity requires that we try to eliminate the differential risks and to prevent the excess illness those experience. Otherwise the burdens and risks of illness will fall differently on different groups, and the risk of impaired opportunity for those groups will remain, despite the efforts to provide acute care. Care is not equivalent to prevention. Some disease will not be detected in time for it to be cured. Some is not curable, even if it is preventable, and treatments will vary in efficacy. We protect equal opportunity best by reducing and equalizing the risk of these conditions arising. The fact that we get an equal chance of being cured once ill – because of equitable access to care – does not compensate us for our unequal chances of becoming ill.

For these reasons, the fair equality of opportunity account places special importance on measures which seek the equitable distribution of the risk of disease. Some public-health measures, such as water and waste treatment, have the general effect of reducing risk. But historically, they have also had the effect of equalizing risk between socio-economic classes and between groups living in different geographical areas. Many other environmental measures, such as recent clean air laws and pesticide regulations, have both general effects on risk reduction and specific effects on the distribution of risks. For example, pollutants emitted from smokestacks have a different effect on people who live downwind from those who live upwind. Gasoline lead emissions have greater effect on urban than rural populations. But other health-protection measures primarily have an effect on the distribution of risks: the regulation of workplace health hazards is perhaps the clearest example. Only some groups of workers are at risk from workplace hazards. The general implication of the fair equality of opportunity account is that stringent regulation in all of these ways must be part of the health-care system.

There is also much evidence that life-style choices impose differential risks of disease – smoking, diet, exercise all have a major effect on morbidity and mortality. For example, if we correct for differences in longevity, almost all of the difference in cancer death rate between 1930 and 1980 – some 40 per 100,000 – can be attributed to the rise in lung cancer rates, which in turn is primarily the result of increased smoking (Weinberg 1983: 82). So far, public measures aimed at prevention have been restricted largely to educational efforts. Smoking is not prohibited, only warned against. Fitness programs are not compulsory, but are promoted in ways it is profitable to do so. It is interesting to note that the preventive efforts themselves may have a differential effect on the elimination of risk: the largest reduction in smoking and the greatest emphasis on fitness has been in the upper-middle classes.

A striking feature of public interventions in the domain of life-style choices – following the US Prohibition era – has been the concern not to run afoul of individual liberty. Self-affecting behaviors, however harmful, tend to be seen as falling within a sphere of individual freedom or autonomy. The public interest in reducing the risk of disease must be tempered by this conflict with liberty. I will say more about this conflict with lifestyle choices briefly in later sections of this chapter, but my main concern here is a different conflict between individual liberty and the search for equity – namely, in the workplace. This focus needs explanation.

Prevention and OSHA regulation

In this chapter I will discuss preventive health-care measures in an institutional setting, the workplace. In part, I choose this focus because the regulation of workplace risks is clearly mandated by and emphasized by the fair equality of opportunity account, which urges the equalization of the risk of disease. But I also choose this focus because the workplace is a context in which actual regulation and not just education, as in matters of life-style choice, has been initiated. This regulation has been the object of great public controversy, largely because it has forced employers to bear the considerable costs of cleaning up workplaces. Without such cleanup, the costs are 'externalized'; they are borne by workers, in the form of increased disease and disability, and by society, which pays the resulting increased health costs in the form of higher insurance premiums. The fair equality of opportunity account points toward the need for rather stringent hazard regulation. Its goal is to protect fair equality of opportunity, which implies that the significantly increased risks of disease faced by particular groups of workers are to be avoided to the extent it is possible to do so. Moreover, the fact that there may be significant costs to protecting equal opportunity in this way, or that such stringent protection may not be economically efficient, does not override the requirement of justice in this regard. The priority we give to fair equality of opportunity means that we must be willing to accept some economic losses of this kind.

Though much of the public debate about health hazard regulation has focused on costs, there is another, extremely important issue which also is raised as an objection to stringent regulation, and thus to my account. The objection is that the account comes into conflict with other requirements of justice, namely the protection of individual liberty. Specifically, it threatens the liberty of workers and employers to contract, through hazard pay, to distribute the benefits and burdens of risk-taking to their mutual advantage. Stringent regulation seems unduly paternalistic, perhaps valuing workers' health more highly than workers themselves value it. It is in this context, then, that there arises a sharply defined conflict between equality – in the form of stringent prevention efforts – and liberty – in the form of eliminating consent to risk as a method of distributing the burdens and benefits of risk-taking.

The regulation of hazards – and risk-taking – in the workplace thus illustrates a general and classic problem my account faces, the reconciliation of demands for equality and liberty within our concerns about justice. In the last chapter, I pursued this issue in a different direction, arguing that the demands of my account do not conflict with legitimate physician liberties or economic entitlements. In this chapter (and the next) I continue the process of showing that my account does not involve internal conflicts among competing demands of justice. Thus what follows is less an effort to elaborate the implications of the fair equality of opportunity account than it is to show that its general implications are compatible with other concerns for justice, specifically, our concern that individual liberty or autonomy, e.g., to take risks for compensation, such as hazard pay, is not undermined. The rather detailed and very narrow discussion that follows, focused as it is on a fine point about the stringency of Occupational Safety and Health Administration (OSHA) regulations, should be seen as illustrative – and hardly exhaustive – of a more general issue.

The form my discussion will take is to consider a rather restrictive form of health hazard regulation, one that might well be required by the fair equality of opportunity account. The task will be to determine if such restrictive regulation, viewed as an 'upper bound' on stringency, can be justified without violating legitimate concerns for the protection of individual liberty. The upper bound to be considered is not hypothetical: it is the *actual* criterion for regulative standards embodied in the Occupational Safety and Health Act of 1970, namely, the 'technological feasibility' standard. If this actual standard can be shown to respect individual liberties, then it is plausible to think that the fair equality of opportunity account will be consistent with those components of the general theory of justice which protect individual liberty.

This focus of my discussion needs further explanation because there is an asymmetry between acute and preventive care which is relevant here. A just health-care system provides equitable access to medical services which are themselves equitably allocated – but it remains an individual's decision whether to use such services. The social obligation is to protect opportunity by providing the institutions which make individual consumption of these services possible. There is an elaborate doctrine of *informed consent* which intervenes between the framework of services society makes available and individual choices about consumption. Risk-taking, including the risks of medical treatment, is generally viewed as a matter which should be left for individual decision: deep strands of liberal political philosophy coalesce to form a protected space within which the individual is to be sovereign in his self-regarding decisions. But in preventive contexts, especially where groups are protected, as in the workplace, the issue of consent arises in a much more complicated form. The central issue in this chapter will be to reconcile the demands of justice – that we provide a just distribution of preventive health services through stringent regulation of exposure to health hazards – with these concerns about individual liberty. In the next chapter, I shall examine how variation in individual susceptibility to risk raises a different problem of consistency within the theory of justice, namely the complaint that the principle of fair equality of opportunity may be in conflict with itself.

The OSHA 'feasibility' criterion: in search of a rationale

The Occupational Safety and Health Act of 1970 requires the US Secretary of Labor to set *standards* for dealing with toxic or harmful materials in the workplace. Such standards specify permissible exposure levels and require various practices, like the wearing of air masks, and means, like monitoring devices, for insuring that exposure does not exceed these levels. But when is a standard a good standard? How much protection should a good OSHA standard afford, assuming full compliance and enforcement? A centrally important feature of the 1970 Act is the *criterion* it specifies for acceptable standards: a standard should 'assure, *to the extent feasible*, on the basis of the best available evidence', that no employee will suffer material impairment of health.[1]

Challenges to the criterion and to specific standards, like the cotton

[1] The OSHA act of 1970, Pub. L. No. 91–596, 84 Stat. 1590, is codified at 27 USS pp. 651–78 (1976).

dust standard, have focused on the sort of feasibility involved. OSHA has taken 'feasibility' to mean *technological (or technical) feasibility*. A standard must protect workers to the degree it is technologically feasible to do so. In fact, however, OSHA must make a modest concession to economic considerations: the costs of compliance with the standard should not result in putting a whole industry out business, though it may drive out marginal producers.[2] In this discussion, I shall ignore this economic concession and shall refer to the criterion as the *strong* or *technological feasibility criterion*. Issues of enforcement aside (and they are aside throughout this chapter), the strong feasibility criterion has teeth. It compels the stringent regulation of hazards and is therefore seen as an essential feature of the OSHA Act by many proponents of public-health regulation.

A recent US Supreme Court decision (American Textile Manufacturers Institute *et al.* v. Donovan, commonly referred to as the Cotton Dust Case) upheld the technological feasibility criterion. Textile manufacturers had demanded that OSHA employ a cost-benefit analysis to demonstrate the *economic feasibility* of the cotton dust standard. Though there might be different ways to use such an analysis, the minimal intention would be to show that there is a net benefit, measured in dollars, to all effects of instituting the standard; standards which yielded a net cost would be rejected. Alternative economic feasibility tests might concentrate on the inflationary impact of the standards or its impact on the international competitiveness of US employers. Though a number of justices were clearly worried about abandoning economic feasibility criteria (*US Law Week* 1981a: 3524), the majority found Congress quite clearly intended to impose the technological feasibility criterion.

The findings in the Cotton Dust Case bear further scrutiny. The Court held that, 'The plain meaning of the word "feasible" is "capable of being done," and thus Sect. 6 (b) (5) directs the Secretary to issue the standard that most adequately assures that no employee will suffer material impairment of health, limited only by the extent to which this is "capable of being done".' But the argument of the Court hardly rests on this semantic assertion. Rather, the Court suggests that the technological feasibility criterion is the one that Congress justified by its own higher-

---

[2] OSHA's economic constraints have been hammered out in a series of court cases. For a review of this history, see United Steelworkers v. Marshall, 647 F. 2nd 1189 (1980); also Industrial Union Dept, AFL-CIO v. Hodgson, esp. 499 F. 2nd at 478; also AFL-CIO v. Brennan, 530 F. 2nd at 123; and American Iron and Steel Inst. v. OSHA, 577 F. 2nd at 836.

order weighing of costs and benefits. As Justice Brennan put it, 'In effect, then, as the Court of Appeals held, Congress itself defined the basic relationship between costs and benefits by placing the "benefit" of worker's health above all other considerations save those making attainment of this "benefit" unachievable.' The Court suggests this balancing of costs and benefits by Congress is clear in the Act's legislative history: 'not only does the (legislative) history confirm that Congress meant "feasible" rather than "cost-benefit" when it used the former term, but it also shows that Congress understood that the Act would create substantial costs for employers, yet intended to impose such costs when necessary to create a safe and healthful working environment' (*US Law Week* 1981b: 4721).

Of course, the Court is not asserting that any *formal* cost-benefit analysis was carried out by Congress, one that showed that the strong feasibility criterion always yielded standards which resulted in net benefits and thus in potential pareto improvements.[3] Such a formal procedure would have involved the adoption of an explicit methodology, including a way of assigning dollar values to life-years (or 'quality life years') saved, and Congress used no such procedure and endorsed no such methodology. Rather, the suggestion is that Congress *informally* assessed the benefit of maximally protecting worker health and safety and then judged that it outweighed the costs of compliance with the strong feasibility criterion.

Put in this way, the Court's argument seems open to an important objection. The Court suggests that Congress itself intended to assess the merits of OSHA regulation by a cost-benefit criterion, weighing the benefits of worker protection against the costs of compliance. Congress, then, concluded that the benefits of following the strong criterion always outweighed (or generally outweighed) the costs. But, so the objection goes, if Congress intended costs and benefits to be so weighed, then why should OSHA not be required to make a more careful and direct assessment of each proposed standard, by calculating its benefits and costs? Moreover, in making such assessments, why should it not employ the most respectable cost-benefit methodology available? Doing so would only be appealing to the underlying justification Congress itself endorsed.

[3] An equilibrium point is *pareto efficient* if no one in it can be made better off without someone being made worse off. Intuitively, a policy with net benefit has a 'surplus' which, in principle, *can be* distributed in a pareto efficient way; thus it contains a *potential pareto improvement*. Clearly *actual* distributions of net benefits may not be pareto efficient.

Another way to put the point is to ask why OSHA should not test the accuracy of the Congressional conclusion about the relative weight of costs and benefits by using cost-benefit analysis to assess each standard? If Congress was merely attempting a generalized weighing of costs and benefits, then there is nothing to be feared from seeking to maximize net benefits at the margin by eliminating standards which individually are too stringent to be cost-beneficial. Doing otherwise would seem to be worshipping the 'rule-of-thumb' that vigorous protection of worker health is cost-beneficial. If the technical feasibility criterion is indeed cost-beneficial in general, it would prove to be so were we to test it by using cost-benefit analysis to delimit standards. So, the Court's own rationale for its ruling does not in principle show why OSHA should not design, or be required to design, standards by reference to a cost-benefit criterion.

There are two ways to respond to this objection. A legalistic response is to urge that the Court is right in placing ultimate authority with Congress to carry out the weighing of costs and benefits in the design of its legislation. Congress may err in its judgment, or have its judgment overruled by cost-benefit analyses of individual standards. But then the remedy is clear: the public should urge Congress to reform its charge to OSHA. The second response is philosophically more interesting. According to it, Congress judges the importance or value of worker protection to be so great that standard cost-benefit methodologies are bound to fail to match the Congressional conclusion. And so much the worse for these methodologies! Here, too, of course, there is a legalistic corollary at hand: if Congress is wrong in this judgment, then it is up to Congress to correct its error. But the second response remains philosophically interesting because it invites an examination of the underlying justification for the Congressional judgment.

Thus the Court's argument leaves important philosophical issues unresolved because it does not specify the grounds for the Congressional judgment about benefits. For example, is the protection of workers, to the extensive degree required by the technical feasibility criterion, *a matter of justice*? Are such protections moral entitlements derived from important rights, for example the right to be free from assault, or from matters of fairness and equity, as on my fair equality of opportunity account? Is this the sense in which we must hold worker protection immune to direct cost-benefit analysis? Or is there another basis for believing worker health to be such an important good that Congress, *acting beneficently* to promote the public welfare, imposed the stringent feasibility criterion? In any case, the stringent health hazard regulations made possible by the feasibility standard themselves raise questions of justice, for they involve constraints on autonomy, for example, the autonomy to consent to certain risks. These constraints may be unduly paternalistic, violating basic liberties. Notice that Congress may have constitutionally based *legal* powers to regulate in ways that so constrain autonomy, but there may still be *moral* objections to such powers and constraints.

So the philosophical task that remains is to try to dig deeper than the Supreme Court's judgment about constitutionality and Congressional intent and to search for a plausible moral justification for stringent health hazard regulation, or for a demonstration that there is none. At least we must show what issues the decision about the feasibility criterion leaves unresolved. As will become apparent from my discussion, I do not intend a detailed treatment of the OSHA standards or their governing criterion,[4] nor of the Court's ruling in the Cotton Dust Case. Rather, I use the issue raised by this stringent standard to explore the moral foundations for health hazard regulation of the sort approved by the Court. If no such foundation can be found for this criterion, then we would know that the fair equality of opportunity account would also be restricted to less stringent preventive measures. We are examining a question about the limits of my account.

The feasibility criterion: beyond market regulation

One way to see the issues raised by the Supreme Court defense of the feasibility criterion is to notice how the criterion moves OSHA beyond the role of mere 'market adjustor'. Suppose we held the view that the task of government is to intervene in markets where individuals exchange goods only when the markets depart in specifiable ways from the conditions that define ideal or fair market conditions. The goal of such intervention is to adjust conditions in the direction of the ideal. We might then look at the 'market' for such commodities as health-care protection and willingness to take risks (daring) and ask if the exchanges workers and employers make in this market take place under fair or ideal market conditions. To the extent that they do, we would be assured that the

---

[4] A full discussion would note the rather different technological feasibility criteria that result from adopting different background economic constraints. For example, the current criterion requires 'technological forcing' within an industry; a much weaker criterion would result if such forcing was not required. See references in n. 2 above.

resulting distributions of risks and benefits are both efficient and *fair*. They are fair because the market process which led to these outcomes is fair, and well-known optimality theorems prove they are efficient.

Where ideal market conditions or prerequisites are not met, however, we would authorize interventions to reestablish them or we would impose compensatory mechanisms which mimic their presence. For example, the market model presupposes that exchanges between employers and workers, such as the buying of daring with hazard pay, take place with adequate or full information about the nature of the risks involved. If there is a systematic absence of relevant information, or if access to the information is systematically unequal, then a regulatory intervention is needed to ensure that only informed exchanges take place. Uncertainty would otherwise undermine both efficiency and procedural fairness. Similarly, markets will be efficient and procedurally fair only if the commodities in them are priced at their true social cost. To the extent that many of the costs of health damage to workers are *externalized* and not priced in the health hazard market, since the bill for illness and disability is picked up by society as a whole, the market will be neither efficient nor fair in its outcomes. Such a 'free' market would embody a form of free-loading. In it advantageous bargains would be made between workers and employers at the expense of non-consenting third parties outside the market. To restore the market to ideal conditions would require a mechanism compelling the internalization of the externalized costs.

To the extent that the health hazard 'market' in fact fails to provide for *informed* exchanges and fails to price all factors of production *at true social cost*, a major role would be provided for OSHA as a market adjustor. Such a role would have to be agreed to by any who accept the underlying rationale for the fairness and efficiency of ideal markets themselves. In this case, OSHA would have the role of guaranteeing that information is provided to all parties involved in the exchanges – and this task would involve many of the monitoring, research, and notification requirements incorporated in current OSHA standards. Indeed, it might involve more vigorous protection of workers' 'rights to know' than we now find in practice. Similarly, OSHA would have the task of making sure the market properly priced the commodities exchanged in it. Of course, there are many possible ways to promote the internalization of externalized costs: instead of standards defining permissible dose exposures, forcing the costs of cleanup on the company (at least initially), there might be taxes imposed on relevant employers, the revenues from which would be earmarked to defray the externalized costs. Presumably, these taxes would no longer be available to employer and worker as part of the pie that they divide among themselves. But another way of internalizing costs might be to use a *cost-benefit* feasibility criterion in the design of protection standards. Such a criterion would force the internalization of externalized costs only when, and to the point where, further 'internalization' was counter-productive from the point of view of third parties.[5]

But now it should be clear just how the stricter, feasibility criterion pushes OSHA well beyond the role of mere market adjustor or regulator. The effect of the standard is to eliminate completely the market in which daring is exchanged for hazard pay, at least for all hazards that it is technologically feasible to eliminate. Ideally, there would be no hazards left to bargain about. But if this is the effect of upholding the technological feasibility criterion, why should we single out this market for such drastic intervention, indeed elimination? Why not allow exchanges within the modified, adjusted market that would result from a weaker OSHA, one which merely provided information and which internalized externalized costs? *We need an argument to show that health protection in this setting is so special that it should not be treated to any degree as a market commodity.* So the shift from a cost-benefit to a technological feasibility criterion is more than a mere question of degree. Unfortunately, the Cotton Dust Case blurs this issue with its talk about Congressional weighing of costs and benefits.

The 'specialness' of health protection and the problem of consent

I have suggested that the technological feasibility criterion seems to commit us to some very strong views about the special importance of health protection. Such strong views might be needed to save the argument in the Cotton Dust Case and to justify the virtual elimination of a market for risk-taking under OSHA regulation. Are there bases for such strong views?

---

[5] A cost-benefit feasibility criterion is not to be identified with one aimed only at internalizing externalized costs; for our purposes, I shall use the former to indicate where the latter is an efficient policy. In my discussion, I shall not comment on the many critiques of cost-benefit analysis and its uses in these settings, since I am interested in the question whether we should regulate more stringently than even an acceptable cost-benefit methodology would recommend. For an exposition of cost-benefit methodology, see Stokey and Zeckhauser (1978) or Mishan (1976). For critiques of its use in regulatory settings, see Baram (1980).

One possible basis involves an appeal to individual rights, specifically a right to bodily integrity and freedom from assault (Gewirth 1980). Just as my bodily integrity is violated by a punch in the nose, so too it is threatened by toxins and carcinogens others place in the environment, including the workplace. Just as I have right claim against those who would punch me in the nose, so too I have one against those who would batter my lungs, liver, or DNA with hazardous materials at work. Just as I may need the help of police and the courts to protect my rights against assault and battery of my nose, so too I may need OSHA to protect me against battery of my DNA.

Whatever the strengths and weaknesses of such a rights-based account in general, it falls dramatically short of helping us with the problem we are considering, namely, the justification of the technological feasibility criterion. To use the individual rights model to justify the strong criterion, one would have to supplement it with two features, neither of which is intuitively plausible. First, one would have to assert that the only, or most satisfactory, way to respect these individual rights is to bar exposures to the degree required by the criterion. But it is not clear that these rights fail to be adequately respected by other combinations of measures, for example by combining a cost-benefit feasibility criterion with special insurance protections against the contingency that health is damaged, or with special liability protections, such as an enhanced Workman's Compensation program, or even with a more liberal approach to torts for these cases. Second, one would have to treat the right as non-waivable.[6] Yet, I can waive my right not to have my nose punched. Indeed, were I a world-class boxer, I might be able to get $10 million for doing so. So too, it would seem, I should be able to consent to have my DNA assaulted, especially if I feel the compensation I get (with costs internalized) for taking that risk is worth it. Only if it can be shown why my consent and waiver is to be ignored in just the cases OSHA regulates can we resurrect the rights view in support of the technological feasibility criterion. Moreover, what will be doing the philosophical work here is *not the appeal to the rights* themselves, but the *supplementary theory* that explains the extent of the right and the limits of consent in these particular contexts.

Support for the special importance of health hazard protection might derive from an argument from fairness which requires that there be equity in the distribution of risks. To see the force of the argument, we

---

[6] Mark McCarthy (1981–2:782–7) makes these and other objections.

must first ask a more general question. When do the risks I impose on another through various activities I engage in give rise to claims for compensation? After all, as Charles Fried (1969) points out in his discussion of this argument (see also Nozick 1974: Chapter 4 and Rabinowitz 1977), if I drive to the corner store to buy a newspaper, I impose risks on others all along the route, risks to which they have not explicitly consented. Do they have a right claim against me to refrain from imposing these risks? The answer depends on pointing out that there is reciprocity in the imposition of such risks: my neighbor *normally* imposes them on me, just as I do on him. Since the pursuit of our ordinary, otherwise non-proscribed activities is *roughly reciprocal*, we ought to accept the balance of threats and risks that emerges as the price for collectively living normal, reasonable lives. The 'risk pool' that results ought to be consented to, even if it is not usually the object of explicit consent. Tolerating these 'normal' reciprocal risks is a fair way for each of us to 'use others' to advance our own ends.

But if the argument from fairness justifies the imposition of some unconsented-to risks, it does so only if a central presupposition is met. As Fried notes in his discussion, the risks must be *roughly equally distributed*. If risks to health and safety are unequally distributed, then simple arguments from fairness will count *against* their acceptability to those facing the greatest risks. A paradigm case of such unequal distribution of avoidable risk is the health risk imposed by hazards in the workplace – at least in societies where we do not all rotate our jobs periodically. This argument from fairness implies, then, that workplace hazards are not part of socially acceptable risk pool, and workers have a claim against their being imposed.

Viewed as a vehicle for justifying the technological feasibility criterion, the argument from fairness founders on the same rocks as the rights-based view. Though workers may have a claim, based on fairness, against having unequal health risks imposed on them, the argument does not specify how they are to be protected or compensated for their loss. Some form of compensation may be all that is needed to meet the fairness argument. More importantly, the claim of such workers is only against risks to which they do not consent. If workers are willing to face the risks in exchange for other benefits (assuming they actually can bargain for benefits and keep them in the long run), the fairness argument becomes irrelevant, or so it would seem. If consent is not a reliable risk-distributing mechanism in these contexts, we will have to know why, and it is *this* explanation, not the fairness argument above, that will be needed to justify the strong feasibility criterion.

Perhaps the argument from fairness fails because it is too general: it pays too little attention to what is *special* about health and therefore about the protection of health. The fair equality of opportunity account is just such an account: it shows why health-care needs are of special importance and why they give rise to social obligations to provide needed services. Does it also show why protecting worker health is so important it warrants the strong feasibility criterion?

I think not. The fair equality of opportunity account also falls short of providing a direct and clear rationale for the strong feasibility criterion so central to the OSHA Act. Health may be special or important from the perspective of a theory of justice because of its impact on opportunity, and this importance may give rise to social obligations to protect health. But nothing in this view makes health protection *so* overriding a concern that we may deny individuals the autonomy to take risks that endanger life, liver, and lungs. Consequently, it cannot be just the special importance of health that justifies the strong feasibility criterion Congress imposed. Rather, there may also be something special or peculiar about the context in which these risks to health arise that justifies the imposition of the strong criterion. If so, our search for a justification will compel us to examine what is distinctive about the context.

More protection than I want: a libertarian lament

To focus our problem it may be useful to consider the lament a libertarian worker might make against the technological feasibility criterion. Of course, few actual workers would be likely to argue in this fashion. Indeed, most have sought stringent government regulation (Berman 1978). Nevertheless, however unusual or hypothetical the lament, it forces us to face squarely an important moral issue.

Imagine, then, that the lament is voiced by a libertarian moral philosopher, driven by market conditions out of academe into the industrial workforce. Having been forced to flee the safety of academic life, Bob, we shall call him, suddenly discovers his willingness to take risks. Indeed, it is one of his few marketable talents. More accurately, it *would* be marketable except that OSHA's technical feasibility criterion almost eliminates the market for such daring in regulated contexts. Bob can negotiate for hazard pay only with regard to a residue of ineliminable risk. In contrast, an economic feasibility criterion, say one that merely guaranteed the internalization of costs, would leave him a greater range of risks for which he could negotiate hazard pay and would increase the market value of his daring. In fact, the more stringent criterion, with its greater compliance costs, might mean fewer jobs and less job security than would be possible in a market which allowed employers and workers room to negotiate a distribution of burdens more congenial to them.

Bob's complaint, then, is that protection from risks is being valued more highly than he values it, given the relevant information. Bob's lament is that his liberty to exchange daring for dollars or greater job security is unnecessarily restricted. What is worse, the restriction is completely out of keeping with our other practices regarding autonomy and the regulation of risks. People take risks with their health, and are allowed to do so, in other contexts, in work, in play, and in everyday living. Why, then, these stringent restrictions in selected work settings?

Consider, for example, the inconsistency between stringent OSHA standards and the autonomy granted in other work contexts. Many workers, ranging from specialists, like stunt drivers and test pilots, to policemen, firemen, and ironworkers, face great risks in their work. They are permitted to negotiate hazard pay for the full range of these risks, and no government agency intervenes to insist that risks be eliminated to the extent technologically feasible. Of course, there are safety rules and regulations in most of these contexts, some imposed by the government, some initiated by unions. But no such restrictive standard as the technical feasibility criterion plays a role. Indeed, economic considerations often directly affect worker safety. The recent tax cuts due to Proposition $2\frac{1}{2}$ in Massachusetts led to the closing of fire stations and the layoffs of firemen in Boston. But reduced response time (older, bigger fires are more dangerous ones) and extensive team support are critical factors affecting the risks to firemen.[7]

Second, many life-style choices bring with them risks to health of greater magnitude than risks from many workplace health hazards. Yet people are not prohibited from smoking, drinking excessive alcohol, failing to exercise, or eating too much fatty meat. Nor are they prohibited from hang-gliding, scuba diving, driving without seat belts (in the US),

---

[7] We would be left unhappy, I think, with an explanation that said the externalized costs of health risks to public workers, like firemen and policemen, can be internalized only at public cost, so there is no point to internalizing costs, and we might as well let them negotiate for hazard pay without constraint.

or sun bathing. Indeed, the very workers we refuse to allow to face even modest exposure to carcinogens in the workplace we still allow to drive to work with cigarette in mouth and seat belt unhooked (even if we require auto makers to install the belts).[8]

Any rationale for the strict feasibility criterion must be responsive to the libertarian lament, and be consistent with the autonomy we allow in these other contexts.[9] Of course, one response would be to restrict autonomy in the name of health protection in these contexts as well. But such intrusive and extensive paternalism would be difficult to justify, at least to reconcile with other widely held views about autonomy. (In any case, Congress and the Supreme Court would hardly countenance this way of saving the strong feasibility criterion.) Rather, any plausible justification would have to turn on finding something distinctive about either (1) the *type of risk-taking* involved in OSHA-regulated contexts or (2) the *contexts* in which these choices would be made. The distinctive feature would then have to be capable of explaining why we may restrict autonomy to the degree we do in the OSHA-regulated contexts. Only if we can flesh out such an account can we reconcile the unusual restrictiveness of the strong feasibility criterion with plausible views about the importance of protecting health, such as those generated by the fair equality of opportunity account.

It is important to see how the argument just presented precludes one kind of defense of the strong feasibility criterion. It might be suggested that the issue of paternalism does not arise at all because the strong feasibility criterion is Congress's response to the will of the majority of workers in the affected workplaces. If the majority wants such stringent regulation, and if the regulation is passed in response to that majority will, then the minority is not being protected paternalistically at all. The (libertarian) minority is being protected, despite its own wishes, for the sake of others, not itself. Variants of this defense might also claim that a cost-benefit alternative to the feasibility criterion is either too inconvenient administratively or too vulnerable to employer bias in

[8] The Johns-Manville company banned all smoking by workers at all of its asbestos facilities in an effort to reduce synergistic effects. But the US Court of Appeals struck down the ban as its Dennis plant arguing, 'the danger is to the smoker who willingly courts it . . .' (Johns-Manville Sales Corp. v. International Association of Machinists, Local 1609, 621 F. 2nd 759 (5th Cir, 1980), cited in Lavine (1982:36)).

[9] Indeed, it is often argued that OSHA standards are assessed by a more stringent criterion than is used in other health and safety regulative contexts, e.g., by Consumer Product Safety, by the Environmental Protection Agency, by the Nuclear Regulatory Commission, etc. Whether there really is inconsistency here, despite differences in the standards, is itself a complicated question.

supplying estimates of compliance costs. That is, these variants say the majority wants adequate protection and it is better or more convenient to err on the side of greater protection rather than less.

But this defense and its variations are not fully responsive to the libertarian lament. The heart of the matter is whether the autonomy of the minority with regard to these choices is a liberty that is fundamental or important enough to be viewed as a right, rather than as a matter of privilege. If, as the lament points out, we vigorously protect analogous liberties in other similar contexts, we have some strong, if not conclusive, evidence that the liberty is at least currently respected as a right. We should not compromise it for mere matters of administrative convenience. So the burden of the argument shifts to those who challenge autonomy. (Or even if the burden does not really shift here, we can learn something by being sympathetic, for the purpose of argument, to the libertarian, and act as if the burden is shifted.) They must show why the restriction of choice here is not a violation of an important liberty, one we should view as a right. (I shall remark on this issue about liberty again later.)

Autonomy, paternalism, and risky life-style choices

So far I have rejected the suggestion that the special importance of health protection alone provides an adequate rationale for OSHA's strong feasibility criterion. That defense seemed unduly paternalistic in view of the risk-taking we otherwise permit both in work and play. Consequently, either we must find those distinctive features of OSHA-regulated *risks* or *contexts* which justify the strong or we must abandon this strategy for defending it. We may derive some clues from our inquiry from a brief look at the related problem of risk-taking in life-style choices.[10]

Though most of us would agree that promoting health life-styles is an important social goal, we are also justifiably hesitant about permitting too much social intrusion into individual decision-making about life-styles. We seek to promote autonomy in the definition and pursuit of our conceptions of the good life. Of course, we accept some social constraints, such as those justice imposes on our construction and pursuit of individual conceptions of the 'good'. Yet, we resist the suggestion that there is only one acceptable conception of the good, or that self-regarding

---

[10] I am indebted in this section to Daniel Wikler's (1978) fine discussion of these issues.

features of these conceptions must all agree on basic points, for example, in the importance placed on avoiding risks to health. We have no conception of the good life that embodies just one degree of risk-aversion. Nevertheless, even a view that holds the individual to be the best architect of his ends and judge of his interests rests on important assumptions about the *information* available to the agent, the *competency* of the agent to make these decisions rationally, and the *voluntariness* of the decisions he makes. It is because these assumptions are not always met that we require a theory of justifiable paternalism.

One attractive version of such a theory invokes the notion of a social contract (Dworkin 1972). Individuals who value their autonomy must nevertheless realize that sometimes their competency to make rational decisions is temporarily or permanently undermined. They may then engage in self-destructive behavior which runs counter to their 'true' interests. Their 'true' interests are defined counter-factually as the interests they would claim were they competent, informed, and acting voluntarily. It would be rational for such individuals to insure themselves against such harmful outcomes by authorizing others to act on their behalf, even contrary to their expressed wishes, when specifiable failures of competency make rational choice impossible. But it is critical to this theory that the conditions under which paternalism is permitted are well defined and involve failures of decision-making competency, which I here take to include threats to the voluntariness of the decisions.

Notice that this rationale for paternalism imposes constraints on both the *grounds* for interventions and the *kinds* of intervention it justifies. Specifically, decisions which others regard as self-destructive, including decisions that threaten health, do not constitute conclusive grounds for intervention. Only if these decisions are the result of independently defined and detected failures of competency is paternalistic intervention justified. The theory leaves room, then, for informed patients to refuse life-saving medical treatment and for rational suicide. Moreover, interventions should act first to restore, where possible, the diminished decision-making abilities. Only if restoration is impossible is a more direct intervention in the long-term determination of goals and acts permitted.

Clearly this rationale for paternalism has implications for the kinds of coercion or regulation we may use to intervene in life-style choices that affect health. Specifically, health-threatening behaviors – smoking or not wearing seat belts – are not themselves evidence of diminished capacity for rational decision-making. Many of these behaviors, after all, are associated with natural effects – the relaxation of smoking – that are also desirable and whose payoffs individuals may weigh differently. To intervene in these behaviors would require independent evidence that the behavior is the result of diminished capacity to make decisions, or is in some specifiable way not voluntary. Moreover, where there is such evidence, the intervention must be restricted, where possible, to restoring the decision-making capacity; it should not involve permanent prohibition of the behavior. Of course, people may have diminished competency to judge the rationality of these behaviors if they lack relevant information about them (Brandt 1979: 110ff.). But then the preferred intervention is the provision of the information in an effective manner. Only if it is impossible to assure that information will be accessible can we impose more stringent restrictions on outcomes. For example, stringent safety standards imposed by the Consumer Product Safety Commission can be justified on the assumption that we could never guarantee that risk-taking by consumers would be adequately informed (e.g., the consumer or user may not be the purchaser). Such standards insure us against making the uninformed decisions we consumers are likely to make.

We can obtain another clue for our inquiry, one that bears on the voluntariness of decision-making, by looking briefly at a non-paternalistic argument in favor of intervening in health-threatening life-style choices. Indeed, the very factors which weigh against paternalistic intervention to promote healthy life-styles, especially the lack of evidence for diminished competency, might incline us to turn to this argument from equity or fairness. Unhealthy life-styles impose a burden on the portion of society that chooses healthy life-styles, the burden of sharing the costs of the excess illness induced by unhealthy life-style choices. For example, if insurance schemes do not pool risks by reference to life-style choices, then people with healthy life-styles have grounds for complaint. The insurance premiums are not actuarially fair to them, for they involve a cross-subsidy to the risk-takers. There is a parallel here to the point made earlier with regard to hazard pay in contexts where costs are not internalized. 'Free' choices by high risk-takers free-load on the risk-averse. It might then be argued that the burden should be redistributed, say in the form of a differential insurance premium or through special taxes on smoking, hang-gliding, and so on.

Nevertheless, many people are reluctant to accept this argument from 'fairness' for redistributing the costs of risky behaviors (Wikler 1978: 317ff.). One central worry is that many of the life-style choices are not so clearly *voluntary*, or are not ones for which we feel comfortable ascribing full responsibility, even if there is no way to claim diminished decision-making competency. Many factors, such as induced 'false consciousness' through cigarette advertising, exposure to special peer pressures as a teenager beginning to smoke, or the influence of a cultural background which emphasizes the macho image of heavy smoking or drinking, raise questions about the fairness of redistributive measures themselves (Guttmacher 1979). Such measures seem to treat people as more responsible for these decisions than they really are.

If these are indeed ways in which *voluntariness*, and thereby responsibility, is systematically diminished, a distinct argument for protective, paternalistic regulation might be justified, even though the redistributive argument fails. At least the intrusive factors that diminish voluntariness should be attacked. However, the rather minimal step of informing people about the risks of smoking by warnings on cigarette packs and in commercials falls well short of addressing the issue of diminished voluntariness. We are caught apparently by conflicting considerations in our public policy concerning life-style choices. The worry that certain sanctions would be unjustifiably paternalistic stops us in one direction. The worry that redistributive measures would be punishing those not fully responsible stops us in the other direction. These are not inconsistent worries, though there is a slight air of paradox. We compromise by taking minimal steps toward making sure relevant information is present.

Our discussion of paternalism and life-style choices suggests a strategy for trying to defend OSHA's strong feasibility criterion. In general we ought to preserve autonomy: this was the point behind the libertarian lament. But we are not bound to preserve the illusion of autonomy. If unregulated worker 'choices' about risk-taking must fail, or generally do fail, to be *informed, competent*, or *truly voluntary*, then we are not compromising autonomy by intervening. Rather, we are merely avoiding the illusion of autonomy and insuring ourselves against the harms that would result from living with the illusion. Our task, then, reduces to seeing whether choices unregulated by strong OSHA standards would fail to be autonomous in these specifiable ways.

Information and competency

We may be able to motivate two lines of argument in favor of stringent OSHA regulations by noting some contrasts often drawn between *the kinds of risk* faced, by chemical workers, for example, and other risks we do not regulate as stringently. Risks from toxins or carcinogens are not *visible* in the same way that the risks to a fireman of building collapse or smoke inhalation are (see Ashford 1976: Ch. 7). The latter risks are apparent in the work situations in which they arise – no special knowledge or information is needed to make one aware of them. They are familiar. They are dramatic and direct in their action on us. We know exactly what it is to encounter the risk in a particular situation; moreover, each time the fire is put out, we are aware of having survived the risk. That is, their action is immediate. In contrast, the risks from exposure to hazardous materials may be incremental, operating over a very long term. This of course is the case with many of the familiar instances: cotton dust, coal dust, asbestos. Walking out of the mill or mine each day does not mean the danger has been avoided for at least that encounter. To be sure, we can reformulate both types of risks into frequencies or probabilities of disability or death. But it is arguable that the common coin of this reformulation does not remove the difference in the *graspability* of the risks facing the fireman, stunt-driver, or hang-glider as compared to that facing the textile worker.

This difference in the 'graspability' of the risks also suggests a second contrast. The more visible, familiar, direct kinds of risk seem to be apparent to anyone. The invisible, unfamiliar, indirect risks become apparent only when there is access to considerable epidemiological information. But such information is difficult to obtain and is more accessible to employers than workers. So connected to the difference in the graspability of the risks is a potential inequality in access to information about them.

These two differences give rise to distinct arguments about the importance of stringent OSHA regulation of the sort required by the strong feasibility requirement. The first argument expands on the difference in the graspability of these risks and claims that there is diminished competency to make rational decisions about the less graspable risks. Indeed, our risk-taking competence developed primarily around the more visible, direct kinds of cases, so we have some reason to rely on our normal competency in these contexts; but we have no comparable reassurance about competency in the other instances. Since the information about these other risks must be couched statistically, and generally it is in the form of a low risk of a serious outcome, we have even more reason to worry about individual competency. A recent body of psychological literature has shown that we are notoriously unreliable and inconsistent 'rational deliberators' about just the kind of risk-taking decisions imposed on us by the invisible, long-term risks (see Tversky and Kahneman 1981). Consequently, to rely on individual decision-making in a hazard pay market for these risks would be to rely on a competency we have definite reason to think is diminished. Moreover, merely supplying more statistical information may not compensate for the deficit in graspability and thus lead to improved competency. The 'autonomy' a hazard pay market for these risks involves is thus illusory, and regulation eliminating such illusory choice-making is not a threat to autonomy.

The problem with this argument is that it seems to prove too much. The same sort of invisible, indirect, 'low-graspability' risks are part of the fabric of our everyday life-style choices. Thus the decisions to accept the risks of smoking, or not exercising, or eating too much fatty meat – all seem to involve decisions very much like the risk-taking involved in exposure to cotton dust or benzene. If we want to challenge competency in one domain, consistency requires we do so in the other, unless there are still other countervailing differences. Our problem then, is that this argument fails to meet the conditions of adequacy on a successful rationale imposed by the libertarian lament. Though we have found a difference between OSHA-regulated risks and some other risks in which we allow autonomy, the difference does not generalize to cover the relevant cases.

The second argument draws on the potential for inequality in access to information about the risks. In effect, it says that even the best efforts of a regulatory agency which concentrated on making information accessible to all parties to hazard pay agreements will fall short of giving reasonable assurance that decisions are adequately informed. But if no such assurance about the adequacy of information is achievable merely through regulation, then we have no assurance that autonomy will be real and not illusory in agreements between workers and employers. This argument is thus similar to a rationale often given for stringent safety regulation of consumer products. The argument there turns on the fundamental inequality in information between the manufacturer and retailer, on the one hand, and the consumer on the other. There seems to be no way to make sure that a consumer is informed when he makes his purchase; moreover, purchasers of products are not always their users, so there is even more room for failures of information, which thus leads to the imposition of unconsented-to risks. The result is that products must be held to some measurable safety standard, and we cannot rely on the mechanism of consent to distribute the benefits and burdens of risk-taking.

The difficulty with this argument is that it again fails to steer the proper course among the obstacles illuminated by the libertarian lament. Why should not the same argument about information apply to consumers of cigarettes, alcohol, cholesterol, and so on? Indeed, it seems more likely that we could take steps to insure equality of access to information in the relatively determinate employer–employee relationship than that we could in the highly diffuse relationship between cigarette manufacturer and consumer. In this regard, the former relationship more closely resembles the doctor–patient relationship than does the latter. And even though there is inequality in power or authority, as well as in access to information, in the doctor–patient relationship, we rely on an ideal of informed, competent, voluntary consent to make sure that autonomy is preserved, at the same time we allow risk-taking by individuals. Of course, the analogy is not exact: inequality in power may be greater in the employee–employer relationship than in the doctor–patient one; and there is no traditional ethic governing the 'agency' relationship in the former, as there is in the latter.[11] Still, there seems to be more potential for correcting problems in access to information between workers and employers than there does between smokers and cigarette manufacturers. So if it is information, or the lack of it, that is at the heart of the rationale for OSHA's strong feasibility criterion, we have not cleanly met the libertarian challenge.

Intrinsic and extrinsic rewards of risk-taking

There is another relevant set of differences between the risks faced by workers handling toxins and carcinogens and other risks we do not regulate so stringently. In general, the risks OSHA is supposed to regulate stringently lack three desirable effects which can be associated with various less stringently or unregulated risks. First, workplace toxins and carcinogens are not associated with natural effects that are themselves desirable, as cigarettes are the satisfaction smokers experience. Second, exposure to workplace toxins and carcinogens is not

[11] There is some common law precedent for the notion that an employer has specifiable duties to protect his employee (or slave or apprentice) against certain hazards. Still, whatever the history of recognition of such duties and the entitlements they engender, we still want to have a rationale for them. In any case, these duties seem only to establish a liability of employers. They leave unspecified the mechanism for distributing costs. Specifically they do not show why strong standards of prevention are mandatory.

directly connected to consequences of obvious moral significance, like the protection of life and property by firemen and policemen. These direct moral consequences mean that a certain prestige attaches to the risky work, and some people are attracted to the work by a 'calling' to perform this sort of social service. In contrast, the beneficial, safety effects of asbestos on brake-linings are so indirect that the social significance of the risk-taking is negligible; few are likely to feel a calling to be asbestos workers (McCarthy 1981–2: 779–80). Third, some risk-taking is psychologically gratifying because of the kind of skill, talent, or immediate bravery – and training – it requires. Special prestige may be attached to those who visibly accept such challenges, and various forms of 'macho' camaraderie may arise to give psychological support to those who persevere in facing these risks. But the handling of workplace toxins and other hazardous materials usually does not involve special skills or talents or such visible daring. It may involve only the breathing of cotton dust or benzene fumes, – unpleasant, insignificant, and undramatic parts of one's daily work routine. And where a 'macho' attitude arises, it is more likely to be viewed by others as a pathetic and morbid form of false consciousness.

All three of these differences make it easier to see why people might want, for reasons based on their underlying desires, to take those risks associated with desirable consequences. Accordingly, it is more difficult to intrude paternalistically where people taking risks actually value the direct consequences associated with them. Since the handling of work-place toxins or carcinogens is unconnected to any such desirable consequences, it might seem easier to justify intervention: the risk-taker cannot really want to do what he is doing, it seems. The very taking of the risks appears to be evidence in these cases for incompetent or irrational decision-making.

But the problem with this argument is that risk-taking with carcino-gens or other hazardous materials can be associated with *extrinsic* rewards, even if it is not naturally or socially connected to directly desirable consequences. A system of hazard pay establishes just such extrinsic rewards, and these rewards are motivating and connect to underlying conceptions of the good or individual utility functions. The only way to save the argument for paternalism here would be to show that these extrinsic rewards are suspect in a way not true of the more direct, desirable consequences associated with other risks. And whatever the grounds for such suspicion about extrinsic rewards, the argument must leave room for the fact that extrinsic rewards are also attached to risk-taking in cases where the intrinsic rewards are demonstrably greater – for example, the high pay of Hollywood stuntmen.

One line of argument to show that the extrinsic rewards are suspect is to suggest that they may be particularly sensitive to factors that affect the *voluntariness* of the risk-taking decisions. For example, the extrinsic rewards might be thought enticing only because the range of available alternatives makes them so. Where risk-taking is associated with certain intrinsic rewards, we can imagine particular personality types attracted to them. Such individuals plausibly can be viewed as choosing the risky job because it reflects a definite preference; it is deliberate in a relevant way. Where the rewards of risk-taking are all extrinsic, however, e.g., in the form of hazard pay or increased job security in the short run, then we are led to think the risks are accepted only because there is no more attractive alternative available. Moreover, such a restricted choice is *typical* for a broad class of workers. And if the lack of alternatives is the result of a coercive exclusion from alternatives, or even an unfair or unjust denial of alternatives, then we have reason to be suspicious about the voluntariness of the risk-taking decisions.

A number of observations may motivate such an argument. The class of workers which handles the hazardous materials OSHA regulates tends to have fewer skills and less training than other parts of the workforce. In many places, the affected industries are dominant employers. In any case, the affected jobs comprise a significant portion of the available industrial employment in an economy which has high levels of unemployment. These observations suggest that the mobility of workers likely to be faced with the choice of handling hazardous materials is restricted. The bitterness and despair of workers who have fought against risks in the workplace – which is evident in the struggles of coal miners and textile-mill workers – is further evidence of such constraints on alternatives.

In what follows, I shall consider two lines of argument that develop these worries about the voluntariness of the choices workers make when they trade daring in handling hazardous materials for hazard pay. Both lines of argument provide somewhat different rationales for OSHA's strong feasibility criterion. Moreover, they capture a concern frequently expressed in the literature, that the existence of a hazard pay market for these risks does not imply that the risk-taking is really voluntary. The inference from market exchange to voluntary exchange is faulty (McCarthy 1981–2: 780; Ashford 1976: 333–6).

Coercion

Is it *coercive* to propose that a worker take hazard pay for accepting certain technologically reducible risks in handling carcinogens or breathing dust? It is tempting to look for an argument that shows coercion would be present in any such hazard pay market, or the one we are likely to encounter. Such a result would clearly imply the kind of diminished voluntariness needed to justify the paternalism involved in OSHA's strong feasibility criterion. In contrast, arguments that depend on showing that the range of choices open to workers is unfairly or unjustly restricted are likely to be weaker in either of two ways. Even assuming their premise, that choices are unfairly or unjustly restricted, we still get only a controversial inference to diminished voluntariness in choices about risk-taking. Moreover, the premise itself is likely to be controversial, for different theories of distributive justice will produce different judgments about the fairness of the range of choice. So, whereas coercion might be viewed as a *prima facie* wrong by anyone, controversy about justice will undermine confidence in the soundness (validity aside) of arguments in which we infer diminished voluntariness from restricted ranges of choice.

Nevertheless, I think it is difficult to establish any straightforward claims about coercion in the relevant cases for our argument. The reason is that the concept of coercion is itself complex and controversial in ways that make its application to the health hazard context complex and controversial. Indeed, we lack a persuasive, dominant philosophical analysis to which we may appeal in such applications. It is worth seeing that this is the case, since it always helps to know why we must settle for less, as I think we must here.

Consider a central case of coercion, the mugger who threatens, gun in hand, 'Your money or your life!' The standard analyses all agree that the coercion consists in the fact that (1) the mugger changes the range of options open to the victim, and (2) the change makes the victim much worse off than he would be in some relevant baseline situation.[12] Much of the difficulty in providing an account of coercion derives from the problem of specifying the relevant baseline. Usually, the specification will involve appealing to a complex counterfactual judgment. For

---

[12] Other conditions concern the relative payoff of the alternatives. In general, the utility of a victim's doing the coerced act will have to be much greater than his suffering the consequences of his not doing it. Thus the victim generally much prefers paying to dying. There are complexities here I shall ignore. I am indebted throughout this section to David Zimmerman (1981); also see Nozick (1969).

example, the baseline in our example would be defined by reference to the options that would have been available to the victim had the mugger not acted at all. But there are complexities even here: suppose that if mugger A had not acted, mugger B, lurking in the shadows of the very next doorway, would have acted instead. Do we specify the victim's baseline options by reference to the *local counterfactual* involving only mugger A, or do we refer to the *global counterfactual* which includes the shadowy mugger B as well? If we include B in specifying the baseline, then A is not reducing the victim's options, and, by (1) and (2), seems not to be coercing him. If we do not include B in specifying the baseline, we fail to characterize the victim's real options were A not to act. Consequently, the 'normally expected' baseline of options would be arbitrarily and misleadingly drawn.

Let us look more directly at these difficulties as they arise in the case of health hazards in the workplace. Suppose we take the case of a worker who has a 'clean', non-risky job. His employer wants to change the work process and proposes, 'Accept hazard pay for these increased risks or lose your job.' Is the proposal coercive? Our first problem is to specify the 'normally expected' course of events. But here we face a problem similar to that in the mugger example. Shall we construe the normal course of events quite *locally*, as the continuation of the clean job now held by this worker? Or should we specify the normal course of events by reference to a more *global* baseline, the normal practices and prerogatives of employers, which include the powers to hire and fire in accord with decisions about the profitability of production processes?

If we construe the baseline *locally*, the proposal begins to look coercive. The employer's proposal changes the particular worker's options in a way that makes the worker much worse off. But this result is quite sensitive to the actual array of alternatives (and their utilities) open to this particular worker. It does not just depend on the employer's action. If there is ready access to comparable clean jobs elsewhere, and shifting jobs entails no great losses of benefits, pensions, and so on, then we may just have a case of an *unpleasant*, not a coercive, offer. The 'lose your job' part of the employer's proposal loses its sting, and the employer has not really seriously altered the worker's options for the worse. That is, conditions (1) and (2) of the standard analysis fail to obtain, so the proposal is just an (non-coercive) offer. However, if the alternatives really are 'starve your family (go on welfare) or accept hazard pay for cancer risks', then the proposal again meets conditions (1) and (2) and may well be coercive.

Notice how specific this result is to the details of our example. If the worker were already unemployed, and the proposal was, 'Accept hazard pay or stay unemployed', then we again have a case that does not meet conditions (1) or (2). After all, the employer's proposal does not worsen the unemployed worker's situation: were the proposal not made, his options would not be improved (just as the victim is no better off if mugger A refrains and B acts). But there seems to be something wrong with an account that makes the coerciveness of the offer depend on whether the employer is proposing unemployment which is new or merely continued. The employer's more explicit causal role in firing rather than not hiring does not seem to be what worries us here. To be sure, the proposal to the unemployed worker might be judged exploitive, even if it is not coercive. But intuitions will differ about whether it is *thereby* coercive (Zimmerman 1981: 133–4). For our purposes, if we could agree the offer was exploitive, we might have grounds for viewing it as morally objectionable in ways that might provide a rationale for the strong feasibility criterion. But then the argument would turn on showing why the exploitive conditions undermine autonomy and not on the narrower, more direct judgment that the employer's offer is coercive.

To avoid the charge that the *local* baseline is unduly sensitive to accidental details of the example (e.g., making hazard pay offers to employed workers coercive, but not those to unemployed workers), we might consider shifting to a *global* baseline. Such a baseline builds into our description of the normally expected course of events an account of normal practices of employers. Specifically, suppose that normally workers are presented with such choices as are embodied in the employer's proposal because the employer's normal practices include the making of decisions which force such proposals. Though our employed worker now faces an unhappy choice, between taking unpleasant risks or not having work, and though his particular options are worse than the ones he happened to enjoy before the proposal, they are not worse than the normally expected options specified by the global baseline. That is, workers normally have such poor options, and the employed and unemployed workers are treated similarly. However, conditions (1) and (2) are now not met in either case, and the offer is not coercive on the standard account.

Unfortunately, in making the baseline less sensitive to putatively irrelevant details, such as whether new or continued unemployment is threatened, we have also made it hostage to the status quo. If the general practices defining the baseline are, intuitively speaking, coercive, proposals which are no more coercive than these practices will be camou-flaged: they will blend in and will not appear coercive at all. Indeed, proposals which (intuitively) seem coercive may be welcomed by people who 'normally' suffer from practices that are part of a 'coercive' (global) baseline. Nozick (1969: 450) discusses the examples of a slave owner who beats his slaves daily. One day he proposes that the slave can avoid his usual beating if he does something disagreeable that the slave master wants done. The proposal seems coercive, but we cannot show it is by appeal to a baseline of normally expected options: the change from the baseline is here welcomed by the slave. So, if we do not modify or supplement our account of the 'normally expected' baseline, we cannot accommodate this kind of example. And yet, this is the kind of example that seems most relevant to our case: the offer of hazard pay for facing cancer risks is most likely to be welcomed by the otherwise unemployed worker.

There are two main ways to supplement the account of the baseline to accommodate the example of the slave. The first, which Nozick and others adopt, is to suggest we need a *second* baseline, specified by what is *morally required*. In the slave example, it is morally required that the slave not be beaten, or not be a slave at all. By reference to this pre-proposal baseline, the master's proposal is coercive, even if the slave welcomes the offer. The second approach, adopted by David Zimmerman (1981), is to search for a *non-moral* way to specify relevant baseline.

The two-baseline theory faces some serious difficulties. First, where the normally expected and morally required baselines conflict and yield different judgments about the presence of coercion, we need to know which baseline to use, which is problematic in some cases.[13] Second, and more important from our perspective, is the fact that the two-baseline theory makes the concept of coercion an intrinsically moral one (Zim-merman 1981). That is, on this view, we cannot decide whether a proposal is coercive or not unless, in key cases, we can agree on other judgments about what is morally required. For these cases, our judg-ment about the coerciveness of the proposal is no more basic and no more secure than our judgment about what is morally required at the baseline.

Consider the effect of this point on our hazard pay example. Nozick

[13] For example, Nozick (1969:451) considers the example of the drug supplier who proposes that he give an addict his usual dose for $20 only if the addict, in addition to paying, performs a disagreeable task. Nozick suggests the proposal is a threat because here the addict's *preference* is for the normally expected baseline (the $20 dose), not the morally required baseline (no drug). We need to know why the addict's preference is here (always?) decisive. See Zimmerman (1981:129).

would probably believe that the normal – unregulated – hiring and firing practices of employers do not violate the morally required baseline. Such practices break no prohibitions derived from what is morally required, since they are within the employers' rights, as specified by Nozick's (1974: 263) view of individual rights (see Zimmerman 1981: 121–2, 129–30). Others, however, would argue that if the distribution of income or other social goods, like opportunity, is not fair or just, despite compliance with a framework of Nozickian property rights, then hazard pay proposals will make workers worse off than what is morally required. Of course, the background injustice may not be the result of actions by the *particular* employer making the proposal at all: they are *systematic* and *institutional* in origin. Notice what has happened: by making coercion a moral notion, we are required to make judgments about justice. The result is that we cannot hope to appeal to agreement on coerciveness, and its prima facie wrongness, to undercut or short-circuit moral disagreement about these other issues. Thus we lose one of the advantages, noted earlier, of seeking a rationale for strong OSHA standards that rests on claims about coercion.

There is a related point here as well. The invocation of a second, moral baseline threatens the explanatory simplicity of the analysis of coercion (see Zimmerman 1981: 127–30). That is, we might have hoped that whatever made a proposal coercive by reference to the non-moral baseline has something to do with making it coercive by reference to the moral baseline. Thus David Zimmerman suggests that a correct account should yield the right sort of explanation of the prima facie wrongness of coercion, and that, intuitively, this wrongness will have something to do with the way in which coercion undermines freedom. Where the morally required and normally expected baselines diverge, on the two-baseline account, the relevant pre-proposal situation in general is picked out by the victim's *preferences*. But this suggests that it is the frustration of the victim's preferences which makes acquiescence to the proposal a case of 'unfreedom' and therefore a prima facie wrong (Zimmerman 1981: 129).

Because of the difficulties with the two-baseline account, Zimmerman suggests we adhere to the 'normally expected' baseline in all cases, though we then need a new account of the normally expected. Specifically, he suggests that an *offer*[14] to a person Q is coercive 'only if Q would

---

[14] In general a proposal is an *offer* only if the person to whom it is made prefers moving from the pre-proposal situation to the proposal situation, as does Nozick's slave and (presumably) our unemployed worker. A proposal is a *threat* if its victim strongly prefers not making this move, as, presumably, does our employed worker. See Zimmerman (1981:129).

prefer to move from the normally expected pre-proposal situation to the proposal situation, but he would strongly prefer even more to move from the actual pre-proposal situation to some alternative situation' (Zimmerman 1981: 132). We must obviously limit the class of relevant alternative proposals, for all of us can formulate pre-proposal situations (e.g., winning the Irish Sweepstakes) by reference to which the actual offer becomes coercive. Zimmerman proposes that P's offer to Q is coercive only if he actively prevents Q from being in the alternative, feasible pre-proposal situation Q strongly prefers. Intuitively, for P to be coercing, he must be doing the limiting or undermining of Q's freedom. On this account, exploitive offers differ from coercive ones because the proposer is not *causally responsible* for the victim's frustrated desire to have an alternative pre-proposal situation.

Even if the account were successful over all,[15] it becomes apparent that the effort to show that hazard pay offers for reducible risks are coercive is misplaced. On Zimmerman's account, some such offers are probably coercive.[16] But whether they are or not depends critically on the specific actions taken by employers to block realization of the preferred, pre-proposal baselines. If the hazard pay offer is from an employer who supports legislative or administrative efforts to weaken OSHA, it is coercive. If an employer who is politically inactive makes the same proposal to a worker with the same degree of 'unfreedom' (caused by others), the proposal is not coercive. Yet it is the unfreedom in the *situation* the worker finds himself in that is worrisome from our perspective, not the extra blame we would ascribe to an employer who plays an active role in creating the unfreedom. From the worker's point of view,

[15] Zimmerman's note (1981:136 n. 22) gives reason to worry. Similarly, the businessman who is *forced* out of business – say he must accept a takeover proposal – when he would have preferred to keep control may not be able to make the stronger charge – that he was coerced. Zimmerman can use no moral notions to narrow the class of relevant pre-proposal baselines; but the mere causal agency of the proposer makes any *competitive* victory a *coercive* one. Thus Zimmerman's account is too broad, finding coercion where it does not exist. As I suggest above, it may also be too narrow, not finding coercion where it may well exist.

[16] If OSHA regulations embodying the strong criterion do not put most industries out of business, they constitute a feasible pre-proposal alternative. Even workers who might accept hazard pay were it offered might strongly desire this alternative. Moreover, we can get the baseline by both act-type ('offering hazard pay for reducible risks') subtractions and act-token ('this employer offering this worker this hazard pay for these risks') subtractions. Finally, most employers have fought against strong OSHA regulations and continue to oppose them in various ways. So Zimmerman's prevention criterion is satisfied in general. This result is interesting in light of Zimmerman's discussion of capitalist wage offers in general: at least a large class of capitalist wage offers will count as coercive even if wage offers in general do not (say because the feasibility condition is not satisfied).

the context of restricted choice and the frustration of the strongly desired pre-proposal situation is what results in claims of diminished voluntariness. Thus the coerciveness of certain offers, as Zimmerman's account defines it, should not be the focus of our argument. We would be ignoring all the other ways in which automony may only be illusory in such unfree contexts.

Voluntariness and justice

I shall now sketch an argument which, I believe, both provides a plausible rationale for OSHA's strong feasibility criterion and successfully steers its way around the obstacles erected by the libertarian lament. The argument has a resemblance to arguments which justify paternalism under certain conditions, but the argument straddles a fence between an argument from justifiable paternalism and an argument from justice. The reason it must sit on this fence derives from the considerations in the last section, where we saw the difficulty of making clear-cut, uncontroversial attributions of coercion to cases of the sort we are considering. Despite the argument's plausibility, it is not without its problems, which I note in the next section.

To state the argument I will introduce a bit of terminology which will help us capture the underlying intuition. Let us call a proposal *quasi-coercive* if it imposes or depends on a restriction of someone's alternatives in a way that is *unfair* or unjust; that is, a just or fair social arrangement would involve a range of options for the individual both broader than and strongly preferred to the range in the proposal situation. Some quasi-coercive offers will turn out to be straightforwardly coercive ones: it will depend on *how* the unfair or unjust restriction of options emerged. For example, if the person making the proposal or other relevant persons acted outside their rights, Nozick (1969) suggests, we will have a case of coercion. But, contrary to Nozick's view, systematic injustice in social arrangements does not always derive from explicit acts of individuals who go beyond their rights. These forms of injustice may lead to proposals which count here as quasi-coercive.

The intuition underlying calling unfair or unjust restrictions of options 'quasi-coercive' is that they involve a diminished freedom of action of the same sort which is glaring in the central cases of coercion. A central difference may be the mechanism through which freedom of action is diminished. We do not have the direct and invasive intrusion into the 'choice-space' of the individual which is present in the central cases of coercion, for example, when the mugger exceeds his rights by pointing a gun at my head. Instead, we have an indirect, yet pervasive, erosion of that space as a result of unjust or unfair social practices and institutions. The two share the feature that the restriction is *socially caused*. It is not the kind of restriction that results merely from misfortune; it is an act or institution of man, not God or nature, that produces it. Moreover, there are just, feasible alternatives.

Notice an important fact: like the slave in Nozick's example, people who standardly suffer from an unfair or unjust restriction of their options may welcome a quasi-coercive proposal. That is, from their perspective, it may represent an offer and not a threat. Locally considered, the proposal may advance their interests. Moreover, its quasi-coerciveness may even seem invisible. Not everyone living under an unjust arrangement may be aware of its injustice. Some may even deny its injustice, say through 'false consciousness'. Indeed, against the background of a familiar and psychologically accepted range of options, however unfair or unjust it is, jumping at the new 'opportunity' embodied in such a proposal, say by trading daring in handling carcinogens for hazard pay, may seem the essence of autonomous action. After all, no one is holding a cocked pistol to my head or threatening prison if I do not take the offer. The quasi-coerciveness of unjust arrangements works in a more subtle, but still restrictive, fashion.

There is another way in which the quasi-coerciveness of some proposals may be hidden: it may be only potential, not actual. That is, if we imagine institutionalizing such proposals, then their effect *over time* will be to produce, or to contribute to, actual quasi-coerciveness, even if initially, and viewed locally, there seems to be nothing worrisome about them, and they seem to be the essence of autonomous exchange (Cf. Rawls 1977: 159–65; Nozick 1974: 204–13). There is just such a worry about a hazard pay market for certain kinds of risk when the market is aimed at workers with a severely restricted range of options. Such proposals might seem unquestionably fair at one time: they are the local manifestation of a process of market exchange which seems procedurally fair under certain circumstances. But such markets will tend to greater inequality over time, especially where there is substantial inequality in bargaining power because workers have highly restricted alternatives. Workers who might at one point be able to sell their daring at a relatively high price – as do, say, movie stuntmen – will find that it is worth little or nothing over time. Risk-taking then becomes a condition of getting a job at all, a price only one with an unfair or unjust range of options – one who is quasi-coerced – would accept. This outcome has historically been the lot of the textile-mill worker involved in the Cotton Dust Case, and other low-skill workers whose typical work choices involve exposure to health hazards.

The argument of OSHA's strong feasibility criterion can now be sketched as follows: (1) Hazard pay proposals for technologically reducible risks in the contexts OSHA regulated are quasi-coercive or would tend to be over time. (2) Eliminating such proposals (and the market for them) protects workers from harmful consequences, viz. the destruction of their health at a price that only someone under quasi-coercion would accept. (3) Though hazard pay proposals of the sort involved here may be offers welcomed by certain workers, the autonomy embodied in accepting them is only illusory, for quasi-coercion undermines true autonomy in much the same way coercion does. (4) Just as people would reasonably contract to permit paternalistic interventions which protect them against the harmful decisions they would make when they are not, or cannot be, adequately informed, competent, or free to make autonomous ones, so too they would reasonably contract to protect themselves against quasi-coerced decisions of the sort involved here. Thus, (5) OSHA's strong feasibility criterion can be viewed as a social insurance policy against quasi-coercive proposals to trade health for other benefits.

I shall restrict my defense of this sketch to comments on several of its controversial features. One issue of considerable concern is that the argument not prove too much: we do not want to trip over the obstacles illuminated in the libertarian lament. Specifically, the claim about quasi-coerciveness, or potential quasi-coerciveness, assuming we can apply it to OSHA contexts, should not extend readily to hazard pay proposals involving some other kinds of risky work, where we endorse no such stringent regulation. Does the argument cover the right cases?

Earlier (pp. 162ff.), I noted that the risks we are most concerned with, the handling of toxins, carcinogens, and other hazardous materials, are not risks which are likely to be chosen for their intrinsic desirability, for the satisfaction that might derive from facing danger or using special skills to survive, or for their instrumental connection to highly desirable consequences, for example saving lives. Rather, the motivation to take these risks derives entirely from the extrinsic rewards associated with them, rewards like hazard pay or steady employment in areas of limited employment opportunity. Partly as a result of this difference, the choice to be a fireman or stunt-driver is *exceptional*, reflecting a high degree of self-selection: such choices could readily have been foregone for many other kinds of work. In contrast, the choice to be a miner, mill worker, or industrial worker facing health hazards subject to OSHA's strong criterion is *typical*. For a large class of workers, these are the primary forms of available employment. Indeed, these are the typical options, or the sole or most attractive ones, facing a class of workers with a significantly restricted range of options. The restrictions on workers' options are the result of various factors: their limited educational opportunity, their array of marketable skills and talents, accidents of geographical location, or their limited economic resources for financing job mobility.

Moreover, this narrowness of the range of options open to the typical worker is compounded by another factor. The riskiness of exceptional jobs (stunt-driver, fireman) can be viewed as stable over time: the worker knows more or less what he is getting into over a standard period of employment. But in 'typical' jobs, changes in manufacturing processes can expose workers to risks not anticipated at the inception of an employment period. To impose the burden of dodging these risks on the worker, given possible losses in benefits, pensions, family disruption, is to overestimate his effective options, to assume he has job mobility where it does not exist.

What this point about exceptional versus typical choices means, then, is that hazard pay proposals in one setting, made to one group of workers, may be, or will tend to be, quasi-coercive without all hazard pay proposals being so. The difference will depend on judgments about the range of alternatives open to one group, rather than the other, and on the reasons for the restricted options. Thus the argument does not force us to treat dissimilar groups similarly.

Moreover, nothing in this argument for strong OSHA regulation implies we ought to intervene similarly in life-style choices affecting health, even though by doing so we might prevent comparable harms. Like the stuntdriver's choices, these life-style choices are also not generally or potentially quasi-coerced.[17] Earlier I expressed some worries about the voluntariness of certain life-style choices, noting, for example, the effect of strong sub-cultural influences. But these threats to autonomy are different from quasi-coercion, and arguments based on these more diffuse kinds of influence are not likely to justify comparable interventions. Indeed, they are just the sorts of influence we are fearful of undermining if we respect diversity.

The argument sketched here for the OSHA criterion thus appears to

---

[17] The poor elderly who have to eat dogfood may be a case of quasi-coercion.

avoid the worries of the libertarian lament. It turns out that only the appropriate hazard pay proposals are quasi-coercive, or potentially so. It is important to remember that the argument does not require that we think the range of options open to regulated workers is already unjustly or unfairly restricted. It is sufficient that we believe the restricted range of options such workers enjoy, though fair or just now, would tip in the direction of injustice and unfairness over the long run. Moreover, we should be concerned that the 'tipping' might be hard to detect and therefore that the quasi-coerciveness would remain hidden and invisible to many participants in the hazard pay market. Consequently, we should be reluctant to rely on our perceptions of fairness once faced with such situations. Just as some incompetent or uninformed individuals may not be in the best position to detect their diminished capacity for making autonomous decisions, so too we should not wait till we are quasi-coerced to protect ourselves against diminished autonomy. Rather, it is prudent to impose prior, protective constraints on the framework of markets built on exchanges between workers and employers. These constraints are designed to ensure that market changes remain within the requirements of justice or fairness.

An important objection to this argument sketch is connected to a point made earlier, that the argument straddles a fence. The appropriate reaction to complaints about an injustice, or potential injustice, in the distribution of social goods should be to alter the fundamental institutional arrangements which lead to the unjust distribution. Yet our argument leads us merely to intervene narrowly to block one sort of consequence of such (potential) injustice – the harm that might result from quasi-coerced decisions. This intervention seems to add insult to injury, if the premise about quasi-coercion is correct. We leave all the factors intact which create, or tend to create, the unjust, quasi-coercive setting. Instead, we intervene to stop a vulnerable class of individuals from exercising its own discretion. This paternalism seems vexing because it leaves intact the background conditions which seem to make the intervention necessary. The objection, then, is that worries about injustice should not lead to narrow constraints on autonomy. If the objection is correct, step (4) of the argument sketch is dubious.

I should like to make three points in response to this objection. First, the autonomy that is restricted here is only an illusion if the claim about quasi-coercion is correct. To be sure, the interventions may remain offensive to those who want to accept the offers involved, but if the discussion in earlier sections is correct, we have reason to think the voluntariness of quasi-coerced decisions is diminished in morally significant ways. Second, contrary to the premise of the objection, arguments from justice often involve restrictions on free exchanges among individuals: the restrictions take the general form of restricting some free exchanges to preserve the fairness of others. Does a market which permits quasi-coerced exchanges respect liberty more than one that restricts some exchanges in order to make all exchanges free from quasi-coercion? I would suggest not, but the answer would take us afield into some central questions in the general theory of justice.[18]

My third point is that the modification of distributive institutions involved in OSHA regulations does have an effect on distributive justice, at least if arguments I have made elsewhere about the nature of health care as a social good are at all plausible. No doubt, the importance of health might be argued for in various ways, all of which might justify viewing the trading of health for too low a price as unfair. But on my own view, health is of direct relevance to worries about justice because it contributes directly to the distribution of opportunity in society. Compromising health through quasi-coerced hazard pay bargains thus compromises the ability to maintain fair equality of opportunity in a society. The restricted opportunity range of poor or worst-off classes of workers would act, in hazard pay markets, to further undermine fair equality of opportunity. Earlier, I argued that claims about the special importance of health or health care will not show *by themselves* why we should not rely on consent to distribute risks to health: health is not *so* important we refuse to let people compromise it in various contexts. The argument sketch for the strong OSHA criterion shows, however, why certain hazard pay proposals would depend on a highly questionable form of consent, consent under quasi-coercion, and that is the crux of the rationale offered here.[19]

Worries and conclusions

There is a deeply troubling consequence of the argument offered in the last section, one that is important to bring out in the open. The rationale I

---

[18] See the debate between Nozick (1974:204–13) and Rawls (1977:159–65) on the basic structure as the subject of justice and the light it throws on the plausibility of Nozick's claims about side-constraints. For an argument bearing directly on freedom in the market, see Scanlon (1977).

[19] Whether this argument sketch also tells us how to supplement a rights-based account, making it clear when we should not accept certain waivers, is a question I cannot discuss here.

offered turned on concern about the actual or potential quasi-coerciveness of certain hazard pay proposals. The quasi-coerciveness of the proposals depended on the fact that the class of workers facing such proposals has, or is likely to have, unfairly or unjustly restricted alternatives. But what if we could agree that the distribution of income and opportunity were really fair or just, and that the distribution would not be tipped toward unfairness over time through the operation of a market for such risk-taking. Suppose, that is, that we lived in a just social arrangement, one that were stable over time. If the rationale for OSHA's strong criterion depends on the claim about quasi-coerciveness, then there would be no need for the strong OSHA feasibility criterion. Perhaps the class of workers receiving these hazard pay proposals might still face a range of options more restricted than more fortunate groups of workers or professionals, but the inequalities here are no threat to justice (we are supposing). In such circumstances, we would still have a role for OSHA: guaranteeing that adequate information is present for informed decision-making about risk-taking, and guaranteeing that costs are internalized, so that hazard pay bargains do not free-load on other parties. But the strong OSHA criterion now lacks a rationale.

Some proponents of the strong OSHA criterion might readily agree to this restriction on its applicability: for them, the rationale I have offered would seem to capture their underlying moral view. But some proponents of strong regulation might feel uneasy about the restriction: indeed, I feel uneasy about it myself. It is not clear to me just what follows from this sort of unfocused uneasiness. It could be that there are other components to a rationale which are not captured in this argument from justice. Yet, it is not obvious at all what they are. On the other hand, the problem may lie with this methodology for testing a philosophical argument. Intuitions or considered moral judgments about the rightness of a practice, like stringent OSHA regulations, arise in a particular social setting, one which has many forms of injustice or threats of injustice. It is notoriously difficult to clean up and make the principles underlying these intuitions explicit merely by forming counter-factual test situations in which to deploy them. To be sure, this is standard philosophical method, but its results are often less clear than what we take them to be (see Daniels 1979c). Nevertheless, if one cannot show why one is dissatisfied with the kind of 'test' of the rationale this hypothetical case involves, then the dissatisfaction will linger to infect the rationale itself. This result should worry proponents of strong OSHA regulation, who must offer an alternative, or more complete, rationale than the one sketched here.[20]

The rationale I have offered, despite these deeper worries that there are still *other* components needed for a complete account, does carry weight wherever we have reason to worry about quasi-coerciveness in our own society. That is, we *do* get a plausible argument for the OSHA criterion as long as we have reason to worry about the fairness or justice of the distribution of options available to the workers most likely to receive the hazard pay proposals in question. But, of course, just such worries are themselves controversial. And differences in moral judgment here depend not only on different estimates of empirical facts, but on different underlying conceptions of what is just or fair. So my rationale also has the strength of locating clearly a source of controversy about the acceptability of the OSHA criterion itself. My rationale will be controversial just where moral controversy about regulation is sharpest in our society. The rationale cannot by itself resolve this dispute. Still, it may help make it clearer what might be needed to do so, given the source of conflict.

Does OSHA protect too much? The answer depends on other moral judgments we make about the justice and fairness of choices open to workers in certain hazard pay markets. My belief is that such stringent regulation is appropriate in our society, and this conclusion has definite implications for the acceptability of the fair equality of opportunity account. Specifically, it shows us how to define the *limits* on the fair equality of opportunity account set by liberty-regarding principles of justice. Stringent regulations of the sort OSHA *in theory* is mandated to provide will be required by my account of just health care wherever there is reason to think consent is an inappropriate mechanism for the distribution of risk, since the consent is quasi-coerced or may become so

[20] My worries about the rationale I have offered are not deep enough to make me embrace a suggestion offered by Mark McCarthy (1981–2). He suggests that certain 'public values' must be invoked to explain (and presumably justify) such practices as OSHA's stringent regulation of health hazards. Indeed, he argues, once we note the 'conceptual' difference between individual risk-taking and group risk-taking, the former involving uncertainty and the latter certainty about outcomes, we will see why society may judge the acceptability of outcomes in group contexts (all workers facing certain risks) differently from the way in which individuals judge the acceptability of risks to them. For example, 'public values' may mean that numbers count, that group outcomes will be unacceptable because of the magnitude of death and injury, whereas individuals might be willing to take the corresponding risks. But we still need an account of just what 'public values' play a role here, why they are acceptable, and how they cohere with the rest of our moral framework. We would be unsatisfied if we get an answer of interest only to a moral anthropologist: 'This society simply does invoke these values in this context, though there is no coherence with its other practices or underlying rationale.' We seek a justification, not merely a description.

over time. Where we can assume quasi-coercion will not arise, the fair equality of opportunity account will only justify less stringent forms of health hazard regulation.

This conclusion about how to reconcile the demand for equality central to the fair equality of opportunity approach with a concern for liberty may not generalize directly to other contexts. I already noted that less stringent preventive measures may be in order in the case of life-style choices, since these are not in general quasi-coerced. The stringent preventive measures the fair equality of opportunity account endorses in other preventive contexts, e.g., environmental protection, may not face the same libertarian objections. The risks in these contexts are in general not ones we consent to. But one can imagine increased efforts to put decisions about issues of the stringency of environmental protection to public referenda, seeking thereby some form of consent to risk. The recent effort by the US Environmental Protection Agency to seek a community vote on how stringently arsenic emissions should be regulated at a Tacoma, Washington smelter, can be viewed as an effort to obtain consent to risk. I am not sure how to extend the account I have given, based on the notion of quasi-coercion, to these contexts. Still, I think the approach I adopt illustrates the kind of analysis we need if we are to reconcile demands for equality with distribution mechanisms that rely on consent to risk. I have addressed the issue in one well-defined, illustrative context, but I cannot explore all of its variations.

8 · Risk and opportunity

Safe workplaces and safe workers

Individual variation in sensitivity to risk

A theory of just health care must be compatible with other components of our general theory of justice. In particular, where such a theory pursues equality in a vigorous fashion – for example, through a principle guaranteeing fair equality of opportunity – it must be compatible with the liberties we ought to grant providers, patients, and recipients of preventive care. In chapters 6 and 7, I explored these limits on the fair equality of opportunity account of just health care. In this chapter I examine another such limit on my account. I consider a context in which the demands of fair equality of opportunity for access to jobs may be in conflict with the requirement of the fair equality of opportunity account that we provide stringent health protection in the workplace. In a sense, there is a threat that the equal opportunity principle is in conflict with itself. This conflict requires some explanation.

The fair equality of opportunity account of just health care implies that it is important to seek equity in the distribution of the risk of disease, not just its treatment. Such equity will be possible only if there is stringent regulation of exposure to health hazards in the workplace, for such exposure imposes substantial risks on particular groups of workers. In Chapter 7, I considered this implication of the theory with reference to a particular feature of health hazard regulation in the United States, namely, the requirement that the Occupational Safety and Health Administration reduce worker exposure to hazards to the degree it is technologically feasible to do so. I argued that this stringent form of regulation is morally justifiable under the conditions that exist in our society. Specifically, we cannot rely on workers' consent to risks in the workplace, say through hazard pay negotiations, wherever workers choices may be unjustly or unfairly restricted ('quasi-coerced').

But the argument in Chapter 7 abstracts from an important fact: not all individuals are equally sensitive to exposure to workplace hazards. Even when protective standards meet the 'technological feasibility' criterion, some workers will remain at excess risk because, for a variety of reasons, they are especially sensitive to hazards. If we can identify them through new technologies that allow us to determine their individual susceptibility, should we remove them from the workplace? With or without their consent? Here the principle of equal opportunity may be in conflict with itself: if we remove them to protect their health, and thus their fair equality of opportunity, then we interfere with their opportunity to compete for jobs and careers. Is the obligation to protect equal opportunity through preventive health care in conflict with the obligation to insure equal opportunity in the pursuit of jobs and careers?

This question is not merely hypothetical. It is an actual and pressing public policy issue because new biological monitoring and screening techniques allow us to look inside workers' bodies and cells in order to measure their degree of sensitivity to risk. Some older techniques, such as testing for blood lead levels, are already in use. They allow us to measure individual variation in the body burden of hazardous materials, which is an indicator of the risk of further damage. Some newer and more controversial techniques, such as cytogenetic screening, look for sub-clinical effects of past exposure, with the intention of predicting degree of risk. Other techniques aim at detecting individual variation in the physiological ability to tolerate certain hazards. These include screening individuals for enzyme or other genetic markers for such deficiencies. More generally, medical surveillance and pre-employment physical examinations and tests can detect prior or developing medical conditions – including habits, such as smoking or drinking – which affect individual susceptibility to workplace hazards. Many of these techniques may be used in either pre-employment screening or on-the-job biological monitoring and medical surveillance.

All of these varied techniques bring to the fore one general ethical issue: What is the moral relevance of individual variation in susceptibility to risk? Obviously, knowledge of such variation gives us certain options we do not have without it. We can merely inform individuals of their particular risks. We can afford special protection to individuals at 'excess' risk, whether they want it or not. We can exclude them, with or without compensation, from risky contexts to protect their health or for the benefit of others, for example, to reduce the costs of liability for employees or society as a whole. Controversy about these options lies at the center of much recent debate in Europe and the United States concerning the use of biological monitoring and genetic screening. But which of these options are morally acceptable alternatives? Do considerations of fairness or justice make some options preferable to others? For example, do we violate worker rights to equal opportunity if we exclude them from certain jobs in which they are at excess risk? If so, then these rights may act as limits or constraints on the equal opportunity account of preventive health care. Thus the general question about the moral relevance of individual variation is closely connected to my concern that the equal opportunity principle may be in conflict with itself.

The problem posed here by detectable individual variation in susceptibility to workplace hazards is part of a far more general issue. After all, people also vary in their susceptibility to disease and thus in their probable claims on curative parts of the health-care system. Some people will be highly susceptible, compared to the average person. The source of this extra susceptibility varies: it may be genetic background, past disease or trauma, or other environmentally induced sensitivities, including those voluntarily imposed, say through smoking. If we cannot detect this variation and distinguish individuals by the risks they face, uncertainty eliminates the problem. All individuals will appear to be in the same risk pool. But if we can distinguish individuals actuarially and divide the population into subgroups of distinct susceptibilities, then we face a general moral question: What is the moral relevance of detectable individual variation in susceptibility to disease? The question about the moral relevance of individual susceptibility to workplace hazards seems to be just a special case of this more general question.

It is quite striking that in the curative context, for example, in the design of our acute-care insurance schemes, we generally pool people of detectably different actuarial levels of risk. Employee group plans, for example, do not separate risk subgroups, say by careful screening using good predictors of disease or disability, before admitting people to group health plans, although employer screening of prospective workers may have some of this effect, if not this intention. (Of course, private insurers may well try to market their coverage selectively to low-risk populations, but this is a different issue.) Similarly, in systems with national health insurance schemes, there is a common risk pool and no differential tax or premium rate depending on differences in susceptibility to disease. Pooling risks in this way means that low-risk subgroups subsidize high-risk subgroups. In effect, this amounts to treating detectable variation in susceptibility to disease as a morally irrelevant basis for distributing the burdens of financing curative health care.

This practice of ignoring detectable differences in susceptibility to disease is given a justification by the fair equality of opportunity account. Specifically, it is a result of granting (lexical) priority to the fair equality of opportunity principle over distributive principles governing other economic advantages. Protecting fair equality of opportunity is given priority over allowing some individuals to gain economic advantages from their biological good fortune. Thus, the protection of opportunity is provided to all who are threatened, regardless of the likelihood of threat imposed by the 'natural lottery'. The costs of that protection of opportunity are to be borne by all. It is a collective, not individualized, burden. Doing otherwise might well threaten the chance of really protecting the opportunity of the high-risk groups. In particular, their greater susceptibility to disease should not work to the economic disadvantage of those most likely to be ill.

If special sensitivity to workplace hazards is but a special case of special susceptibility to disease, then it seems there is no unusual problem here. It seems we are enjoined to assume collectively the burden of protecting the health of the most sensitive workers, just as we finance the acute care of the most susceptible patients. But this issue is more complex than it appears. There may be plausible reasons for not treating individual variability the same way in preventive and curative contexts. For example, some view the greater durability of some workers as a market-able skill. To them, individual variation in susceptibility has a different moral relevance in these job placement contexts, and equal opportunity is defined against a background which assumes this variability. Whether this view is correct or not is a question of intrinsic interest. Without addressing it, we cannot respond to the other question which motivates this chapter, whether the fair equality of opportunity account is consistent with other requirements about equal opportunity.

To answer these questions about the moral relevance of variation in susceptibility to risk we must examine the problem of special workplace sensitivities in concrete settings where public policy issues arise. This warrants a warning to the reader. The philosophical reader will have to be patient, for philosophical issues are not always easy to dissect away from the tissue of legislation and regulation. We will have to examine some features of actual practice in more detail than elsewhere in this book – sometimes only to make it clear that issues of principle have not been clearly addressed or resolved in existing regulatory practice. To carry out this investigation I have had to make some arbitrary choices: I have restricted my discussion to certain workplace contexts in which individual variation in sensitivity to risk forces policy choices. This narrow window on our problem will not distort our view, even if it allows us to see but one context in which individual variation is a problem.

Two strategies for achieving health protection in the workplace

The fact that individuals vary in their susceptibility to risk means that we have two main strategies available for meeting the goal of making the workplace as safe as is technologically feasible. (The technological feasibility criterion is explained in Chapter 7.) The first strategy is to *modify the workplace* so that it is safe for the workforce. It involves eliminating or reducing the exposure of workers to various hazards, barring the use of some, and requiring engineering controls or modified work practices to reduce exposure to others. The workforce, however, is taken as a given. The second strategy is focused on *modifying the workforce* so that it can better tolerate the hazards of the workplace (see Lappe 1982: 5). The second strategy does not take the workforce as a given. It is premised on the claim that workers vary in their abilities to tolerate hazardous materials and it seeks to establish a workforce resistant to workplace hazards. The variation in individual 'resistance' to risk comes from several sources: prior medical conditions, genetic variation, vulnerability of reproductive functions, prior body burden, degree of subclinical damage, age and life-style factors. Consequently, implementing the second strategy would involve a combination of pre-employment screening techniques and on-the-job biological monitoring techniques intended to reduce the likelihood that workers at 'excess' risk appear or remain in the workplace.

I have characterized the two strategies in an extreme way in order to represent polar attitudes toward the relevance of individual susceptibility to risk. In fact, the strategies are neither exclusive nor incompatible. In practice, no one promotes one to the complete exclusion of the other, and existing standards combine them in various ways. Thus we might clean up the workplace to the technologically feasible limit, and then identify and remove workers at greatest risk. The lead standard has features that combine the strategies in this way. Alternatively, once we identify and remove workers at greatest risk, we might then seek to redefine the level of safe exposure for the modified, more resistant workforce. The Supreme Court decision in the benzene case seems to leave room for this combination to be pursued (see Lappe 1982: 5). If a modified, more resistant workforce faces no significant risk at a proposed exposure standard, then there may be a basis for arguing the standard is more restrictive than need be. Many other combinations are possible.

Ethical implications of the two strategies

Each strategy, and each combination, carries with it moral implications and presuppositions. Consequently, disagreement about acceptable public policy in this area not only reflects obvious conflicts of interest among the affected parties, but it reflects moral disagreement about the implications and presuppositions of the different strategies. One way in which the strategies differ is the degree to which they 'collectivize' or 'individualize' the burdens of providing health protection.

The strategy which emphasizes modifying the workplace rather than the workforce *collectivizes* the burdens of providing worker health and safety in ways which have important moral implications. As embodied in current OSHA regulations, this strategy imposes clear legal obligations on the employer to make the workplace as safe as is technologically feasible. The level is determined by OSHA. Though the costs of meeting this obligation are initially borne by the employer, they are in large part transferred to broader segments of society through tax deductions, consumer price increases, and reduced wages to the workforce, which can no longer negotiate hazard pay except for the residue of ineliminable risks. Three features of the strategy are of moral relevance:

(1) The strategy leaves little room for relying on worker consent to risk as a method of distributing the benefits and burdens of risk-taking. At issue is the degree to which the collective decision about the level of acceptable risk is compatible with the respect for individual autonomy of choice shown in other work and non-work settings (see Chapter 7).

(2) The strategy combines all workers into a common 'risk pool' without drawing actuarially relevant distinctions among subgroups which face different risks. This 'community rating' of the combined risk pool increases the costs of making the workplace safe for workers who are better risks. Thus lower-risk workers, and society as a whole, pay a 'higher premium', which includes a cross-subsidy, to ensure that the workplace is safe (for any given level of protection), than would be required if we agreed to 'insure' only the most resistant, durable workers. At issue is the moral justification for community rating the insurance scheme we call OSHA regulation. Specifically, as I noted earlier, can we appeal to the same justification we might use for the community rating of curative insurance schemes?

(3) The strategy involves making minimal distinctions among workers, so that we have to know less about each worker. It collects diverse workers into an average worker, who is the 'given' or fixed variable held constant while the workplace is modified. Consequently, we do not need to risk invading the privacy of individuals to gather the biological information needed to implement the alternative strategy. At issue is the amount and kind of information we can require workers to make available as a condition of future or continued employment.

In contrasting ways, the strategy of modifying the workforce 'individualizes' the burdens of making the workplace safe. It uses medical and biological information about individuals to distinguish subgroups of workers at differential risk for a given level of exposure to a workplace hazard. Acquiring this information, however, may involve compromising individual privacy. Moreover, using this information individualizes the treatment of different subgroups of workers in either of two ways. First, we may seek 'consent' to higher risks from certain workers. At issue here, however, is the moral relevance of consent in these conditions, which was a central focus of discussion in Chapter 7. Second, we may exclude workers at higher risk from certain work settings. In this case, the issue is the moral acceptability of excluding workers on the basis of this biological difference. In individualizing the treatment of workers are we discriminating against a subgroup of workers in a morally objectionable way? Have we compromised their equality of opportunity in an unjustifiable way?

My central task in this discussion is to examine whether equality of opportunity is threatened by the uses of biological monitoring which involve the strategy of modifying the workforce. This way of posing the question about the moral relevance of individual variation in sensitivity to risk will help us answer the question which motivates this chapter, whether there is possible conflict of the equal opportunity principle with itself. To focus the issue further, I will examine the analogy which has been drawn between special sensitivity or susceptibility and those kinds of physical and mental handicaps protected by the US Rehabilitation Act of 1973 (Rockey, Fantel, and Omenn 1981; Hogan and Bernacki 1981). I shall argue that underlying controversy on the issue of discrimination is a deep philosophical uncertainty about the proper classification of biologically based special sensitivity. Is it a morally suspect distinction for job placement purposes, like race, sex, and some physical handicaps? Or is it to be assimilated to morally relevant individual differences, such as differences in talent and skill, which constitute the background variation against which equality of opportunity is defined? Whether the fair equality of opportunity account risks internal inconsistency depends on resolving this prior question.

Before addressing these central issues, however, it will help to make them concrete by considering the use of biological monitoring embodied in an existing OSHA standard, the lead standard. This discussion of the lead standard is useful for two reasons. First, it shows how the two strategies have been combined in actual regulatory practice. Second, it shows that the central moral issues that concern us have been skirted in the design of these regulations. As a result, features of the use of biological monitoring found in the lead standard are *not readily generalizable as models* for the design of standards for other hazards. To go beyond the lead standard will require addressing the moral issues it skirts. (The fact that OSHA dodges these moral issues does not imply it has shirked its moral duty, a point I return to later.)

Biological monitoring in the lead standard

Features of the lead standard involving biological monitoring
The OSHA lead standard has been reviewed extensively by the courts and central features involving biological monitoring have been substantially upheld.[1] The standard provides us with one working model for combining the two strategies of modifying the workplace and modifying the workforce. Since I am concerned with the ethical import of the biological monitoring provisions, I undertake no complete review of the lead standard. I will, however, be interested in aspects of the standard which reflect special properties of lead as a health hazard, for these affect our ability to generalize from the case of lead to the design of other standards.

Five features of the standard are of greatest concern to us:

1   *Biological monitoring tied to ambient monitoring ceilings.* When ambient monitoring reveals worker exposure to airborne lead levels greater than 50 micrograms per cubic meter (the 'permissible exposure limit' or PEL), employers must make available free

---

[1] 43 FR 5295, 14 Nov., 1978. Cf. United Steelworkers of America, etc. v. Marshall, 647 FR 2nd series: 1189 (1980); cf. Revised Statement of Reasons on the Feasibility of the Workplaces Standard on Lead (46 FR 60758, 11 Dec., 1981). Major provisions of the standard have been in effect since 1 March, 1979, and engineering control provisions went into effect 29 June, 1981. It will be necessary to comment briefly above on some recent (July 1982) OSHA proposals to revise (weaken) the standard.

biological monitoring (blood lead tests) and physician consultation and surveillance to provide a full medical assessment of worker health status.[2]

2   *Voluntary participation.* Worker participation in the biological monitoring and cooperation with the medical surveillance is voluntary.

3   *Compulsory temporary medical removal.* If a worker's blood lead level exceeds 40 micrograms per 100 grams,[3] the employer must temporarily remove the employee from his job or institute other measures that restrict exposure, as determined by a physician review of the blood tests and other examination results.

4   *Medical removal benefit protection.* Employers who must temporarily remove workers must also provide complete wage and benefit protection for up to 18 months. Whether the worker is on reduced time or laid off or transferred, he must be paid his full wages, given all normal raises, and be credited with all seniority. Once final medical determination is made that his blood lead levels have returned to safe limits, he must be returned to his old job with all benefits intact. These benefit protections may be made contingent on cooperation with biological monitoring and medical surveillance.

5   *Notification and confidentiality.* Workers are to be notified of the results of all monitoring, both ambient and biological. Adequate, permanent records are to be kept. Physicians involved in the medical surveillance process must respect confidentiality of workers with regard to any findings unrelated to lead exposure.

Ethical issues raised by biological monitoring features of the lead standard

My examination of the biological monitoring features of the lead standard will focus on one central question: Underlying the design of these features, is there a unifying moral position governing how we may treat individual variation in susceptibility to health hazards in the

---

[2] Specifically, if ambient monitoring detects exposure levels in excess of 30 micrograms per cubic meter (the 'action level'), employers must undertake further monitoring to see if any worker is actually exposed to more than the PEL. If so, employers must comply with requirements calling for engineering controls and altered work practices which reduce exposure levels. The biological monitoring involves tests for blood lead level (proposed tests for zinc protoporphyrin have been stayed by the courts).

[3] The blood level ceilings are phased in over a five-year period, beginning at 80 micrograms/100 grams in the first year of implementation.

workplace? Does the design of the standard reflect considerations of justice, or other moral considerations, which constrain our treatment of such individual variation? If such an underlying moral view could be abstracted and defended, it might show us which features of the lead standard can serve as a general model for other uses of biological monitoring. Unfortunately, as we shall see, no such general position is implicit. Though certain features of the standard imply a reluctance to shift the burden of protecting workers to those workers who are at greatest risk, the arguments for these features often reflect special properties of lead as a hazard and not general moral principles. Consequently, we will still face the philosophical task of seeking a moral framework which can guide the design of OSHA standards and the use of biological monitoring techniques.

To focus discussion, I shall consider four questions of moral significance raised by particular features of the lead standard. First, does the use of the blood lead test and the temporary medical removal of workers who are at excess risk shift the burden of protecting workers to the shoulders of a minority of them? Second, is denying workers with high blood lead levels the option of 'consenting' to their excess risk a form of justifiable paternalism? Third, can we justify making worker compliance with the biological monitoring and medical surveillance voluntary by appealing to a worker's right to privacy? Is the voluntary compliance consistent with the compulsory removal from work of those known to have high blood lead levels? Fourth, does the provision of benefit protection during medical removal depend on acknowledging any worker rights or entitlements to such protection? We shall consider these questions in turn.

The relationship between biological monitoring and the PEL

The requirement that an employer use engineering controls and other work practices (e.g., respirators) to keep exposure levels of all workers to airborn lead within certain limits is part of the strategy of modifying the workplace to keep the workforce safe. The requirement that biological monitoring and medical removal be used to protect workers at greatest risk is part of a strategy of modifying the workforce to achieve a goal of worker protection. So clearly the lead standard involves a combination of strategies. To determine the moral assumptions behind this particular combination requires knowing how the critical blood level (measured in micrograms/100g) and airborne lead limits (measured in micrograms/ m^3) were chosen and what they achieve. Specifically, we want to know whether the 50 micrograms/m³ PEL represents the maximal level of protection it is 'technologically feasible' to provide. If it does, then temporary medical removal for those with unsafe blood lead levels represents an effort to provide additional protection to those who are unavoidably at excess risk. But if the PEL is itself the result of a trade-off between the economic costs of modifying the workplace and the burdens imposed on subgroups of workers most susceptible to risk, then we have a very different view of the role of individual sensitivity to risk.

For our purposes, it is sufficient to examine the defense OSHA provides for its standard in the Federal Register, a defense generally substantiated by the courts.[4] OSHA seems to have pursued the following course in designing the standard. First, it sought to determine if there is a 'safe' blood lead level which represents no significant health risk to workers. The level of 40 microgram/100g is the level at which subclinical effects on levels of the important enzyme ALA are detectable, though it is associated with only rare clinical symptoms of lead toxicity. Still, it is not a level 'safe' for reproductively active male or female workers, or their fetuses; nor is it safe for workers with certain medical conditions, like anemia or renal deficiency (United Steelworkers v. Marshall 647 FR 2nd series: 222). Only blood levels kept below 30 micrograms/100g would be 'safe' for all subgroups of workers. Second, OSHA needed to determine (1) what level of exposure to airborne lead was associated with keeping blood levels safe, and (2) what PEL it was technologically feasible to achieve. The low 30 micrograms/100g blood level is not achievable unless we keep airborne lead levels well below the PEL of 50 micrograms/m³. But setting a PEL below that level is not 'technologically feasible' (43 FR 52972). The 50 micrograms/m³ PEL, however, is technologically feasible, through engineering controls and revised work practices. It would be adequate to keep the great majority of workers at blood lead levels below 40 micrograms/100g. Still, the margin of safety is small. Even at the 50 micrograms/m³ level, some detectable minority or workers (about 6%) will still exceed the 40 micrograms/100g blood level (43 FR 52972–3). Moreover, since it is not feasible to implement the 50 micrograms/m³ PEL except over a period of years, some workers will remain at relatively high risk. Consequently, OSHA urged supplementing the strategy of

---

[4] A complete discussion would involve assessing the scientific evidence and history of the legislation, which goes beyond my purposes here. If OSHA's presentation of the case is misleading, and the PEL is not the technologically feasible limit of airborne protection, then the original standard begins to look more like the position taken in the July 1982 proposals for revision, discussed below.

modifying the workplace with biological monitoring and temporary medical removal, a 'last-ditch, fall-back mechanism' (43 FR 54449) to protect the most sensitive workers.

If this interpretation of OSHA's intent is correct, it seems that there was considerable reluctance to shift much of the burden of protecting worker health to the shoulders of the more sensitive workers. Indeed, two other features of the standard tend to reinforce this view. The temporary medical removal will, after all, be only temporary for most of the workers affected. Consequently, there will be little over-all effect on their opportunity to work. Moreover, the affected workers are cushioned against economic loss by the benefit protection provisions of the standard.

Together, these features seem to present a rather different attitude than the one reflected in the proposals for revising the lead standard advanced by OSHA in July 1982 (*Legal Times* 1982: 1). These proposed revisions called for raising the PEL significantly, to 150 micrograms/m³, and continuing to use biological monitoring and medical removal to protect those workers not adequately protected by the standard. Such a proposal, in contrast to the current standard, seems to shift more of the burden of protecting health in the workplace to more sensitive workers. At the higher PEL, for example, it is far more likely that a larger number of the most sensitive workers would not be able to maintain blood levels safe enough to permit them to return to work. The costs to them of loss of work and employment opportunity have been traded for the economic gains to employers, to other workers, and to society of instituting a less costly PEL. The existence of the 1982 proposals suggests that the issue of who should bear the burden of protecting sensitive workers has not been resolved finally.

The inference that the current OSHA standard reflects an underlying moral view about individual variation in susceptibility must thus be taken with a grain of salt. First, there is no explicit expression of any such principle or view. In fact, several of the features of the standard which incline one to look for such an implicit view are actually defended on rather special grounds. For example, the temporary medical removal provision is defended as a *preventive health measure* because of the *reversibility* of lead damage at the 40 micrograms/100g blood lead level. If we were involved with a hazard to health which produced irreversible damage, as we are with asbestos, for example, we would not be able to defend a medical removal provision as a preventive health measure. Similarly, for other hazards, it is far less likely that removal will be temporary, where it is justifiable at all. The particular kind of increased sensitivity some workers show for certain hazards other than lead would imply permanent removal of them from the workplace and screening them prior to entry into it. Moreover, as we shall see in more detail shortly, the protection for benefits provided in the lead standard is defended on grounds that depend on special properties of lead as a hazard. To make medical surveillance effective, workers must cooperate and report early symptoms of lead intoxification. Benefit protection is intended to make workers willing to cooperate; it is not defended on the grounds that there are any considerations of justice which entitle workers to benefit protection.

Finally, the lead standard itself works in ways that allow individual variation in sensitivity to play a role as part of an over-all strategy for protecting worker health. Some workers will not be able to return to work because they cannot maintain safe blood levels even after extended temporary removal. In fact, some features of the standard give employers an incentive to use biological screening techniques to keep more suscep-tible workers out of the workplace. Simple blood lead tests could serve as a pre-employment screen to exclude workers whose prior body burden of lead makes them more likely to exceed blood lead limits on further exposure. More refined techniques might detect the physiological basis for screening out workers who have trouble eliminating lead at normal rates. The point is that the lead standard, and the arguments for its features, remain silent on moral issues that bear on these natural extensions of practices already embodied in it.

Compulsory medical removal

As a possible alternative to the provision calling for the protection of wages and benefits during medical removal (MRP), OSHA considered the option of letting workers decide what the outcome would be if their blood lead levels exceeded safe limits (43 FR 54440, 54451). That is, workers would be given the option of 'consenting' to higher risk or accepting some form of medical removal. Given that the worker would control the outcome of biological monitoring and medical surveillance, it might be argued, any reluctance to cooperate should disappear. OSHA rejected this alternative on the grounds that, 'far too often, workers who should be removed from further lead exposure would choose not to be', and employers would not be able to utilize 'removal in situations where it was imperative'. These results 'are inconsistent with the preventive purpose of the Act, and thwart the level of health protection which temporary medical removals can provide' (43 FR 54440, 54451). Elsewhere in its defense of the standard, OSHA documents the degree to which workers are quite willing to trade their health for continued employment, given their fear of the immediate option of unemployment or reduced wages. Workers have been reluctant to comply with medical surveillance features of other health and safety standards because of real and justified fears about the way in which employers will react to any evidence of increased liability.[5]

It is clearly not enough for OSHA merely to argue that workers are willing to trade risks to health for economic security in order to justify denying them the option of consenting to risks. Consent is a mechanism we rely on for distributing the benefits and burdens of risk-taking in other work and leisure contexts. Moreover, if we imagine that protection against airborne lead exposure is maximal, that is, at the technologically feasible limit, then the residue of risk left here should perhaps be construed as an 'ineliminable' risk. Yet all workers who work under OSHA standards may be exposed to such a residue of ineliminable risk, to which we might imagine they can 'consent' through negotiations for hazard pay. Is OSHA being unjustifiably paternalistic when it insists on denying lead workers the option of consenting to a residue of excess risk?

To answer this point, it is necessary to show why OSHA is justified in ignoring the mechanism of consent to risk in this context. Fortunately, such an argument is available. It is a natural extension of the more general argument developed in Chapter 7, which showed that the 'technological feasibility' criterion for acceptable OSHA standards is not itself unjustifiably paternalistic. In Chapter 7 I argued that consent is an inappropriate mechanism for distributing the burdens of risk-taking in the contexts OSHA regulates. In these contexts, the range of options open to the typical worker is unjustly or unfairly restricted. As a result, choices made in these contexts are 'quasi-coerced'. Over time, for example, hazard pay bargains which start out being attractive are likely not to remain so. It is reasonable then to protect workers against the illusion that truly voluntary consent will be reflected in their hazard pay

---

[5] 43 FR 54442–6. 'The Battery Council International (BCI), the major trade association representing battery manufacturers (Ex. 137, p. 1), recommends that workers either be discharged or permanently transferred (with no maintenance of earnings) whenever their blood lead levels repeatedly exceed 80 micrograms/100g . . . At one plant, workers are permanently laid off and barred from any lead job upon the second occurrence of an elevated blood lead level (with seniority determining whether or not individual workers are able to secure non-lead jobs in the plant).' This BCI policy clearly shows how the lead industry would prefer to shift the burden of protecting worker health to those workers at greatest risk.

negotiations. In effect, the technological feasibility criterion permits consent only to ineliminable risk.

If this argument is acceptable, then we might try to apply it to our problem: Should we accept the consent of workers with high blood lead levels to the residue of 'ineliminable' risk which is not technologically feasible to eliminate? A relevant fact is that the excess risk faced by those with higher blood lead levels is *avoidable*, even if it is 'ineliminable': We simply find such workers and remove them. To accept the consent of such a worker at excess risk would be to trust his 'quasi-coerced' consent even though we refuse to trust the 'quasi-coerced' consent of other workers to even lower risks. The general argument for the technological feasibility criterion thus justifies compulsory removal.

Even if this defense of OSHA's position is acceptable, it points to another problem. OSHA's argument for compulsory removal turns critically, like the general argument just sketched, on the fact that the removal is a *preventive* health measure. That is, it depends on the reversibility of the damage that lead involves at the levels we are discussing. Where a biological monitoring technique indicates irreversible damage, particularly the initiation of a disease process not necessarily accelerated by further exposure, OSHA's argument for compulsory removal would not apply. Removal would not protect or preserve the worker's health, even if it might reduce employer liability for subsequent medical or disability costs. That is, by overriding consent where health protection is possible, at least the *benefit* of protection, as well as some of the *burden*, accrues to the employee. But where the monitoring detects a condition for which protection is no longer an issue, overriding consent to risk involves imposing only the burdens of removal with no direct benefit to the worker. In such a case we are no longer justifying paternalism. Once again, the features of the lead standard do not generalize to other cases: key arguments turn on special features of lead as a hazard.

Voluntariness of worker participation in biological monitoring
As an alternative to the benefit protection provided by the MRP provision of the existing standard, OSHA considered the option of mandating that workers participate in biological monitoring and surveillance. OSHA rejected mandatory participation on the basis of three quite distinct lines of argument. We shall have to assess their relative importance. One line of argument is that the government should not compel workers to undergo detailed medical examinations when this may

involve 'clashes with legitimate privacy and religious concerns' (43 FR 54450). For example, reproductive activity is particularly sensitive to the hazards of lead, and medical surveillance would require 'inquiries into the most private aspects of the lives of American workers' (43 FR 54451). But this argument is barely developed by OSHA, and it is immediately qualified by the remark that 'Governmental coercion in this context would often prove counterproductive to the goal of achieving meaningful worker participation in medical surveillance' (43 FR 54451). Indeed, as OSHA couches this argument, privacy considerations apply only to governmental coercion: nothing is said about the permissibility of employers mandating such monitoring. And evidence in the Federal Register indicates such compulsory measures have been taken by employers for both on the job monitoring and preemployment screening.

In raising the question of privacy rights solely by reference to rights against government intrusion, the central issue may well not be addressed. Rights against government invasion of privacy will not protect the worker who refuses monitoring and faces firing or job transfer as a result of employer policy. Are there rights to privacy that protect the worker who exercises them against employer sanctions? If a prospective employee is required to undergo biological screening techniques as a precondition for employment, his privacy right may be exercised only at a significant cost to him, his exclusion from consideration for the job. The point can be put another way: seeking informed, voluntary consent from someone undergoing a diagnostic or therapeutic medical procedure is our standard way of protecting the individual against invasion of his privacy (among other things). But how voluntary is 'consent' given by employees or prospective employees who must agree to monitoring or screening as a condition of continued or future employment? (This issue is clearly broader than the focus given it here: employers often require psychological tests, disclosure of criminal records, and other information which might be thought to invade privacy.)

This issue is by no means easy to resolve. Consideration of it carries us to the same problem of 'quasi-coercion' to which I referred in the last section and in Chapter 7, when I raised the problem of consent to risk. Whatever is problematic about consent to workplace risk is likely to be problematic about consent to monitoring, and so a general solution to one problem will hold the key to both.

OSHA's silence on the question of *non-governmental* invasion of privacy gives us reason to wonder how much weight it really wants to give this appeal to worker privacy rights against the government. Indeed, one can be suspicious that, were the facts about lead different, OSHA might have argued that the importance of public health protection overrides privacy considerations, as it does in other public health law. For example, were blood tests the only way of guaranteeing the over-all protective level of engineering controls and work practices, it might be argued that a worker's refusal to permit biological monitoring poses a threat not just to himself but to others. It is not obvious how successful such an argument might ultimately be, but the point is that OSHA does not develop the argument from privacy rights as its primary argument because it may not be happy with its consequences in other settings. (This is, admittedly, speculation.)

OSHA's second line of argument seems much closer to the heart of its case. It argues that compulsory participation would not yield the quality of medical participation needed to make participation in medical surveillance meaningful. For example, male sperm count and quality is particularly sensitive to exposure to lead. Males considering having children should undergo examination to detect possible reproductive effects and might require temporary medical removal. But, OSHA argues, without MRP (benefit protection), a worker might decide to face health risks rather than face risks to job security or economic loss. Unfortunately, OSHA's example only points to the importance of benefit protection *whether or not* there is compulsory monitoring. It does not show that benefit protection combined with mandatory participation would fail to produce 'quality' participation. This point aside, granting OSHA its conclusion about the importance of benefit protection, the argument applies only to a special range of cases. If a monitoring and surveillance program did not depend for its success on the 'quality' of participation – because of facts about the particular health hazard involved – then OSHA's argument is irrelevant. Once again, it is hard to generalize from the features of the lead standard to other cases because OSHA's position does not ultimately rest on strong moral claims, e.g., about rights to privacy, but on particular features of lead as a hazard.

It is worth noting that the *compulsory removal* of workers with high blood lead levels and the *voluntariness of submission* to biological monitoring raise an issue of consistency. A worker may refuse biological monitoring because he suspects that if he has a blood test he will be removed from his job, and he may prefer not to be removed even though MRP protects him against immediate economic loss. Perhaps he suspects he may never be able to return to work. Why should we allow him the option of refusing monitoring when we deny him the option of refusing removal?

One way of responding to the worry about consistency would be to say that privacy rights of workers are so important to protect that we must pay the price in loss of health protection in order to preserve them. Whether or not this line of argument could be developed, OSHA does not pursue it far enough to convince us that it would use this line of defense. Unfortunately, the argument that 'quality' of cooperation would be diminished if participation in medical surveillance was mandatory affords only modest protection against the charge of incon-sistency. As I noted earlier, quality of cooperation may be compromised if MRP is not present, but there is little reason to think that quality would be compromised if benefit protection was provided *and* participation was mandatory. Indeed, OSHA might be advised to trade some loss of cooperation under these conditions to gain the greater coverage provided by mandatory monitoring.

A third argument OSHA offers is as follows:

Mandating worker participation would not affect the issue of appropriately allocating the costs of temporary medical removals. Temporary medical removal is fundamentally a protective, control mechanism, and OSHA has determined that the costs of this control mechanism should properly be borne by employers. This judgment is unrelated to whether or not workers voluntarily participate in medical surveillance, thus OSHA would include MRP (medical removal bene-fits) in the final standard even if total worker participation were somehow assured without MRP. 43 FR 54451

To see that this argument involves a *non sequitur*, it will be necessary to turn to OSHA's arguments for the benefit protection provisions of the lead standard. We need to see why OSHA thinks the costs of benefit protection should be construed as part of the cost of the temporary medical removal provision of the standard.

Wage and benefit protection

The central argument OSHA offers for the medical removal benefit protection provisions (MRP) of the standard can be paraphrased as follows (43 FR 52972–3; 54440–54450): The thin margin of safety provided by the PEL means that biological monitoring and medical surveillance are necessary if maximal protection of worker health is to be provided. But medical surveillance in the case of lead will not work without full worker cooperation, indeed cooperation at a high level of quality. Such cooperation will not be forthcoming unless benefit protection is provided, for workers' fears about job insecurity and economic loss are widespread and justified, given the ways in which employers have used monitoring and screening procedures in the past.

At no point in the argument for MRP is it ever asserted or implied that workers have rights or entitlements to the kinds of protection involved. (Nor is there a denial there are such rights. In fact, OSHA is enjoined from creating or extending rights which should be the results of collective bargaining or legislation.) No claims are ever made that the MRP provisions are required by considerations of justice or fairness – for example, that it is necessary to protect equality of employment opportunity. But then it seems the costs of MRP can be considered as part of the costs of temporary medical removal only because of the necessity to motivate workers to cooperate with medical surveillance. But this suggests that the claim OSHA makes in its third argument for the voluntariness of biological monitoring, quoted in full above, is not supportable given the framework of OSHA's own defense of MRP.

OSHA does offer one more specific argument about the costs of MRP being among the costs of temporary medical removal, but appeal to this argument again compromises the generality of the lead standard as a model for biological monitoring. Two costs are associated with temporary medical removal: costs of dislocation to employers and costs to workers of lost wages, benefits, and job security. OSHA suggests that all of these costs can be construed as 'costs of doing business' once we accept the necessity of temporary medical removal as a 'protective, control mechanism' (43 FR 54449). That is, since temporary medical removal is necessary to protect worker health, its costs should be construed as among the costs of doing business and should fall on the shoulders of the employer. This argument *depends critically on the fact that lead damage is reversible* at the blood lead levels anticipated when the PEL is generally observed. Workers are generally only temporarily displaced from their usual jobs: the costs are the costs of temporary displacement. But where other hazards are involved, the facts will be quite different. Then OSHA's argument will be very difficult, if not impossible, to generalize.

I have suggested that the biological monitoring features of the lead standard seem to reflect an underlying principle, namely the principle that we should refrain from shifting the burden of health protection to the shoulders of those most at risk, those with special sensitivities, at least until all more 'collective' steps have been taken to minimize risks. The general relationship between the 'technologically feasible' PEL and the monitoring and medical removal provisions is consistent with such a principle. But though it is tempting to think that such a principle is *implicit* in the central features of the lead standard, it is never argued for directly. In fact, the actual features of the standard are never defended in ways that appeal to any such principle, or to underlying considerations of justice which might support such a principle. Rather, the features of the standard are defended in ways that turn critically on special properties of lead as a hazard and the kinds of steps adequate to meet those hazards.

This discussion is not intended to suggest OSHA should have tried to defend features of the lead standard on the basis of such moral arguments. Indeed, it is an important legislative constraint on OSHA that its standards not extend worker rights or entitlements in ways that go beyond its charge to provide protection. Consequently, appeal to more general moral principles would be legally inappropriate. But we are still left with the philosophical task of trying to find a moral framework which does give guidance to the design of OSHA standards and to the use of monitoring techniques. Since we cannot abstract that framework from the 'model' contained in the OSHA lead standard, we shall have to look more directly at some complex issues in the theory of justice which bear on the distribution of the burdens of health protection.

Individual variation in sensitivity and discrimination in employment

Practices bearing on variation in sensitivity to risk
The central question is whether workers who are specially sensitive to certain risks are treated unjustly or unfairly if they are excluded from or removed from jobs they are otherwise competent to perform. This question underlies any attempt to determine what the balance should be between the two protective strategies, modifying the workplace and modifying the workforce, noted earlier. It is the question that must be answered before we can decide if the fair equality of opportunity account risks internal inconsistency. I have argued that this issue is not resolved in any general way by the provisions of the lead standard or by the arguments OSHA offers for them. Moreover this central question has relevance to diverse practices which involve the use of new technologies for biological monitoring. Specifically, the question cuts across two quite different uses of such technologies, in on-the-job monitoring and in preemployment screening. To be sure, different constraints on their use apply in these different settings, because there may be special duties that

arise from the existence, rather than the mere prospect, of an employer–employee relationship. Still, both kinds of uses have an effect on the range of job opportunities open to individuals and thus on our concern to protect equality of opportunity.

In addressing this general question, I shall not be concerned with differences in the *sources* of sensitivity. Variation in sensitivity to risks can come from prior medical condition, genetic variation, prior body burden, or life-style factors. For example, synergistic effects of smoking or alcohol consumption on sensitivity to workplace hazards are well known. It seems probable, at first glance, that different moral considerations may be relevant to assessing how we may treat special sensitivity to risk depending on its source. Prior medical condition and genetic variation seem to be the results of chance, a 'natural lottery', whose fateful outcomes we may want to protect people against with some form of social 'insurance'. But prior body burden and life-style choices seem to involve the agency – and therefore the responsibility – of individuals, either employers or the workers themselves. How responsibility in either of these categories is to be clearly assessed is a very complex question, which I shall not address here. All my subsequent discussion, then, must be qualified by the fact that it abstracts from consideration of the source of individual variation in sensitivity.

To address the bearing of sensitivity to risk on equality of opportunity, I shall first consider the analogy that might be drawn between extra sensitivity and the kinds of mental and physical handicaps afforded special protection by the Rehabilitation Act of 1973. This analogy is suggested by a number of writers (Rockey, Fantel, and Omenn 1981; Hogan and Bernacki 1981), and seems promising. If a special sensitivity is a handicap covered by the Rehabilitation Act, then the law may constrain policy options and we may be able to develop a moral argument to defend the legal practice. But the analogy must be examined carefully, and the applicability of the Rehabilitation Act to this issue is controversial. To show why it is controversial, I shall examine the philosophical framework which underlies our legal apparatus for protecting equality of opportunity. One might hope that even if the legal apparatus has questionable application to individual variation in sensitivity, the philosophical model will be clear enough to guide our practice. Unfortunately, there is deep controversy about how to fit sensitivity to risk into the philosophical apparatus defining equality of opportunity.

Sensitivity and handicaps

The Rehabilitation Act of 1973 imposes various obligations on employers not to *discriminate* against *qualified handicapped* individuals seeking employment or job placement. To examine the applicability of this Act to the problem of worker sensitivity to risk, we shall have to know what counts as a handicap, when a handicapped worker is qualified for a job, and what counts as discrimination. Controversy appears to surround each notion, though I shall not discuss 'discrimination' in any detail here.

When 'handicap' is defined in the Rules and Regulations published in the Federal Register, we find the following. An individual is 'handicapped' if he has a 'physical or mental impairment which substantially limits one or more major life activities', or 'has a record of such impairment' or is merely 'regarded as having such an impairment' (45 FR 66710). 'Physical or mental impairment' is defined broadly to include physiological disorders affecting a broad range of body systems, and it is certainly plausible to argue that physiological conditions increasing sensitivity to risk could be included. Though sample diseases and conditions are listed, and though the list does not include sensitivity to workplace health hazards, it is not intended to be inclusive. Quite importantly, 'substantially limits' is defined to include effects on the individual's employability. It might seem that sensitivity to workplace risks does not impair other life activities and acts as a handicap only if employers treat it as one. But the definition of 'handicap' includes individuals who are merely 'regarded as having' an impairment, and someone is 'regarded as having an impairment' even if the impairment limits major life activities, namely employment activities, 'only as a result of the attitudes of others toward such an impairment'. Indeed, someone is regarded as having an impairment even if he does not, 'but is treated as if' he does (43 FR 66710). This broad definition has been noted by others, who argue that workers screened out of certain jobs on the basis of low-back injury, for example, are being treated as if they have a disqualifying handicap when they do not (Rockey, Fantel, and Omenn 1981: 212–14).

But even if we can apply the concept of handicap to extra sensitivity to workplace risks, we still face a problem with the requirement that a handicapped individual be 'qualified' to perform a job. An individual is 'qualified' to perform a job if he can perform its 'essential functions' once 'reasonable accommodations' are made for the handicap. 'Reasonable accommodations' would include, for example, access ramps to work sites or some modest revisions of the job description. A worker with extra sensitivities to risk will thus be able to perform the essential features of his job.[6] But there is also the requirement that the individual *be able to perform the functions of the job safely*. And a medical examination may be used to determine if an individual has the 'ability to withstand various working conditions and environments' (45 FR 66713).

These qualifications concerning 'safe performance' and 'ability to withstand various working conditions and environments' go right to the core of the issue. The Rehabilitation Act does not seem to protect a handicapped worker against hiring or placement decisions that reflect a concern for the *safety* of the individual. The Rehabilitation Act does bar employers from speculating about the long-term course of a handicapping condition and potential safety risks: the medical assessment must be restricted to the ability to perform the essential tasks *in the current time-frame*. But it is certainly arguable that extra sensitivity to risk is a problem in the current time-frame, even if the consequences of exposure to certain hazards will not be manifest for a long time. So it is not unreasonable to take the problem of 'safety' broadly to include occupational health hazards and not just risk of injury; the language of the Rules and Regulations permits that extension. But then the Rehabilitation Act fails to protect workers who are specially sensitive to environmental conditions at just the same point at which the Act fails to protect other handicapped individuals who cannot be assured of 'safe performance' of their jobs.

This safety proviso and its implications for the problem of specially sensitive workers have been noted by some writers. Hogan and Bernacki (1981), for example, consider several cases in which medical screening or biological monitoring might reveal individuals who are at 'excess risk' when they encounter certain environmental hazards. Specifically, they note the extra risks that face smokers who encounter asbestos, those with cirrhotic conditions when they are exposed to chloroform, and those with arhythmic heart disorders who encounter trichloroethylene. They sug-

---

[6] Daniel Wikler has suggested to me that the notion of 'essential' job tasks, by reference to which handicapped workers are judged to be 'qualified', is problematic. Suppose a mildly retarded worker can perform the 'essential' tasks of a certain low-skill job. He is then protected against being refused employment in contexts where a normal worker is not so protected and might not be hired. Employers do take non-essential tasks into account in routine hiring decisions, and so, ordinarily, workers compete for jobs in ways that make their ability to perform non-essential tasks important to their success. Just how serious this problem is cannot be explored here, but it suggests that protecting the equality of opportunity of some workers carries with it some costs to other workers and may disguise the real costs to poorly endowed normal workers of the usual workings of our economic system.

gest that once we cannot reduce further any factors which affect individual susceptibility or levels of environmental risk, then we should consider changing workplace assignments.[7] The clear suggestion of their article is that the Rehabilitation Act cannot be invoked to protect workers at irreducible excess risk from job reassignment. The authors do not make clear, however, just what constraints should be imposed on the process of job reassignment or exclusion from the workplace. Does concern about equality of opportunity still require that some extra steps be taken to make sure that the burdens of health protection do not fail primarily on those most at risk?

To address this question I shall step back from the legal framework of the Rehabilitation Act and examine the underlying philosophical issues.

Equality of opportunity

Philosophical model

Recent work in the theory of justice has focused attention on the concepts of equality of opportunity and meritocratic job placement (see Rawls 1971: Sect. 13, 14; Nozick 1974: 213–39; Daniels 1978: 206–23; also see Chapter 3 above). In part, of course, the interest in the philosophical literature reflects social action and legislation to rectify hiring and job placement practices which are morally objectionable and discriminatory. I will attempt no literature review of these questions here. Rather, I will describe a philosophical model of various traits and their relevance to job placement decisions. The model underlies much of this literature, and, though some features of it are controversial, other features seem not to be. I shall determine what light – if any – the model throws on the question of special sensitivity to health hazards in the workplace.

The model is an attempt to answer the question: Which human traits are morally relevant, and in what ways, to the important social task of assigning people to jobs (or offices)? The task is of fundamental social importance because significant extrinsic rewards are generally associated with job assignments. Though people are motivated to choose careers and seek jobs partly because of intrinsic features of the jobs – it is what they think they would like to do – they also seek the rewards, money, or prestige, associated with them. For the moment, let us dissociate the problem of rewards that a given society associates with its jobs: what

[7] Hogan and Bernacki (1981:469–75) suggest the term 'safe' should be interpreted to mean the absence of excess risk to an individual either immediately or over time. They cite legal support for the interpretation in E. E. Black, Ltd v. Marshall, USDC Hawaii, No. 79–0132, 5 Sept. 1980.

schedule of rewards and what inequalities it might include we shall treat as a separate question of justice. Instead, let us ask the question, from a social perspective, what features of persons and what features of jobs do we have an interest in matching to each other? And what is that interest?

One obvious point is that different jobs require or involve the performance of certain skills and the use of certain talents in various combinations. Indeed, rewards aside, this is partly what constitutes one job as different from another. Moreover, persons have different combinations of such talents and skills. There is a gain in *productivity* from matching – within certain limits – the abilities of persons to the requirements of jobs. We can distribute this social gain in various ways. Some want an *individual's* talents and skills and the contribution they make to determine directly his share of the gains of social cooperation. Others want to treat the pool of skills and talents as a *social* asset: the benefits of its use should be distributed in a way that helps everyone, especially its worst-off members. To some extent this characterizes the debate between John Rawls (1971) and Robert Nozick (1974: 216–32).

Despite this debate about how to divide the rewards of variation among persons in talent and skills, there is much agreement that the proper basis for the placement of persons in jobs is the match between abilities and job requirements. There is disagreement about how 'tight' this fit must be: Must we always give a job to the person with the highest qualifications, as measured by some local matching of skill measurements to job requirements? Or may we look more broadly at the way over-all productivity can be enhanced by the fit of persons to jobs (see Daniels 1978: 209–16)? But this disagreement does not detract from the main point of the model. That is, because of our deep social concern to enhance productivity through social cooperation, skills and talents are a relevant basis for assigning persons to jobs.

In contrast, other features of persons are clearly irrelevant to the process of assigning persons to jobs. Specifically, features of persons which seem to have little or no direct bearing on their ability to perform a job are viewed as irrelevant. It is at this point that the notions of meritocratic (i.e., ability-connected) placement and equality of opportunity come together. People have *equality of opportunity only if irrelevant features of persons do not interfere with ability-based placement.*

The central examples of irrelevant features are paradigmatic because of facts about our social history. We live in societies which have used class background, race, religion, and sex as important categories for the provision of social rewards – largely through the connection of those rewards to placement in jobs. But there is also a more complex interaction between the irrelevant traits and the relevant ones. Through social practices, e.g., education, a society can shape the development of the relevant traits, skills, and talents, by differentially treating individuals who have irrelevant ones. One important disagreement, noted in Chapter 3, concerns the degree to which we must take steps, in the name of equality of opportunity, to rectify the disadvantages in skills and talents that some people suffer because of racist, sexist, or class-biased practices. Some individuals merely want equal opportunity to be defined *formally*, as the refusal to allow irrelevant traits to play a legal or quasi-legal role. Others want equal of opportunity to be *fair*, requiring the use of social resources to rectify the effects of past discrimination.

The central point is that equal opportunity, whether fair or formal, *takes as a given individual variation in talents and skills* (see my use of this fact in Chapters 2 and 3). Even fair equality of opportunity does not commit us to eliminating this variation among individuals, which remains relevant to the process of job placement. Impairments of equal opportunity will derive, directly or indirectly, from the effort to use 'morally irrelevant' traits of individuals as a basis for assigning to them jobs or offices.

Classifying special sensitivity

I shall discuss our central question with reference to the Table (p. 206): just which traits are *relevant* and *irrelevant* in the appropriate ways? The extremes of column I are clear: race and sex, at the top, are paradigmatic examples of morally irrelevant traits for purposes of job placement. Using them interferes with equal opportunity. In contrast, skills or abilities and talents, at the bottom of column I, are relevant traits: equality of opportunity is defined against a background which assumes them relevant. Handicaps and special sensitivities to workplace risks fall in between. To the extent that physical or mental handicaps nevertheless leave a person 'qualified' to perform the 'essential' tasks or functions of a job, there is moral agreement, reflected in law, that we have a morally irrelevant trait. Indeed, a handicap is relevant only when it directly prevents the competent performance of the central tasks of a job – we then say the individual is not a *qualified* handicapped individual (but see n. 6). As we noted in the last section, however, there is an important proviso on the applicability of the law: if a handicap interferes with the

I	II	III
Type of trait	Direct relevance to job performance	Cost of treating trait as irrelevant
1 Race	None	Effects through attitudes of other workers (generally minor)
2 Sex	Some possible effects; Burden of proof to show relevance to safety, 'business necessity'	Effects through attitudes of other workers; Possible effects of some job redescription (generally minor)
3 Physical and Mental Handicaps	No effect on 'essential functions', possible minor effect on other functions; Burden of proof to show safety or 'business necessity' effects	Effects through attitudes of other workers; Cost of 'reasonable accommodation' to handicaps (e.g., access and job redesign effects) (possibly modest)

4 Special sensitivity
  a) prior medical condition
  b) body burden
  c) genetic variation
  d) life-style factors
	Generally none	Long-term health costs, effects on turnover rates, disability costs (modest to significant)

5 Talents and abilities	Major relevance	Major productivity losses

safe performance of a job or is clearly incompatible with an individual's tolerating the conditions of the work environment, then there are special grounds for placing him in contexts that impose less risk.

There is an important matter of classification here which is also critical to our understanding of the problem of special sensitivities. One alternative is to insist that *an implicit requirement of any job* is that individuals fall in the normal range for ability to perform the job safely or to withstand the hazards of the work environment. That is, we ordinarily take it for granted that each person has the requisite capacity to perform safely, which is why we do not generally make the requirement explicit in job descriptions. We make the requirement explicit only when there are special reasons to think it may not be met, such as when individuals have certain physical or mental handicaps. What is assumed by this method of classification is that the 'talent' of *being in the normal range for safe performance* is a relevant trait for job assignments. Consequently, the decision to exclude someone lacking the 'talent' of normal resistance from certain jobs does not deny him equal opportunity. The individual's fair range of opportunities is defined by reference to his talents and skills, and he lacks the 'talent' to perform certain jobs safely.

The other alternative is to deny that sensitivity or durability is a talent at all. In favor of this alternative is the fact that sensitivities resemble such morally irrelevant traits as sex and race in that they are *unrelated* to the standard list of central skills or talents required to produce the product in a given job (the product may be a service). The worker with special sensitivities to an environmental toxin is still a competent worker as judged by the usual standards of competency. His special sensitivity does not mean his work product is compromised in any obvious way, but ability to produce the standard work product is just what we think of as most central to employer decisions about placement. This resemblance is noted in column II of the Table: the first four items show that the respective traits are not connected to the standard features of job performance, as judged by its product.

Sensitivities resemble race, sex, and physical handicaps in another way, which is indicated by the entries in column III of the Table. We can think of the costs noted in column III as the inefficiencies introduced into our productive schemes when we treat certain traits as irrelevant to job placement. There are costs to protecting equality of opportunity even with regard to our paradigmatic cases of traits that should play no role in job placement. For example, in our society there are indirect costs associated with integrating the workforce which result from workers not cooperating adequately because of racist or sexist attitudes. Or the costs may be direct ones, like the costs of affirmative action programs intended to overcome a history of departures from equality of opportunity. In general these costs are likely to be minor and to diminish over time. More significant costs may be involved in bringing the workplace, or educational and other public institutions, into compliance with the laws guaranteeing equal opportunity to handicapped individuals. But even here these costs, though initially directly assessed to some employers, are eventually distributed to broader segments of society, through higher prices or special uses of public funds. Such costs are the social price of guaranteeing equality of opportunity, especially in a society which has a history of denying it.

Very similar costs would be involved protecting the equal opportunity of individuals with special sensitivities. Giving priority to a strategy of modifying the workplace rather than modifying the workforce has such costs. The 'extra' cost of establishing the 50 micrograms/m³ PEL in the lead standard, rather than relaxing it and removing more workers permanently from the workforce, can be construed in just this way. It is a social cost of protecting the equality of opportunity of lead-sensitive workers. Though these costs may in some cases be significant, they are comparable to costs incurred when we protect opportunity with regard to other traits – sex and race – which also not relevant to one's ability to produce the product or deliver the service involved in a given job.

Despite these important similarities between special sensitivities and our paradigmatic cases of morally irrelevant traits, there is also an important difference. When we ignore race or sex in job placement decisions, treating them as morally irrelevant, we do the individual no harm. Respecting equality of opportunity in this way does the individual only good, not harm. However, ignoring sensitivities in placement and hiring decisions – in the name of equal opportunity – may involve doing harm to the very individual whose opportunity we are protecting. (This point will need qualification in light of later discussion.) This very difference between sensitivities and the paradigmatic cases is good reason for putting them in a separate category (on the Table) and not merely assimilating them to race and sex.

Still, this difference between sensitivities and race or sex does not automatically push sensitivities into the category of talents and abilities either. Nor does it mean that we need not be concerned about compromising equal opportunity. First, we might allow individuals who have special sensitivities to consent to their extra risks. Then the cost of protecting their equal opportunity is the cost of allowing them to work in risky contexts. These costs may be the costs of extra workplace modification, or the costs of special insurance policies to cover their increased health care. If we reject this option, because we are still concerned that such consent might be 'quasi-coerced', then we have other policy options. We might offer individuals with special sensitivities special training programs. The intention would be to expand their range of opportunities in ways that compensate them for the loss of opportunity involved when we exclude them from risky work settings. Or we might afford them priority placement in other, low-risk jobs. The costs of these or other compensatory programs are the price of protecting equal opportunity in this setting.

Adopting special policy options such as these is morally obligatory, on the line of argument we are considering, only if sensitivities ultimately resemble race or sex more than talents and abilities. Unfortunately, our philosophical model pulls in two directions. We are led to contrast sensitivities with talents and abilities relevant to job placement because sensitivities do not affect a worker's ability to produce the product or deliver the service characteristic of a given job. From this narrow, product-oriented perspective of what counts as a job, sensitivities have a strong resemblance to race and sex. But this resemblance is not conclusive. It is also not implausible to think normal 'durability' is similar to other abilities we definitely treat as relevant to job placement decisions. In fact, if we consider the *whole job performance*, and not merely its product or outcome, we might well think that safety and maintenance of health are 'part of the job'. From this broader perspective, the normal ability to withstand risks looks as if it is – and should be – one of the requirements for a job, even though we do not usually pay attention to it unless we have special reason to. If there is plausibility to viewing the whole work process, and not just the product, when defining jobs, then there is some basis for ignoring the resemblance between sensitivity and traits like race and sex. The philosophical model itself does not tell us how to resolve the tension between these opposite pulls.

Adopting the broader perspective in defining jobs has clear risks. It makes it easy – too easy – to build into the description of a job many factors which provide bases for discriminating against individuals in morally objectionable ways. It is to counter such broad descriptions that the Rehabilitation Act of 1973 insists that only 'essential' or critical features of a job be relevant to assessing whether a handicapped person is qualified for it. Similarly, in US Title VII case law, assessments of competency to perform a job are kept to a fairly narrow product- or service-oriented description of the job for purposes of protecting equality of opportunity. Nevertheless, job practices which have a discriminatory impact on sexes or races may be defended on grounds, such as 'business necessity', which appeal to features of a 'broader' perspective on defining jobs. (In the next section I shall consider the bearing of some recent legal cases on the conceptual and moral issue raised more generally here.)

I would like to consider briefly a quite different kind of argument which may incline some people against assimilating sensitivities to other traits and abilities relevant to job placement. Suppose for the moment that we do make such an assimilation: job placement decisions will reflect 'natural lottery' outcomes for sensitivities as well as other talents and skills. I noted earlier that there is fundamental disagreement among moral theorists about how to constrain the inequalities that follow from using natural lottery outcomes in job placement decisions. Rawls's (1971) Difference Principle requires that basic institutions in a society should admit only those inequalities which make the worst-off individuals maximally well-off, as measured by an index of primary social goods. In effect, the principle treats the natural endowment of individuals as a *social* asset and uses the productive effects of social cooperation to enhance the well-being of the worst-off individuals – who are likely to be those with the worst outcomes in the natural lottery for skills and talents. Others, such as Nozick (1974), object to such constraints on the inequalities that result from the natural lottery (see Chapter 3).

Suppose we lived in a society which complied with Rawls's Difference Principle. Then the efficiency that resulted from assimilating normal 'durability' to other job skills would eventually work to maximize the well-being of those whose special sensitivities may have kept them from better jobs. Under such conditions, we might be consoled by realizing that those with special sensitivities are as well off as they can be. But here is the rub: in *our* social system, no such principle of distributive justice actually applies. As a result, losers in the natural lottery, including losers with regard to special sensitivities, will not benefit maximally from the most efficient ways of assigning individuals to jobs. But what is acceptable when there is conformance with a general principle of justice may not be acceptable when arrangements are not just. In fact, it might seem we could *ameliorate* the general injustice for a certain class of individuals by refusing to assimilate special sensitivities to other job skills. We thus afford them special protection through our concern for their equal opportunity. An argument of this type, if not of the same detail, may underlie the concern of many for the *vulnerability* of workers who turn out to have special sensitivities. This concern might not be felt were the system as a whole more just, that is, considerate of those who fare poorly in the natural lottery.

Whatever the appeal of this argument, we should note that it does not help us with the general question we have been discussing. It does not turn on pointing out a morally relevant conceptual difference between sensitivities and other abilities. Rather, it seems *ad hoc*, affording special protection to one group, which fares poorly in the natural lottery, though not to others. Such *ad hoc* decisions may well be morally acceptable and yield an arrangement in some degree preferable to the alternative. But we must look elsewhere to resolve the problem of classification we have been considering.

Impact of sensitivity on suspect classifications

My discussion of how to classify sensitivity to risk has so far been inconclusive. Sensitivity to risk has an important resemblance to sex and race – all are traits which have no bearing on the ability to produce the product or service involved in a job. Yet, if we take job performance to include safe and healthy job performance, it is also plausible to treat sensitivity to risk as a trait relevant to job placement. Consequently, the underlying philosophical model of equal opportunity does not answer our central question: Does excluding workers from jobs because of special sensitivities interfere with equal opportunity? In this section I shall look very briefly at some recent case law involving Title VII protections against sex discrimination. The theory underlying this case law has a bearing on the question we are considering, though it is less direct than we might have hoped. Of course, no comprehensive review of this extensive case law is possible here. Rather, I shall try to draw some inferences from one recent case, Wright v. Olin Corp.[8]

Wright v. Olin Corp. is of particular interest because it focuses on the 'fetal vulnerability' program instituted by Olin in 1978. The program creates three job classifications, restricted, controlled, and uncontrolled jobs, which are distinguished by the degree to which the job exposes a worker to abortifacient or teratogenic agents. All women age 5(!) through 63 are assumed fertile and can be placed in restricted jobs only if medical consultation establishes infertility. Pregnant women can work in controlled jobs, which have very limited exposure, only after case-by-case evaluation. Other women must sign consent forms indicating they are aware of the extra risk involved. Olin encourages women in controlled jobs to bid for transfer to unrestricted jobs if they become pregnant. Plaintiffs in the case charged that the fetal vulnerability program clearly violates the equal opportunity protections afforded to women by Title VII, especially as amended in 1978. That 'pregnancy amendment' makes it clear that a classification based on the ability to become pregnant is classification based on sex and is to be covered by Title VII provisions (42 USC 2000e–2(a) to 2000e–2(c)).

The central issue, according to the court, was to establish the proper conceptual framework within which to carry out a legal analysis. All parties admitted the differential impact on women employees, but the

[8] Wright *et al.* v. The Olin Corporation, United Paperworkers International Union, Local No. 1971, and United Paper Workers International Union, AFL-CIO; Equal Employment Opportunity Commission v. Same, Nos. 81–1229 and 81–1230, 23 December, 1982, 30 FEP Cases 889–906. US Court of Appeals, Fourth Circuit (Richmond).

problem is to determine what kind of rebuttal of Title VII infringement is appropriate, and then, of course, to assess the evidence within that framework. Olin urged that the proper framework derives from McDonnel Douglas v. Green,[9] and its progeny, most recently the Texas Department of Community Affairs v. Burding.[10] Specifically, Olin contended it was sufficient to show that there was a *legitimate reason* for the policy and that there was *no intention* to treat women less favorably. The Appeals Court rejected this framework, for the intention to treat less favorably is manifest in the fetal protection program.

But if the program involves an intention to treat women less favorably, there are still two lines of justification available. First, in cases of overt discrimination, a defense may be based on showing that the basis for the discrimination is a 'bona fide occupational qualification' or 'b.f.o.q.'.[11] The Appeals Court rejects this framework for this case, partly because the factual claim and the defense actually advanced in the case bear little on it. But it is not implausible to infer that the Appeals Court thought it unlikely that any b.f.o.q. defense could succeed in this type of case because this defense is so narrow. It requires showing that the very qualifications needed to perform the job preclude persons falling in the discriminatory category, which is here the category including all women of child-bearing age. We shall return to this point shortly since it is relevant to our motivating problem.

The Appeals Court concludes that the relevant framework is one which allows the fetal vulnerability program to be construed as 'facially neutral', that is, as not on the face of it having a sexually biased intent. At the same time, the existence of the program establishes a prima-facie case of disparate impact – that is, women bear a special burden under the policy. In insisting on this framework, the Appeals Court argues that it is trying to adhere to a fundamental substantive principle, namely that 'disproportionate consequences of an employment practice, even if unintended or indeed benignly motivated, may, like intentional invidiously discriminatory employer actions, constitute violations of Title VII' (30 FEP Cases 901). A defense against such a prima-facie case requires a judicially developed 'business necessity' defense – an argument that the discriminating practice is necessary for the proper function of the business. Thus this framework allows a broader range of considerations to count as justificatory of an otherwise discriminatory policy

---

[9] 411 US 792, 5 FEP Cases 965 (1973).
[10] 450 US 248, 25 FEP Cases 113 (1981).
[11] See 703(a) of Title VII, 42 USC 2000e–2(a).

than the b.f.o.q. defense. The Appeals Court then sent the case back to lower courts with instructions about how such a business necessity defense would have to be made.

Can the protection of workers' unborn children be considered a 'business necessity'? The answer is not contained in the term itself, nor in case law following the Griggs decision. The courts, have, however, extended the notion of business necessity to include matters of workplace safety. The Appeals Court cites its own view that 'the test is whether there exists an overriding legitimate business purpose such that the discriminatory practice is necessary to the *safe* and efficient operation of the business' (444 FR 2nd series: 798; emphasis added). There remains the question of whose safety may be considered a matter of business necessity: the safety of the women workers themselves, the customers, or others, including fellow workers. It is very important to note that the safety of the women workers themselves does not count as an adequate basis for a business necessity defense. There is a social history to this fact: traditional sexist stereotypes of the vulnerability of women have been a rationale for discriminatory practices. Allowing such defenses would undermine Title VII. Consequently, the courts have held that 'it is the purpose of Title VII to allow the individual woman to make the choice for herself'.[12] This point may have relevance to our central question and I shall return to it.

A business necessity defense focused on the safety of others – fellow workers or service customers – may override the protections to women intended by Title VII. Thus in the Burwell case noted above, the business necessity of providing for passenger safety justified a policy of mandatory pregnancy leaves for stewardesses. The Appeals Court argues that the safety of unborn children falls 'conceptually somewhere between a purpose to protect the safety of workers themselves and a purpose to protect that of customers exposed in the normal course to workplace hazards' (30 FEP Cases 903). The Appeals Court suggests we may think of such unborn children as a special category 'of all invitees and licensees legitimately on business premises and exposed to any of its associated hazards' (30 FEP Cases 903). Such invitees do not have a 'right of choice' as women workers do. On the other hand their safety is not like that of customers, an integral part of the necessity to assure safe and efficient business conduct. Nevertheless, the Court urges assimilating the case of

---

[12] Dothard v. Rawlinson, 433 US at 335 (b.f.o.q. defense); see Burwell v. Eastern Air Lines, Inc., 633 FR 2nd series: 361–71, 23 FEP Cases 949 4th Cir. (1980) (business necessity defense).

unborn children to that of legitimate business customers, suggesting that Congress could not have meant Title VII to deny employers the right to provide protection for such visitors, especially when 'good labor relations' would require protecting members of workers' families. The Court adds that the general basis for the business necessity defense can quite simply be sought in 'the general societal interest – reflected in many national laws imposing legal obligations upon business enterprises – in having those enterprises operated in ways protective of the health of workers and their families, consumers, and environmental neighbors' (30 FEP Cases, n.26).

Consequently, a business necessity defense is in principle possible, and the Appeals Court outlined what kinds of considerations would bear on a successful one. It suggested what kind of expert evidence was necessary, what level of proof was needed, and what evidence concerning the over- and under-inclusiveness of the Olin program would be relevant to rebutting the business necessity defense. This latter issue is of some importance since many toxins, such as lead, threaten unborn children through their effects on both male and female workers. Thus the Olin program may be under-inclusive for its failure to consider effects on males, and it may be over-inclusive since it applies to many women who will not bear children even though they are fertile. But these considerations carry us beyond what is useful to us in this case, and our purpose is not to examine the merits of this decision as it bears on the specifics of fetal protection programs.[13] Rather we are interested in some general features of the argument which have relevance to our question about special sensitivities.

Three points emerge from this summary of Wright v. Olin which have relevance to our central topic. First, the rejection of the b.f.o.q. defense suggests that the courts insist in Title VII cases on a narrow construal of job definitions. The requirements for a job are assessed from a product or service-oriented perspective. Being at no extra or special risk is not an 'ability' or trait relevant to the performance of the job itself. But if such a narrow construal of job requirements is appropriate in the context of race and sex cases, then it is not unreasonable to ask for consistency. A similar narrow construal should be relevant to the question, How should we classify special sensitivities? On the narrow view, special sensitivities are not traits which should render an individual ineligible for performing certain jobs, since he has the ability to perform the job competently.

---

[13] For two excellent discussions of the issues surrounding fetal protection and its impact on women's opportunities, see Williams (1981) and Bertin (1981).

Excluding such a person would clearly infringe his right to equal opportunity – unless we could develop a special justification, e.g., a business necessity justification. But even if we decide there is such a justification, we may still have a basis for providing him with further protections or compensations. That is, we might have grounds for supporting compensatory programs of the sort noted in the last section.

This argument from consistency should be construed as a moral not a legal argument. Title VII does not explicitly include individuals with special sensitivities as a protected category. But even as a moral argument, it is at best only an appeal to make one area of practice consistent with another. It does not ultimately justify the practice in either context.

A second point relevant to our discussion is that a 'business necessity' justification in Title VII cases cannot turn solely on the threat of extra risk to the affected women. There must be a threat to others, and there must be an obligation of the employer to protect those others, e.g., the sort of obligation established by the existence of the OSH Act and environmental protection laws. In such a case, the rights of the women (or any other explicitly protected group) do not extend to preventing employers from protecting the other parties involved. Suppose we were to view individuals with special sensitivities in the way we must treat women whose rights are protected by Title VII. Then, the extra threat *to them* which exclusionary practices might avoid cannot be the basis of a 'business necessity' defense. By analogy, if we treat special sensitivities as morally irrelevant to job placement decisions, because they are irrelevant to the ability to carry out the tasks involved in a job, then, as in the case of sex, we should allow the consent of the affected worker to determine placement. The analogy is not perfect, however.

The special weight given in Title VII case law to a woman's own view of her well-being is warranted by a social history in which women have, on the most generous reading, been victims of unjustified paternalism. There is no such social history in the case of special sensitivities – though some feel we may be about to generate one. There is a difference between Title VII case law, which grants women the final consent to extra risk, and the Rehabilitation Act view of safety for handicapped workers. Handicapped workers may not be 'qualified' if their own safety is in question, and thus their right to choose is different from the rights of workers under Title VII. This variation in legal practice may show the risk in appealing to consistency – we may not have it even where we thought we did.

A third point is relevant to our discussion. A successful 'business necessity' argument must be responsive to the charge that the practice is not unduly over- or under-inclusive, and that there is no better alternative to it, especially one which involves a lesser discriminatory impact. This suggests that exclusionary practices aimed at those with special sensitivities could also be held to the requirement that there be no better alternatives – in particular, none with less discriminatory impact. That is, if we believe the opportunity of workers with special sensitivities is impaired by such exclusions, then we are required to afford them the protection of a policy which actually fits the justification better than any alternative. Specifically, such better alternatives might involve more stringent modification of the workplace, or programs in which excluded workers were given special access to alternative jobs, or special training programs. That is, the 'business necessity' defense does not show that there is no impairment of equal opportunity. It only shows that some impairments are justifiable, given Congress's intent. But the fact that we are dealing with a case of such impairment means we must do everything possible to ensure that there is no alternative that has a less damaging impact on those whose opportunity is impaired.

The bearing of this third point on our original problem, of how to classify special sensitivities, is minimal. It does not tell us how to make that classification. But it suggests that if we have reasons for assimilating special sensitivities to sex and race, and we still find that 'business necessity' may justify impairment of the opportunities of workers with special sensitivities, then at least there are serious constraints on such intrusions. They must be minimal, compared to all feasible alternatives. The burden imposed by that constraint could be substantial in the special protections it affords specially sensitive workers.

The Olin case does not help us resolve, in a direct way, our problem of how to classify sensitivities. Still, the argument in that case suggests some reason, namely consistency with legal practice in other equal opportunity contexts, for adopting a *narrow* view of job requirements. Such a view would in turn incline us to assimilate special sensitivities to traits like sex and race, which are more clearly regarded as morally irrelevant for job placement purposes. We would then have two options. Either we would have to accept the consent of specially sensitive workers to the extra risks they face, as in other applications of Title VII case law, or, if 'business necessity' could be made to justify exclusionary practices, we might have to accept such exclusions as the best available alternative. Consistency with a body of legal practice, whose own moral legitimacy has not been established here, is hardly a conclusive justification for classifying sensitivities with sex and race. But, it may make such a classification seem somewhat more plausible, provided we have no reason to challenge that legal practice.

Inconclusiveness of model

I originally turned to the underlying philosophical model of equality of opportunity because I thought it might provide considerations, at a theoretical level, which would help resolve a matter of moral controversy at the policy level. Specifically, I suggested that we might pursue the goal of protecting worker health through quite different strategies, modifying the workplace and modifying the workforce. Combining these strategies in different ways imposes different burdens on sensitive individuals. But there is moral controversy about the extent to which such burdens may be imposed. And some who resist imposing such burdens argue that the equal opportunity of sensitive workers is compromised if we pursue the strategy of modifying the workforce too vigorously or prematurely. But when I clarified the philosophical underpinnings of this appeal to equal opportunity, the model proved inconclusive at just the point at which we needed help. Classifying sensitivities with 'protected' traits, such as sex and race, is not implausible in light of recent case law bearing on Title VII. But we still lack a conclusive philosophical argument for doing so.

What follows from this inconclusiveness? There are several possibilities. It might be that the model has not been studied carefully enough. Perhaps some refinement of it would reveal a consideration that decisively inclined us to treat sensitivities in one way rather than another. It is also possible that the inconclusiveness does not result from the incompleteness of our effort. Rather, the notion of equality of opportunity, and the model underlying it, is only a crude philosophical tool. Though it may help us to analyze just why there is moral controversy about this issue – it may *explain* the roots of that controversy – it is not a refined enough instrument to resolve disputes about all novel applications. It is even possible that the case at hand is not a matter of justice at all. That is, reasonable policies combining the two strategies in different ways may all be compatible with fundamental principles of justice – which are indeterminate between the two basic alternatives that concern us. Perhaps other social goals or values would decide us between strategies which treat special sensitivities as matters of equal opportunity and those which do not. But the general theory of justice embodied in our standard model of equality of opportunity is indeterminate for this issue.

It is important to be clear about the implications of this inconclusiveness. The result does not rule out claims about the need to protect equality of opportunity: it just suggests that we are missing a clear justification for them. Moreover, it does not rule out other arguments, also based on justice or fairness considerations, which urge that special sensitivities should not be used as a way of shifting the burden of health protection onto the shoulders of those most at risk. Moreover, the analysis still has important implications for other cases. Specifically, if we have a test for a purported sensitivity which is in fact a fairly poor predictor – this charge has been leveled against several forms of cyto-genetic testing, for example – then use of such a test in job placement decisions is highly suspect. We will be compromising the equal oppor-tunity of many individuals in a direct fashion, one challenged by the central features of the model. The philosophical model was inconclusive about how to classify *real* instances of certain sensitivities. But it is not inconclusive about how to classify a trait, like some forms of cytogenetic damage, which is not directly related to sensitivities and is definitely unrelated to the ability to perform a job. Such traits, and thus such tests, are morally irrelevant to job placement and threaten equality of oppor-tunity in a clear way.

Summary and conclusions

What are the implications of this discussion for the fair equality of opportunity account? Is it threatened with internal inconsistency? Does fair equality of opportunity require preventive health measures which themselves threaten equal opportunity in access to jobs?

Answering these questions has been particularly difficult. I began by noting that there is a relationship between special sensitivities to work-place risks and detectable individual variation in susceptibility to disease. The former looks like a special case of the latter. Since the fair equality of opportunity account justifies providing health care regardless of individual susceptibility to disease, it seems the account should also treat the extra burden of protecting specially sensitive workers as a collective one. That is what the priority of the equal opportunity principle requires. In effect, it would treat special sensitivity to hazards as a trait that should impose no extra burdens on those who have it.

But this straightforward conclusion is not so easily drawn because there seems to be a difference between the preventive and acute-care contexts. Specifically, some claim that the durability of a worker is a marketable trait relevant to deciding his eligibility for a job. Specially sensitive workers on this view may not meet minimal eligibility requirements for the jobs at which they face excess risks. Excluding these workers from risky workplaces does not interfere with their equality of opportunity because it is their lack of the relevant talent which keeps them from work, and the equal opportunity principle does not protect one against lack of talents.

To resolve this dispute, I examined carefully two regulatory or legislative frameworks which might have revealed a moral principle or a rationale that could decide the question. My examination of OSHA's lead standard, which contains provisions for biological monitoring, showed that there was some reluctance to shift the burden of protecting health to the shoulders of the most sensitive workers. But no moral principle clearly explained the features of the standard, which were just as well accounted for by special properties of lead as a hazard. My examination of the Rehabilitation Act of 1973 showed that special sensitivities to risks were not 'handicaps' protected by that anti-discrimination legislation, for the Act protects only 'qualified' handicapped individuals (who can perform jobs safely) and what is at issue is whether sensitivity to risks disqualifies one.

Since existing regulatory and legal frameworks do not provide principles to resolve our problem, I turned to the underlying philosophical model governing equal job opportunity. But here, too, there was no clear-cut answer to the question whether special sensitivities should count as lack of talent or as 'protected', morally irrelevant traits for purposes of job placement. The model pulls in both directions. Existing Title VII case law suggests that we generally take 'competency to perform a job' in a narrow way, which would mean special sensitivities should not be treated as talents or skills. But this is not a direct argument for how we should classify special sensitivities, and I have not been able to resolve the dispute about classification. As a result, I have not been able to establish either the symmetry or asymmetry of acute and preventive contexts.

Where does this leave the fair equality of opportunity account? Two points can be made. First, since we cannot show that special sensitivity is a trait which should be morally irrelevant to job placement, there is no firm basis for claiming the equal opportunity account is threatened with inconsistency. Specifically, we cannot definitely say that excluding sensitive workers violates a principle protecting equal job opportunity. Second, and this is the more important point, even if special sensitivities must be treated as 'protected' or morally irrelevant traits, there need be no inconsistency threatening the fair equality of opportunity account. Rather, there are certain limits imposed on the kinds of protective policies that can be imposed in the name of fair equality of opportunity. Specifically, if we deny the chance for specially sensitive workers to consent to their excess risks, we must undertake special measures to preserve their range of opportunities, e.g., by providing them with special training programs or making them eligible for 'affirmative action' as handicapped workers qualified for less risky jobs. Such ways of protecting fair equality of opportunity involve public policy *limits* or *provisos* on the protective health measures that can be carried out in a just health-care system. If such measures are used, there is no need to worry that the equal opportunity account is internally inconsistent.

My conclusion from this discussion and the argument in Chapters 6 and 7 is that the strongly egalitarian fair equality of opportunity account of just health care is neither internally inconsistent, nor incompatible with other requirements of justice. The conflict of the equal opportunity account with provider liberties, I argued in Chapter 6, was largely illusory. The autonomy and powers granted providers in the US health-care system, for example, are not 'basic' liberties protected by requirements of justice. They are privileges and powers US providers have secured for themselves through effective political and economic lobbying and leverage. But this history does not show them to be morally required features of just arrangements. Indeed, insofar as they interfere with the requirements of the equal opportunity account, the opposite is likely to be the case. Similarly, in Chapter 7, I argued that the fair equality of opportunity account is compatible with stringent regulation of workplace hazards wherever the options open to typical, regulated workers are unfairly or unjustly restricted. But these are limits on the applicability of my account, not irreconcilable conflicts with other requirements of justice. We will not be able to reject the fair equality opportunity account of just health care because it leads to injustice.

9 · Philosophy and public policy

Does justice require funding heart transplants?

I remarked in the Preface that applied philosophy is a risky undertaking. It may leave 'pure' philosophers looking for foundations and policy makers up in the air. The utility of the philosophical analyses in this book is probably best judged by others, but I would like to address one question which by now will be on the mind of anyone who looked to this study for moral advice. Does the account developed here help us solve policy problems? Does it help us resolve disputes about the macro questions facing legislators, planners, and the public? My answer, one any Talmudic student would gleefully accept, is, 'Well, yes and no'. An example might show that this answer really is helpful.

In July 1983, state officials in Massachusetts ruled that Medicaid would fund a heart transplant operation for a state resident. Publicity had helped the person raise many thousands of dollars in charitable donations, but the state guarantee was needed before the transplant could be provided at a medical center in another state. Under great pressure because it had refused the funding, Blue Cross/Blue Shield agreed to fund a heart-lung transplant for another patient as an exception to its regular policy, according to which these transplants are experimental, non-reimburseable procedures. The pressure on government and private third-party payers to provide financing resulted from a recent flurry of life-and-death press dramas involving liver transplants for infants and very young children: here the problem was donor location and not just financing. Even President Reagan got into the act by dispatching Air Force planes to 'rescue' transplant patients from their medical need. Blue Cross/Blue Shield in Massachusetts developed a plan to market optional coverage for major transplant surgery to regular subscribers as well as other individuals. The premium depends on how many people want to buy the coverage. Critics argue that the average person could not possibly be expected to judge rationally what it is worth to insure himself against the very low probability of needing such a procedure.

Should the government provide coverage for such transplant procedures? The policy analyst or legislator – indeed the public – might well expect a theory of just health care to tell us what to do about the financing of major transplants. Is it just or fair that these procedures are not available because of financial barriers? This is a macro decision which affects the structure of the health-care institution, and it is one where conflicting claims are strong and persuasive on both sides. Shouldn't the theory help us?

Some argue that we already have a precedent for government financing because renal dialysis is the object of a special government financing program. Those who need help with their kidneys, they argue, should not be given preferential treatment over those who need help with their livers or hearts. An organ is an organ, and we should not permit any bias here. Others complain that the renal dialysis program is a model of how *not* to undertake health planning. It became a feature of our health-care system because of dramatic presentations to Congress: patients who would die without dialysis were wheeled onto the floor as witnesses to the wisdom of the financing.

Precedents aside, the argument for transplant financing can be made directly. Transplants can provide a last chance at a relatively high quality of life for a select number of patients. Unfortunately, a program of financing transplants would deliver a significant benefit to a relatively small number of individuals at a relatively high cost. For example, heart transplants are estimated to cost between $60–125,000, and there may be a natural limit on the number that could be performed because of an estimated ceiling of 10,000 available donor hearts a year. Such a program thus might cost between $1 and $2 billion a year. This is a significant use of health-care resources. Several years ago, Massachusetts General Hospital decided not to institute a heart transplant program because it feared it would drain resources from other important programs. Within a hospital, or the system as a whole, the use of resources for a transplant program must be weighed against other uses of comparable resources. Could equally significant benefits be delivered to a larger number of people if resources were used for other kinds of medical procedures? Could somewhat lesser benefits be delivered to many more people in other ways? The costs of ten or fifteen transplants a year would be enough to finance a prenatal preventive care program that could save two or three times that many babies. Recent cuts in such care in Boston, for example, led to almost a 50% increase in infant mortality between 1980 and 1983 (Knox 1984).

The complaint of some critics who oppose financing such transplant programs is that we are being stampeded by the 'buried coal miner' effect. Transplants present us with life-and-death dramas – we have an *identifiable* victim, often an appealing but jaundiced child, or a young mother or father with dependent children. It is well known that we are prepared to devote vast resources to saving identified victims. At the same time we are much less willing to use the money more effectively to save *statistical* victims, for example by investing in coal mine safety (or preventive prenatal care). There may be an important 'symbolic value' to the expensive rescue made in lieu of less expensive preventive measures, but we are looking to design a system in a rational, principled way, and we do not want symbols to hide from us the real human cost of not investing in alternative programs.

It is now important to notice a feature of the question as it is raised in this public policy debate. Though the question about financing transplants is a macro question, it is raised as a relatively *isolated* problem of resource allocation and financing in response to a very specific kind of political pressure. Many public policy choices are posed in just this way – though not all are. There are occasions, or periods, in which more systematic features of institutions are open to revision and reform. About all these macro questions we can ask, 'What is the just thing to do here?' But it is crucial that we know what kind of macro question we are facing – some macro questions are much more macro than others – before we try to answer the question about justice. There is really more than one kind of question about justice here, and a theory of just health care is more helpful with some of these questions than others.

Frameworks and contexts of compliance

The question of whether justice requires that we finance heart transplants is not a determinate one unless we specify two features of the context in which it arises. First, we must determine what the *framework* for the question is: To what extent are basic features of the institution open to revision? Second, we must specify, for any given framework, whether or not the institution in general complies with acceptable principles of justice. That is, we must make explicit the *context of compliance*. Each of these notions, frameworks and contexts of compliance, needs further explanation.

Consider frameworks first. A framework is determined by how much of the basic or fundamental political, social, and economic institutions we take to be fixed and how much we allow to be revised in the social system under question. The more major changes of fundamental institutions we allow, the more *basic* the framework.[1] An example may help. Suppose our task were to design a set of basic social and economic institutions that yielded a *just income distribution*, and we are free to alter such things as property rights, control over the means of production, institutions that affect job opportunity, and so on. Then our framework is a rather basic one, and the task of designing a just income policy can be captured by the question, 'What principles of justice and priorities among them should we adopt in designing income transfer mechanisms?' (Notice that this framework still presupposes incomes differentiated by jobs.) But we might also formulate a framework that permits much less institutional revision. Suppose we accept as a given the basic economic and social structures within the United States (still allowing some changes of detail). Suppose further, we assume these institutions are resistant or immune to change. We might then refrain from asking any question about the justice of these basic arrangements and instead frame the question, 'What does justice require of us in the design of an income transfer scheme, such as the welfare system, which has a limited role in adjusting income levels for a relatively special class of people in the US economy?' We might imagine even this narrow question to have slightly different frameworks if asked by a legislator and an administrator. Each might be willing to take somewhat different features of the system as fixed.

The general problem that arises, once we note the possibility of different frameworks, is that a question asked about the justice of a reform policy in a distributive institution is really several different questions which have different answers. Consider, for example, a general moral theory like Rawls's (1971), in which constraints are placed on the kinds of inequalities that can emerge through the operation of basic social and economic institutions. Such constraints seem to emphasize the importance of providing adequate income levels to even the worst-off members of society. The same theory may leave room for emphasizing – or it may say nothing about – the role of other principles of institutional design, such as efficiency or merit considerations, once we raise a question in a less basic framework – for example, the framework appropriate to the legislator or administrator. The distinction among frameworks is quite general and can arise within the context of any

---

[1] I introduce the notions of frameworks and contexts of compliance in a discussion of welfare reform proposals; see Daniels (1981). For discussion of what institutions are in general viewed as fundamental, see Rawls (1977) and Bedau (1978).

general moral theory. For example, we might imagine a utilitarian asking, 'Taking certain social and economic institutions as a given, which principles or maxims governing welfare reform and income transfer produce a social order that maximizes net happiness?' The ordering of principles of equality, merit, and efficiency within this less basic framework might be different from the ordering that holds in a more basic framework.

If I am right, a selection of frameworks is presupposed in asking a question about the justice of a given public policy proposal – be it about income transfer or the financing of transplants. We do not face one question about justice but many, each depending on assumptions about the framework. The same theory of justice – either a general theory or a theory of just health care – may give different answers depending on the selection of a framework.

Consider now the notion *context of compliance*. Much recent work in general moral theory, especially theory of justice, is concerned with what can be called *ideal* or full-compliance theory. In Rawls's (1971) construction, contractors select principles of justice they can live with on the assumption that the principles will generally be complied with. On comparable utilitarian theories, rules for regulating the social system are adopted because they would tend to maximize goodness were there general compliance with them. Such ideal theories can be used, so it is argued, to criticize existing institutions and to point us in the direction of better alternatives. I have tried to put my fair equality of opportunity account to just such use in earlier chapters. Still, general theories throw notoriously little light on two critical issues. What is the most effective strategy for moving from noncompliance to compliance contexts? What deviations from ideal principles are permissible in the pursuit of compliance? The first is generally dismissed as a problem in political science. The latter receives scant discussion, e.g., as the issue of 'dirty hands', that is, the problem facing the morally good politician who must compromise his principles or integrity to accomplish his greater goals.

Notice what happens when we put the distinction between basic and nonbasic frameworks together with worries about contexts of compliance. In distinguishing types of framework, I have supposed we could step back from questions about the just design of basic structures and ask about the proper ordering of principles governing the design of less basic frameworks. But, a general moral theory can throw light on principles in less basic frameworks *only if we assume compliance* with appropriate principles of justice for the more basic framework. If we cannot assume such compliance, it is hard to see how we can decide questions about the just design of features of an institution in a less basic framework. Under compliance assumptions, we assume the principles for less basic frameworks are constrained not to undermine more basic principles. In the absence of compliance, we lack even this constraint.

How then do we evaluate the justice of proposals for less basic frameworks? We might aim for the principles that would be ideal were compliance with more basic principles already in effect. Such an approach might have its justification in its value for moral education. The principles would provide us with a living example of the ideal. An alternative approach might lead us to seek priorities for principles which have the effect of moving the whole distribution toward a more just one, that is, toward a distribution that would better comply with the requirements of the more basic principles. Each suggestion faces objections. The former seems insensitive to the deeper injustices that exist in the institution and risks degenerating into a somewhat hypocritical moral scrupulosity. The alternative approach risks using the occasion of isolated reform proposals to try to rectify far deeper injustices, which it may not have the leverage to do at all. The risk is that other inequities emerge.

Let us return to our very impatient legislator or Medicaid administrator, who is still trying to decide if financing major organ transplants is required by my fair equality of opportunity account of just health care. The distinctions I have been drawing should help us explain some of his frustration. My account of just health care would surely be of help if we were raising the question of justice in a basic framework. Clearly the transplants count as meeting a medical need, indeed one that is important given the impact of organ failure on the individual's share of the normal opportunity range. Still, the importance of meeting the need must be assessed from the perspective of a system which protects fair equality of opportunity in many contexts and in the light of resource scarcity. From this broader perspective, the theory might suggest that intensifying the acute-care bias of the US health-care system fails to protect equal opportunity as well as other uses of the resources would. Many other services – personal care, preventive, and other help for the disabled or mentally ill – might be far more effective and efficient ways of protecting the normal opportunity range for a much larger class of people. Reasoning analogous to this might have been the basis for the Massachusetts General Hospital decision to forego establishing a transplant team. If the refusal to finance transplants or allocate resources to them was part of a plan or program to revamp the whole system so that it satisfies the fair equality of opportunity principle, then the theory helps point us in the direction reform must take.

But here is the rub: the impatient legislator or insurance administrator assumes no such basic framework for his question about what justice requires of him. His framework is clearly a nonbasic one. This is true even if he is worried about the precedent financing transplants will set, that is, even if he sees some of the implications of this macro decision for others. The point is that he may not end up responsible for such later decisions, nor need the 'precedent' involved in the current policy actually end up serving as one. The renal dialysis financing scheme may or may not end up a precedent for financing heart transplants. Political pressures may change, new technologies may arise, and the more systematic ramifications of the current decision may never become actual. Unless it is very clear that the macro question is raised in a basic framework and is intended as part of a more fundamental reform of the system, as it might be if we were concerned with proposals to establish a national health insurance scheme or national health service, the question is best understood as arising in a nonbasic framework.

Direct appeal to our theory of just health care may mislead us in a nonbasic framework in any of several ways. If we interpret the theory to say that we should not finance heart transplants, but we continue to finance renal dialysis, then we introduce an inequity: we do not treat cases of similar levels of need, for which we have roughly comparable treatments, similarly. More generally, we are appealing in this instance to a principle, the fair equality of opportunity principle, which may be quite generally violated in the system as a whole. As a result, we may be unfair to the group of patients who are desperately in need of transplants, for we are suddenly scrupulous about a principle we generally ignore. The effect is to make the public policy decision seem arbitrary and indefensible – *ad hoc* at best. If the system as a whole is not in compliance with principles of just health care, it is not likely to be in compliance with general principles of justice as well. We then have the anomaly of refusing to put resources to the beneficial use of supporting transplants, when we put even greater resources to far more questionable uses, say burying nuclear missiles in desert silos. In nonbasic frameworks, we get no reassurance at all that foregoing the chance to provide transplants to patients who need them will yield better uses of those resources inside or outside the health-care system.

It is important to remember that the fair equality of opportunity account does not give us lessons in strategy for reform. Suppose we adopt a strategy of 'hold the line'. We reject funding transplants in order to try to use this example as a lever to produce further changes in the system, to bring it closer to a system which protected fair equality of opportunity in general. The problem is that holding the line here may be a very unlikely starting point for real reform in the system. Moreover, the 'lesson' that might be learned from denying transplants in isolation from general implementation of the fair equality of opportunity principle, might in fact be counter-productive – for all the reasons that make the appeal seem arbitrary. We might think we had evidence for rejecting the theory.

The point I have been making – that it is problematic how to apply a theory of just health care to questions raised in nonbasic frameworks or contexts of partial compliance or noncompliance – is quite general. I used the example of financing transplants, but I could have talked about proposals to control Medicare costs through cost-sharing or hospital costs through new techniques for determining reimbursement rates, e.g., by 'diagnosis-related groups'. All pose the same issues. Indeed, in my discussion of the implications of the fair equality of opportunity account, I had to qualify my remarks in various ways that anticipated problems about frameworks and contexts of compliance. When I argued that rationing by age could be justified if it were part of a unified, prudent social savings scheme, I cautioned against trying to apply this lesson 'piecemeal' to constrain costs in our system. That was a warning against applying the argument in a nonbasic context. Similarly, I cautioned that such rationing would not be acceptable if it only made other economic injustices elsewhere in the system worse. That was a warning against applying the argument in a context of noncompliance with the general theory of justice. My argument justifying the strong technological feasibility criterion for health hazard regulation in the workplace turned on a concern that alternative work choices open to typical workers were unfairly or unjustly restricted. That too involved a claim about the context of compliance.

In raising these issues about frameworks and contexts of compliance, I am not trying to caution philosophers against saying anything about the real world. I have in mind no general injunction against philosophical meddling with the actual public decisions we face, such as the taboo prominent in the middle of this century. Many philosophers then thought that they could speak only about our moral concepts, and they refrained from construction of normative theories or arguments. I have not been so modest. Nor is my caution merely a special instance of the fact that the application of moral theory and principles to particular situations requires an extensive grasp of complex matters of fact – for which philosophers have no special expertise. That very general problem merely shows that philosophers must work hard to understand what they can about complex institutions and work together with others whose grasp of the empirical situation is better.

I am instead saying that the applied philosopher must be clear about what policy question is really being asked and then be sure he knows the limits of his theory and its application. For many macro questions, the theory must be applied with great circumspection, as a critical guide to practice, because the questions arise in nonbasic contexts. But other, very important macro questions can be approached more directly, boldly, and systematically from the perspective of an ideal account of just health care. I have tried to explain why health care is appropriately thought a very special social good, because of its effect on opportunity. The fair equality of opportunity account systematizes that answer and shows the connection between just health care and more general issues of justice. That account does suggest where problems lie in our system and what very general changes in our institutions would be needed to produce a better system.

That my account cannot answer every macro question raised in a nonbasic context points to a very deep feature of applied philosophy. The appropriate response for a philosopher is not to abandon the philosophical vision contained in the ideal theory he articulates. Bureaucrats, whose vision has adapted to survival in nonbasic frameworks, should not expect philosophers to make themselves equally myopic as the price of seeing things in the relevant light. At the same time, it is fair to say that philosophers cannot rest content with claims about the loftiness of their vision. We owe a special effort to develop better philosophical equipment to address questions in a non-ideal world not always bent on basic reform. But that effort was not my intention here, and so my account risks the charge of utopianism. My defense is that I think the fair equality of opportunity account is compatible with deep strands in our moral and political tradition, indeed, with some of the more defensible features of that tradition. That agreement provides a lever it is worth trying to pull. I have no illusions that the lever is efficiently connected to the wheels that drive change. I am not an idealist about history. But I do think that, if people have a good understanding of why what they want is right, they are more likely to strive harder for it.

WORKS CITED

Aaron, H., and Schwartz W. 1984. *The Painful Prescription.* Washington, DC: Brookings Institute

Aday, L. A. 1975. Economic and non-economic barriers to the use of needed medical services. *Medical Care* 13:6:447–56

1976. Response to critique of 'Economic and non-economic barriers to the use of needed medical services'. *Medical Care* 14:8:718–20

Aday, L. A. and Andersen, R. 1974. A framework for the study of access to medical care. *Health Service Research* 9:208–20

1975. *Development of Indices of Access to Medical Care.* Ann Arbor: Health Administration Press

1978. Insurance coverage and access: implications for health policy. *Health Services Research* 13:369–77

Aday, L. A., Andersen, R. and Fleming, G. V. 1980. *Health Care in the US: Equitable for Whom?* Beverly Hills: Sage

Andersen, R. 1978a. Health status indices and access to medical care. *American Journal of Public Health* 68:458–63

1978b. Response to comments on 'Health status indices and access to medical care'. *American Journal of Public Health* 68:1028

Andersen, R. and Aday, L. A. 1978. Access to medical care in the US: realized and potential. *Medical Care* 16:533–46

Andersen, R., Anderson, O., and Kravitz, J. 1975. *Equity in Health Services: Empirical Analysis in Social Policy.* Cambridge, MA: Ballinger

Andersen, R., Anderson, O., and Lion, J. 1976. *Two Decades of Health Services: Social Survey Trends in Use and Expenditures.* Cambridge, MA: Ballinger

Arras, J. 1981. Health care vouchers for the poor and the rhetoric of equity. *Hastings Center Report* 11:4:32

Arrow, K. 1963. Uncertainty and the welfare economics of medical care. *American Economic Review* 53:941–73

1973. Some ordinalist–utilitarian notes on Rawls's theory of justice. *Journal of Philosophy* 70:9:251

Ashford, N. 1976. *Crisis in the Workplace: Occupational Disease and Injury*, Ch. 7. Cambridge, MA: MIT Press

Baram, M. 1980. Safety and environmental regulatory decision making. *Ecology Law Quarterly* 8:473–531

Barry, B. 1965. *Political Argument.* London: Routledge and Kegan Paul

Bayer, R., Caplan, A., and Daniels, N. (eds.). 1983. *In Search of Equity: Health Needs and the Health Care System*, New York: Plenum

Bedau, H. A. 1978. Social justice and social institutions. *Midwest Studies in Philosophy* 3:159–75

Berman, D. 1978. *Death on the Job*. New York: Monthly Review Press

Bertin, J. E. 1981. Testimony before Committee on Science and Technology. US House of Representatives, Subcommittee on Investigations and Oversight, Hearings (14–15 Oct.)

Bishop, C. 1981. A compulsory national long-term-care insurance program. In J. J. Callaghan and S. S. Wallack (eds.), *Reforming the Long-term-care System*, pp. 61–94. Lexington, MA:D. C. Heath

Boorse, C. 1975. On the distinction between disease and illness. *Philosophy and Public Affairs* 5:1:49–68

1976a. What a theory of mental health should be. *Journal of the Theory of Social Behavior* 6:1:61–84

1976b. Wright on functions. *Philosophical Review* 85:1:70–86

1977. Health as a theoretical concept. *Philosophy of Science* 44:542–73

Boskin, M. (ed.). 1978. *The Crisis in Social Security*. San Francisco: Institute for Contemporary Studies

Bowles, S. and Gintis, H. 1976. *Schooling in Capitalist America*. New York: Basic Books

Brandt, R. 1979. *A Theory of the Good and the Right*. Oxford University Press

Braybrooke, D. 1968. Let needs diminish that preferences may prosper. In *Studies in Moral Philosophy* American Philosophical Quarterly Monograph Series, No. 1. Oxford: Blackwells

Brown, P., Johnson, C. and Vernier. P. 1981. *Income Support Policy: Conceptual and Moral Foundations*. Totowa, NJ: Rowman and Littlefield

Buchanan, A. 1981. Justice: a philosophical review. In E. Shelp (ed.), *Justice and Health Care*, pp. 3–21. Dordrecht: Reidel

1983. The right to a decent minimum of health care. In The President's Commission for the Study of Ethical Problems in Medicine and Biomedical and Behavioral Research [1983b], *Securing Access to Health Care*, vol. II, Appendices: Sociocultural and Philosophical Studies, pp. 207–38. Washington, DC: US Government Printing Office

1984. The right to a decent minimum of health care. *Philosophy and Public Affairs* 13:1:55–78

Butler, R. N. 1969. Age-ism: another form of bigotry. *Gerontologist* 9:243–6

Butler, R. N. and Lewis, M. I. 1977. *Aging and Mental Health: Positive Psychosocial Approaches*. St Louis: C. V. Mosby

Callahan, D. 1973. The WHO definition of 'health'. *The Hasting Center Studies* 1:3:77–88

Callahan, J. J. and Wallack, S. S. (eds.). 1981. *Reforming the Long-term Care System*. Lexington, MA: D. C. Heath

Campion, E. W., Mulley, A. G., Goldstein, R. L., Barnett, G. O., Thibault, G. E. 1981. Medical intensive care for the elderly: a study of current utilization, costs, and outcomes. *Journal of the American Medical Association* 246:18:2052–6

Caplan, A. 1980. What are the morals of our treatment of renal failure? In L. J.

Hodges (ed.), *Social Responsibility: Journalism, Law, and Medicine*, pp. 32–50. Lexington, VA: Washington and Lee University Press

Cronin, J., Daniels, N., Krock, A., and Webber, R. 1975. Race, class, and intelligence: a critical look at the IQ controversy. *International Journal of Mental Health* 3:2:46–123

Daniels, N. 1975. Equal liberty and unequal worth of liberty. In N. Daniels (ed.), *Reading Rawls*, pp. 253–81. New York: Basic Books

 1976. IQ, heritability and human nature. In R. S. Cohen, (ed.), *Proceedings of the Philosophy of Science Association*, pp. 143–80. Dordrecht: Reidel

 1978. Merit and meritocracy. *Philosophy and Public Affairs* 7:3:206–23

 1979a. Moral theory and plasticity of persons. *Monist* 62:3:265–87

 1979b. Rights to health care and distributive justice: programmatic worries. *Journal of Medicine and Philosophy* 4:2:174–91

 1979c. Wide reflective equilibrium and theory acceptance in ethics. *Journal of Philosophy* 76:5:256–82

 1980. Reflective equilibrium and Archimedean points. *Canadian Journal of Philosophy* 10:1:83–103

 1981. Conflicting objectives and the priorities problem. In P. Brown, C. Johnson, and P. Vernier (eds.), *Income Support: Conceptual and Policy Issues*, pp. 147–64. Totowa, NJ: Rowman and Littlefield

 1984. Understanding physician power. *Philosophy and Public Affairs* 13:4:347–57

Davis, K., Gold, M. and Makuc, D. 1981. Access to health care for the poor: does the gap remain? *Annual Review of Public Health* 2:10

Derthick, M. 1979. *Policymaking for Social Security*. Washington, DC: Brookings

Dickman, R. 1983. Operationalizing respect for persons: a qualitative aspect of the right to health care. In R. Bayer, A. Caplan, and N. Daniels (eds.), *In Search of Equity: Health Needs and the Health Care System*, pp. 161–82. New York: Plenum

Donabedian, A. 1979. The quality of medical care: a concept in search of a definition. *Journal of Family Practice* 9:2:277–84

Dworkin, G. 1972. Paternalism. *The Monist* 56 (Jan. 1972):64–84

Engelhardt, H. T. Jr. 1974. Disease of masturbation: values and the concept of disease. *Bulletin of the History of Medicine* 48:2:234–48

Enthoven, A. 1980. *Health Plan: The Only Practical Solution to the Soaring Cost of Medical Care*. Reading: Addison–Wesley

Ferber, S. 1973. *Doctors' unions – down and out. Medical Economics* 50 (Sept.):53

Fishkin, J. 1983. *Justice, Equal Opportunity, and the Family*. New Haven: Yale University Press

Fried, C. 1969. *An Anatomy of Values*. Cambridge, MA: Harvard University Press

 1975. Rights and health care – beyond equity and efficiency. *New England Journal of Medicine* 293:5(31 July):241–5

1976. Equality and rights in medical care. *Hastings Center Report* 6:29–34

1978. *Right and Wrong*. Cambridge, MA: Harvard University Press

Gewirth, A. 1980. Human rights and the prevention of cancer. *American Philosophical Quarterly* 17:117–25

Gibbard, A. 1982. The prospective pareto principle and its application to questions of equity of access to health care: a philosophical examination. *Milbank Memorial Fund Quarterly / Health and Society* 60:3

Gibson, R. M. and Fisher, C. R. 1979. Age differences in health care spending, Fiscal Year 1977. *Social Security Bulletin* 42:1:3–16

Green, R. 1976. Health care and justice in contract theory perspective. In R. Veatch and R. Branson (eds.), *Ethics and Health Policy*, pp. 111–26. Cambridge, MA: Ballinger

Guttmacher, S. 1979. Whole in body, mind and spirit: holistic health and the limits of medicine. *Hastings Center Report* 9:2:15–21

Gutmann, A. 1981. For and against equal access to health care. *Milbank Memorial Fund Quarterly / Health and Society* 59:4

Halberstam, M. J. 1973. Unionism: the newest trap for American doctors. *Medical Economics* 50 (16 April): 78

Hart, H. L. 1975. Rawls on liberty and its priority. In N. Daniels (ed.), *Reading Rawls*, pp. 230–52. New York: Basic

Havighurst, C. 1971. Health maintenance organization and the market for health services. *Law and Contemporary Problems* 35:716–95

  1974. *Regulating Health Facilities Construction*. Washington, DC: American Enterprise Institute

  1977. Health care cost-containment regulation: prospects and an alternative. *American Journal of Law and Medicine* 3:309–22

Hogan, J. and Bernacki, E. 1981. Developing job-related preplacement medical examinations. *Journal of Occupational Medicine* 23:7:469–75

Jonsen, A. 1976a. Principles for an ethics of health services. In B. Neugarten and R. J. Havighurst (eds.), *Social Policy, Social Ethics, and the Aging Society*, pp. 97–105. Washington, DC: National Science Foundation

  1976b. Rights of Physicians. Occasional Paper. Washington, DC: Institute of Medicine

Jonsen, A. and Hellegers, A. 1974. Conceptual foundations for an ethic of medical care. In L. Tancredi (ed.), *Ethics and Health Care*. Washington, DC: National Academy of Sciences

Kahneman, D. and Tversky, A. 1981. The framing of decisions and the psychology of choice. *Science* 211:453–8

Knox, R. 1983. Doctors' fees: a new strategy. *The Boston Globe* 224:26 (26 July):45

  1984. Fund cuts are linked to infant death rise. *The Boston Globe* 225:145(24 May):1, 20

Lappe, M. 1982. Ethical issues generated by testing for genetic susceptibility to occupational hazards or monitoring for their mutagenic effects. Dept of

Social and Administrative Health Sciences, School of Public Health, University of California, Berkeley

McCarthy, M. 1981–2. A review of some normative and conceptual issues in occupational safety and health. *Boston College Environmental Affairs Law Review* 9:4:773–814

McCloskey, J. H. 1976. Human needs, rights, and political values, *American Philosophical Quarterly* 13:1

McCreadie, C. 1976. Rawlsian justice and the financing of the NHS. *Journal of Social Policy* 5:2:113–31

MacGreggor, F. C. 1979. *After Plastic Surgery: Adaptation and Adjustment*. New York: Praeger

Macklin, R. 1972. Mental health and mental illness: some problems of definition and concept formation: *Philosophy of Science* 39:3:341–62

Marcus, S. 1975a. Purposes of unionization in the medical profession: the unionized professions' perspective in the United States. *International Journal of Health Services* 5:1:40

1975b. The time has come to bargain for higher incomes. *Medical Economics* 52 (17 March):204

Mishan, E. J. 1976. *Cost-Benefit Analysis*. New York: Praeger

Mollica, R. and Redlich, F. 1980. Equity and changing patient characteristics 1950–75. *Archives of General Psychiatry* 37:1251–63

Morgan, J. N. 1976. The ethical basis of the economic claims of the elderly. In B. L. Neugarten and R. J. Havighurst, (eds.), *Social Policy, Social Ethics, and the Aging Society*, pp. 67–9. Washington, DC: National Science Foundation

Morris, R. and Youket, P. 1981. Long-term-care issues: identifying the problems and potential solutions. In J. J. Callahan and S. S. Wallack (eds.), *Reforming the Long-Term-Care System*, pp. 11–28. Lexington, MA: D. C. Heath

Moskop, J. 1983. Rawlsian justice and a human right to health care. *Journal of Medicine and Philosophy* 8:4:329–38

Nozick, R. 1969. Coercion. In S. Morgenbesser, P. Suppes, and M. White (eds.), *Philosophy, Science, and Method*, pp. 440–72. New York: St Martin's Press

1974. *Anarchy, State, and Utopia*. New York: Basic

Outka, G. 1974. Social justice and equal access to health care. *Journal of Religious Ethics* 2(Spring):11–32

Palmore, E. 1976. Total chance of institutionalization among the aged. *The Gerontologist* 16:6:504–7

Palmore, E. B. and Manton, K. 1973. Ageism compared to racism and sexism. *Journal of Gerontology* 28:3:363–9

Parfit, D. 1973. Later selves and moral principles. In A. Montefiore (ed.), *Philosophy and Personal Relations*, pp. 137–69. London: Routledge and Kegan Paul

Parsons, D. O. and Munro, D. R. 1978. Intergenerational transfers in social security. In M. Boskin (ed.), *The Crisis in Social Security: Problems and Prospects*, 2nd edn, pp. 65–86. San Francisco: Institute for Contemporary Studies

Pegels, C. C. 1980. *Health Care and the Elderly*. Rockville, MD: Aspen

President's Commission for the Study of Ethical Problems in Medicine and Biomedical and Behavioral Research. 1983a. *Securing Access to Health Care*, vol. I, Report. Washington, DC: US. Government Printing Office

1983b. *Securing Access to Health Care*, vol. II, Appendices: Sociocultural and Philosophical Studies, pp. 207–38. Washington, DC: US Government Printing Office

Rabinowitz, J. 1977. Emergent problems and optimal solutions. *Arizona Law Review* 9:1:61–158

Rawls, J. 1971. *A Theory of Justice*. Cambridge, MA: Harvard University Press

1974–5. Independence of moral theory. *Proceedings and Addresses of the American Philosophical Association* 48:5–22

1975. A Kantian conception of equality. *Cambridge Review* (February) pp. 94–9

1977. The basic structure as subject. *American Philosophical Quarterly* 14:2:159–65

1982a. The basic liberties and their priority. In *The Tanner Lectures on Human Values*, vol. III. Salt Lake City: University of Utah Press

1982b. Social unity and the primary goods. In A. K. Sen and B. Williams (eds.), *Utilitarianism and Beyond*, pp. 159–85. Cambridge University Press

Rockey, P. H., Fantel, J., and Omenn, G. 1981. Discriminating aspects of pre-employment screening: low back X-ray examinations in the railroad industry. *American Journal of Law and Medicine* 5:3:197–214

Samuelson, P. 1958. An exact consumption–loan model of interest with or without the social contrivance of money. *Journal of Political Economy* 66:6:467–82

Scanlon, T. M. 1975. Preference and urgency. *Journal of Philosophy* 77:19:655–69

1977. Liberty, contract, and contribution. In G. Dworkin, G. Bermont and P. G. Brown (eds.), *Markets and Morals*, pp. 43–68. New York: Halstead

Scheffler, S. 1976. Natural rights, equality and the minimal state. *Canadian Journal of Philosophy* 7:59

Schulz, J. H. 1980. *Economics of Aging*, 2nd edn. Belmont, CA: Wadsworth

Sidgwick, H. 1907. *The Methods of Ethics*, 7th edn. London: Macmillan

Sloan, F. and Bentkover, J. D. 1979. *Access to Ambulatory Care and the US Economy*. Lexington, MA: Lexington Books

Starr, P. 1982. *Social Transformation of American Medicine*. New York: Basic

Stern, L. 1983. Opportunity and health care: criticisms and suggestions. *Journal of Medicine and Philosophy* 8:4:339–62

Stokey, E. and Zeckhauser, R. 1978. *A Primer for Policy Analysis*. New York: Norton

Stroman, D. 1976. *Medical Establishment and Social Responsibility*. New York: Kennikat

Thibault, G. E., Mulley, A. G., Barnett, G. O., Goldstein, R. L., Reder, V. A., Sherman, E. L., and Skinner, E. 1980. Medical intensive care: indications, interventions, and outcomes. *New England Journal of Medicine* 302:17:938–42

US Law Week. 1981a. 49(27 Jan):3524
   1981b. 49(16 June):4721

Veatch, R. and Branson, R. (eds.). 1976. *Ethics and Health Policy*. Cambridge, MA: Ballinger

Walzer, M. 1983. *Spheres of Justice*. New York: Basic

Weinberg, R. 1983. The secrets of cancer cells. *The Atlantic Monthly* 252:2:82

Western Journal of Medicine. 1975. On the withholding of physicians' services. 123:26:138

Wikler, D. 1978. Persuasion and coercion for health: issues in government efforts to change life style. *Milbank Memorial Fund Quarterly: Health and Society* 56:3:303–38

Williams, B. 1971. The idea of equality [1962]. In H. A. Bedau (ed.), *Justice and Equality*, pp. 116–37. Englewood Cliffs, NJ: Prentice-Hall
   1973. A critique of utilitarianism. In J. C. C. Smart and B. Williams (eds.), *Utilitarianism For and Against*, pp. 77–150. Cambridge University Press

Williams, W. W. 1981. Firing the woman to protect the fetus: the reconciliation of fetal protection with employment opportunity goals under Title VII. *Georgetown Law Journal* 69:641–704

Zeckhauser, R. J. and Viscusi, W. K. 1978. The role of social security in income maintenance. In M. Boskin (ed.), *The Crisis in Social Security: Problems and Prospects*. San Francisco: Institute for Contemporary Studies

Zimmerman, D. 1981. Coercive wage offers. *Philosophy of Public Affairs* 10 (Spring):2:121–45

Zook, C. J. and Moore, F. D. 1980. High-cost users of medical care. *New England Journal of Medicine* 302:18:996–1002

INDEX

Aaron, H., 90, 111
abortion in US, 31–2
access to health care, 11–14, 59–85;
  utilization rate(s), 3; macro level of
  decision in, 35; sources of
  disagreement about, 59 60; equality,
  problem of, 60–3; amenities, 69–71;
  equitable, 141; *see also*
  inequality
access to information, *see* information,
  health hazard; workplace health
  hazards
access to opportunity, 34;
  see also opportunity
access variables, 63–7
acts, legislative, age-bias in, 89
acute care: in basic health-care system, 2;
  overemphasis on, 15, 140; bias toward
  in US, 29; v. preventive, 144, 218–19,
  226; insurance schemes, 182
Aday, L.A., 60–6, 80–1
Aday and Andersen approach, 63–9
adequate care, 81–2; without excessive
  burdens, 78; as beneficence, 82; *see
  also* decent basic minimum
affirmative action, 41, 207
AFL-CIO v. Brennan, 145n.
age criterion for rationing health care,
  90–8
age group(s), 88; health insurance
  scheme, 92–8; transfer of resources,
  92–8; justice between, 94–5; equitable
  transfer schemes, 108–11; *see also* age-
  group competition; age-group
  distribution problem
age-bias: in a distributive system, 86–8;
  in health-care distribution, 86–114; in
  public policy, 89–94
age-group competition, 86–8, 94–8
age-group distribution problem, 94–8,
  100, 107–8
age-relative opportunity range, 88, 103–8
aging, *see* elderly, the
aging and prudence, 98–103
agism *see* age-bias
allocation of resources, 14–15, 54; over
  lifetime, 91–4; effect on treatment

decisions, 135–8; acute v. preventive
  care, 226
amenities, health-care, 61, 80, 83; and
  claims to access, 69–71
American Iron and Steel Inst. v. OSHA,
  145n.
American Textile Manufacturers Institute
  et al. v. Donovan, 145; *see also* Cotton
  Dust Case
Andersen, R., 60–6, 80
Argument From Fair Shares, 20–1
argument from function, 17; in
  utilization rate test, 66–7
Arras, J., 74
Arrow, K., 21n., 43–4
Ashford, N. 160, 164
assignment, workplace, 203; job
  reassignment, 216
autonomy, individual, 142, 173; and life-
  style choices, 154–62; in unregulated
  risky occupations, 154–5; conditions
  for decision under, 156–9; *see also*
  intervention in risk-taking;
  voluntariness in risk-taking
autonomy, professional, *see* professional
  autonomy
autonomy, provider, *see* professional
  autonomy
average use of health care, 77; *see also*
  decent basic minimum

background injustice, 169, 175
Baram, M., 150n.
Barnett, G. O., 87
Barry, B., 60
basic health care, *see* decent basic
  minimum
Battery Council International, 193
Bayer, R., 3
Bedau, H., 224n.
bed-disability days, 64–5; US
  demographic groups, 3
benefit protection, 188–98
benefits-minus-burdens package, 136
Bentkover, J. D., 60, 64, 67, 77
Berman, D., 153
Bernacki, E., 186, 200–3

Index

Index

Knox, R., 87, 124, 222
Kravitz, J., 60, 65–6
Krock, A., 52

Lappe, M., 184
lead, 191–8; blood lead level, 188; blood level, 190; ALA (enzyme), 190; reversibility of damage, 191–2, 198; special features as hazard, 194; see also PEL
lead standard, OSHA, 187–99, 219
Lewis, M. I., 89
liability, employer, 162, 194
liberal political philosophy, 39, 50, 144
libertarian theories, 9; and professional autonomy, 120; challenge to OSHA regulation, 159–62
liberty, 4, 41, 121–3, 142, 143; negative, 7; consent in, 120; v. OSHA regulation, 153–6; see also autonomy, individual
liberty of providers, 115, 119–24
license for reimbursement scheme, 118–19, 121–3
life plan, 27–8, 47, 104–5
life-style choice, 141–2; risky, 154–9; and individual autonomy, 154–62
life-years, dollar value of, 146
Lion, J., 60
lobbying, legislative, 127–8
long-term care, 100–2
low-option plan, see decent basic minimum

McCarthy, M., 151n., 163–4, 178n.
McCloskey, J. H., 26n.
McCreadie, C., 84
McDonnel Douglas v. Green, 212
MacGreggor, F. C., 31n.
Macklin, R., 28n.
macro level of decision, 2–4, 19, 222; access v. utilization decisions, 35
Makuc, D., 65–6
malpractice litigation, 77
Marcus, S., 129–32
market, economic, 19–23, 71–8, 148–50; mechanisms, relying on, 19; needs v. preferences, 20–3; commodity, health care as, 11, 71; account of equitable access, 71–8; failure, 22, 101–2; constraints on job location, 121–3; regulated, 122–3; regulation of workplace hazards, 148–50, 176
market, medical, see health-care market

Massachusetts General Hospital, 87, 222, 226
Medicaid, 3, 12–13, 15, 31, 64, 87, 89, 100, 115, 119, 124, 221
medical ethics, 1–4; dramas in, 1, 221; codes of, 129, 137; traditional, 135–8; see also obligations of providers; and under physician
medical market, 20–3; see also health-care market
medical removal: from workplace, 188–97; benefit protection, 188–98
medical profession, 123–5; collective obligations of, 115–17; entrepreneurial status of, 123; union movement, 124–35; see also economic interests of providers; physician(s); professional autonomy; providers
medical services, see personal medical services; rehabilitative services
Medicare, 8, 12–13, 15, 64, 89, 100, 115, 119, 228
mental illness, 29, 48
minorities (US), inequalities in health care, 3–4
Mishan, E. J., 150n.
modifying worker v. workplace, 184, 217
Mollica, R., 68
monitoring, see biological monitoring
Moore, F. D., 87
Morgan, J. N., 88
Morris, R., 100
Moskop, J., 54
MRP, see benefit protection
Mulley, A. G., 87n.
Munro, D. R., 108

National Labor Relations Board, 126
needs, 23–6; as basis for distributing health care, 12; rare, 21; avoiding talk of, 20–3; course-of-life, 26–8; educational, 46–7
needs, health-care, 19–35; distinguishing basic, 13–14; need for general theory of, 20–3; summarized, 32; expansiveness of, 53; as basis for equity, 66–7; determining, 80
negative right, 6–7
non-homogeneity of health care, 5, 13, 49–50, 59
normal functioning, see species-typical normal functioning
normal opportunity range, 28, 39–42, 51, 103–5, 140–4, 226; fair share, 30; and